↑LEVEL UP!

50 GAME-CHANGING LIFE SKILLS

FOR YOUNG ADULTS+

STEVE M. SCOTT

AR PRESS

Level Up! 50 Game-Changing Life Skills for Young Adults+ (Master a Growth Mindset, Productivity Tools, Healthy Eating, Biohacking, Brainpower, People Skills, Money, Financial Independence, and More)

Library of Congress Control Number: 2024916236

eBook ISBN: 979-8-9909744-0-1
paperback ISBN: 979-8-9909744-1-8
hardcover ISBN: 979-8-9909744-2-5

1. Main category— Self-Help › Personal Transformation › Self Help
2. Other category— Business & Money › Business Culture › Motivation & Self-Improvement
3. Other category— Teen & Young Adult › Personal Health › Body, Mind & Spirit

First Edition

Published by:
AR PRESS, an American Real Publishing Company
Roger L. Brooks, Publisher
roger@americanrealpublishing.com
americanrealpublishing.com

*"Live as if you were to die tomorrow.
Learn as if you were to live forever."*
—Mahatma Gandhi

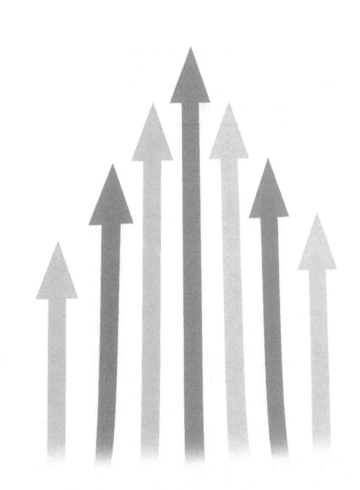

To my family—David, Zachary, Hannah, and my beloved Amy—may your steadfast love, compassionate spirits, and boundless quest for discovery continue to inspire generations with "Eureka" moments.

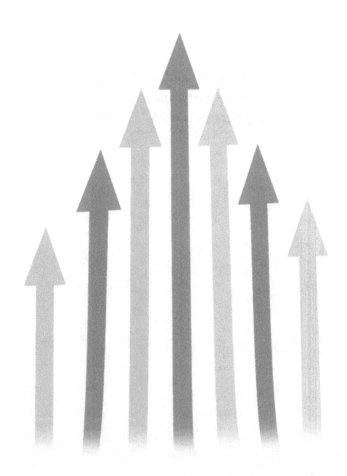

ABOUT THE ILLUSTRATIONS

THIS BOOK CONTAINS ORIGINAL HAND-DRAWN ILLUSTRATIONS by George Miroshnichenko, a twenty-two-year-old artist from Odesa, Ukraine, a rising star in art illustration. His lifelong passion for art led him to complete design art studies, paving the way for his career as an illustrator.

George's vibrant and diverse artistry spans intricate character sketches to expansive landscapes. His fourteen illustrations in this book enrich the written narrative with depth and dimension.

For George, art is an ongoing exploration, a journey he enthusiastically shares with his audience. He says, "Through art, we travel to new worlds. I'm thrilled to bring you along on this adventure."

CONTENTS

INTRODUCTION

THIS BOOK STARTED OUT AS A FINAL LOVE LETTER TO MY family before I boarded a plane. But let me rewind a bit. As the world was watching the crisis unfold in Ukraine during the Russian invasion, I found myself far away, stationed at the US Embassy in Guatemala. One early morning, a colleague from Ukraine reached out, drawing me into a chapter of my life I never anticipated.

The Ukraine Mission was short-staffed in the foreign assistance effort during the summer of 2023—a critical transition time for foreign service staff, and the assistance package was swelling to unprecedented levels. They needed someone with my skill set to help co-manage the program office at USAID through the summer. I'd never been in an active warzone, but I felt a deep urge to help, even if just for a short period, and it was deeply fulfilling.

Before my departure, my colleague, Erin, gave me some sobering advice. She said I should get my affairs in order—including my will, finances, everything—just in case things went south. She was right; with a heavy heart, I hurried to sort everything out. I prepared myself for that summer—mentally, physically, and emotionally. In preparation for this, I started writing letters to my family in case I didn't return home. At the time, my twin boys were seventeen and my daughter was eleven. If I hadn't headed to Ukraine for the summer, I would have spent more quality time exploring colleges and gap-year options with my boys, who were on the cusp of leaving the roost. I wanted to leave all three of them with something encouraging and some life advice.

Writing the letters was difficult. How do you condense a lifetime of advice and love into mere words? There was just too much to say. I timed these letters to send out after my expected return date, but I felt highly unresolved about these letters.

Fortunately, I never had to send the letters. Yet this whole process of writing and reflecting got me thinking—there was so much advice I wanted to pass on to my three children, and I was fully aware that my boys were already becoming young men. So, I just kept writing. Initially, it was for them, but then it hit me—the insights, advice, and skills I wanted to share could help anyone.

That's how the idea for this book came about. It is a no-nonsense compendium of game-changing life skills. It is a practical guide for anybody who wants to enter adulthood skillfully and seize every opportunity to live a richer, more fulfilling life.

Each chapter covers a different pillar of success—developing a winning mindset, goal mastery and productivity, a healthy lifestyle, boosting brainpower, people skills, money skills, and learning to learn and lead. Throughout this book's drafting, I was most fortunate that my children helped me edit my work through thoughtful reviews and dialogue, which was tremendous.

Searching for Gold

Back when my kids were little, we lived on a twelve-acre piece of forested land in rural Virginia. There was a local rumor that there might be gold buried there. David and Zack, my twin boys, would spend hours wandering through the woods and along the creeks on our property, sometimes searching for this rumored gold. Their adventures helped them pick up some excellent skills for exploring the wilderness.

We sold the land before we ever found out if the gold rumors were true. My wife, Amy, and I decided to join the US Foreign Service, and that decision led us to move our whole family to Central Asia, a place entirely new to us. This pivotal moment marked a new chapter for us, turning our family into world travelers. This experience turned out to be a more extraordinary adventure than we ever imagined, a chance of a lifetime that we just could not pass up. Sometimes, the gold we seek is in the seeking, and the prize is beyond our imagination.

Throughout my life, I've been deeply inspired by compassionate idealists and humanitarians—those extraordinary individuals who dedicate themselves to the betterment of our world. They are, in every sense, my soulmates in spirit and purpose. This profound admiration propelled me into the Foreign Service, particularly in the dynamic field of international development. My heart was set on contributing to the global fight against poverty, dedicating my efforts to a cause greater than myself, and genuinely making a difference.

My respect and admiration for my global development colleagues have only grown. These dedicated agents of change tirelessly work toward a world of peace and freedom. Their commitment continues to renew my faith in our shared ability to make transformative impacts worldwide, whether working to end poverty, champion human rights, or enhance global health and education. And, yes, it's some very tough work!

At the root, this job involves helping more people at scale to find and unlock their untapped talents—a different sort of gold. Everybody has inherent worth and a wealth of talent, but sometimes, this innate talent needs to be discovered, unlocked, and cultivated. If you take the time to try new things and invest in yourself, you can discover and use your talents well. Learning, and especially developing the right skills, is key to this.

A skill is an aptitude or ability to do something competently. You can learn skills with sufficient focus, time, and energy. Sometimes, people confuse an acquired skill with a natural quality. Unfortunately, that misunderstanding might be why some people do not invest in improving specific skills. The skills covered in this book all support each other, and together, they can help you live a well-rounded life. There's no silver-bullet solution to living life to its fullest, but developing a range of life skills is a critical part of the equation. Skills acquired are tools that become part of who we are and what we can accomplish.

Some people think they can't change or improve themselves, but that's a limited, fixed mindset. Believing that can trap you in a cycle where you don't even try to get better. But if you shift your perspective, learn new things, and stay open to growth, you can go beyond what you thought was possible.

This book is about learning success life skills—essential skills that will unlock success in all areas of life. We all have different talents, but we discover and develop those talents by developing and applying relevant skills. There is always some skill you can work on improving. You hold the key but must unlock it and walk through that door yourself.

What You Will Learn

Welcome to a comprehensive exploration of fifty game-changing life skills organized by seven chapters marking different levels. Each level builds upon the last to enrich your journey toward a fulfilled, knowledgeable, and empowered life.

- **Level 1: Cultivate a Winning Mindset;** Start your journey by developing a growth mindset, embracing resilience, and igniting your passions for a foundation of success.

- **Level 2: Dream It, Then Do It;** Learn to turn aspirations into achievements with smarter goal-setting and systematic productivity strategies, paving the way for real progress.

- **Level 3: Nourish Your Body and Mind;** Delve into the essentials of physical and mental health, including balanced nutrition, fitness, and stress management for a robust life.

- **Level 4: Boost Your Brainpower;** Enhance your cognitive skills with techniques for memory, creativity, and learning, elevating your innovative thinking and problem-solving.

- **Level 5: Build Bridges, Break Barriers;** Take your interpersonal skills to the next level, from effective communication to empathy, fostering meaningful connections and overcoming conflicts.

- **Level 6: Master Money Matters;** Secure your financial future through savvy budgeting, investing, and planning, guiding you toward financial independence.

- **Level 7: Learn to Learn and Lead;** Conclude your journey by merging the power of continuous learning with leadership, inspiring and equipping you to lead with impact and leave a legacy.

How to Use This Book:
A Guide to Maximizing Your Learning

This book is designed with intentional sequencing to build your skills progressively, but it also accommodates the flexibility to skip around as needed. Think of it as a buffet of vital knowledge—while each skill builds on the previous, feel free to choose what resonates most with you at any given time. The overarching goal is to cultivate well-roundedness to succeed in multiple situations.

Each chapter is an investment in yourself, encouraging you to learn and enhance a specific skill. Each chapter begins with a self-assessment designed to get you thinking about ways to apply the content to your life. Proper pacing is essential for meaningful personal growth. I'm ever-aware that skill-building is a journey of persistence and daily dedication.

Continually honing life skills is a lifelong pursuit, like staying physically fit. Including these skills in your daily life helps keep them sharp, increasingly requiring less effort. Just as regular exercise keeps you physically healthy, using important life skills every day keeps them in top condition. Self-improvement is very much a personal endeavor. Just because I'm writing about them doesn't make me a master at everything; I'm continuously learning, expanding, and honing these skills myself.

Embrace the art of lifelong learning by consistently refining key life skills, weaving this discipline into the very fabric of your existence. Like iron sharpened to maintain its edge, regularly enhancing your core skills ensures peak performance and deeper fulfillment. This relentless pursuit not only sharpens our capabilities but also arms us with the confidence to face life's challenges head-on.

The path of learning and growth should never cease. Each chapter is a lesson and a stepping-stone toward a richer life marked by endless learning, self-fulfillment, and the joy of making the world a better place. *Time to level up!*

LEVEL 1:
CULTIVATE A WINNING MINDSET

L ET'S FACE IT—LIFE CAN BE TOUGH. MAYBE YOUR MIND IS ON constant overdrive, bombarded by the never-ending buzz of social media and the pressure cooker of daily demands, not to mention the big, bold issues of the world. It's a mental marathon out there. How can you make sure you have what it takes?

Do you want to know how you can keep your cool and not just survive but thrive? Welcome to the mental gym of Level 1, where we will level up your mental and emotional game.

We're not just talking about quick fixes here. We're gearing up to build a mind that's as tough as it is flexible, turning you into a confidence powerhouse ready to take on life's curveballs with flair. Ready to transform your mindset? Let's get started!

Self-Assessment

Before diving into the chapter, let's begin with a brief self-assessment to make the most of your reading. Take a moment to reflect on these key questions. Write down the answers to these five questions before starting the chapter.

1. **Skill Strengths:** What life skills are you already good at? Identify your top two strengths.

2. **Improvement Areas:** Which two life skills do you most want to improve or learn?

3. **Motivation:** Why are you motivated to develop these skills? How will they impact your life?

4. **Overcoming Challenges:** Think of a past challenge in learning a new skill. How did you, or could you, overcome it?

5. **Goals:** Set one specific goal for what you hope to achieve by the end of this book.

Keep these reflections in mind as you progress through this chapter. They will guide your journey and align the learning with your personal growth objectives.

SKILL 1:
PAY ATTENTION!

P*AY ATTENTION!* ISN'T THAT AN INTERESTING PHRASE? MOST people wouldn't conflate attention with something you pay, like a currency. Yet, attention is probably the most important currency of all. Your attention span is in short supply as there is a limit to what we can focus on daily. I would argue that nowadays, there is a lot of attention theft. Nowadays, the average human being gets exposed to more information than at any previous point in history, frequently to an overwhelming extent. Your mind is under constant siege as things relentlessly snatch our limited attention away, making it an active battleground in our daily lives. You need to recognize that and learn to reserve your attention for things that truly matter most. In other words, you need to learn how to *invest* your attention.

Allocating your focus is a skill that has grown more difficult as average attention spans have massively withered over the years. Coming from all directions—whether smartphones, advertisements, news, and more—we find ourselves inundated with more and more information daily. As the demands for attention are mounting, our brains have activated a defensive mechanism limiting how much we can take in. Unfortunately, we might miss out on some of the good stuff while letting in "mental junk food."

The first step to being able to invest your attention into what matters most is to recognize when distractions are stealing it away. When you find yourself doom-scrolling, for example, your precious time is wasting away like sand in a bottomless hourglass. You need to exercise awareness in that moment and take back your attention. Then redirect it into something worthy—something that will profit your life, like this book. Be intentional in making good decisions about what you focus on! GIGO (Garbage-In-Garbage-Out) can be a severe problem, so steer your mind away from garbage.

The quality of the content you put into your mind molds your mindset. Focus your mind on things that are true, honorable, right, pure, lovely, admirable, excellent, and praiseworthy.[1] This way, you cultivate a mindset that is not just positive but deeply enriching and constructive.

It takes effort to dedicate focus. I will say that learning to concentrate for more extended periods is a skill that takes practice. Generally, I have a short attention span until I focus on something that interests me. Back in college, for one of my majors, philosophy, I had to read reams of books, and initially, I was not the strongest reader; I found some texts extremely long, dense, and hard to focus on. So, I had to experiment with different ways to get through all the readings, including drinking ample amounts of coffee, listening to instrumental music, and locating myself in a space of no distractions. My level of focus was intentional; I made accommodations to invest my attention, and you know what? I got better at it over time, and it got easier. Like any skill, sometimes it's hard at first, but with sufficient practice, learning, and using the proper techniques, you will be increasingly successful as you develop your skills. Often, this requires the exploration of new approaches. A key is keeping a positive mindset, which is our next skill!

SKILL 2:
BELIEVE IN YOURSELF

"Once you replace negative thoughts with positive ones, you'll start having positive results."
—Willie Nelson

OUR PERSONALITIES AND MINDSETS ARE AS UNIQUE AS OUR fingerprints, but the good news is that positivity isn't just an inherent trait; it's a skill one can cultivate. In a way, a positive mindset as a skill is an application of self-confidence, which requires you to believe in yourself. Believing in yourself starts with recognizing and extinguishing your limiting beliefs.

Consider the tale of a young elephant tethered to a peg. Initially, its strength isn't enough to break free, embedding a belief of powerlessness. This belief persists even as the elephant grows stronger, capable of escaping its bonds. Yet, it remains tethered, not by the peg, but by its limiting beliefs. Similarly, our beliefs about our past can act like that peg, holding us back even when we have the strength to move forward. Some refer to this issue as *learned helplessness*.

On the other hand, a positive mindset empowers you, especially when applied to your past, present, and future. Sometimes, life has significant setbacks, challenges, or situations that can weigh you down. We all have made mistakes. We have all been discouraged by an unkind word in our direction. In accepting that we can move on from our past, we accept that the texture of our past enriches our future. This realization allows us the freedom and confidence to move forward in a positive direction. You are more than the sum of your past; much more!

> **We are more than our history; we are the authors of our next chapter. To fully engage in the present, we must reconcile with our past.**

Our present self-perception, too, plays a crucial role. How we see ourselves today, including our self-confidence, affects our quality of life and performance. Colin Powell once described optimism as a "force multiplier," which is to say that an optimistic view of the future enhances our performance and well-being.[2] Your perspectives along these different timeframes—the past, present, and future—are interconnected.

This shift from criticism to optimism isn't just about how we see ourselves; it extends to how we perceive and interact with others. Imagine what we could achieve if we stopped dwelling on weaknesses or past mistakes. Seeing the potential in others can transform relationships and, by extension, our communities. I think we can all work on this more.

Cultivating a positive mindset is akin to setting sail across the open sea, marked by moments of peace and sudden storms. Like the ocean's unpredictable waves, negative thoughts can threaten to disrupt our balance, with stormy weather tempting us to harbor excuses or cast blame. However, navigating with determination is crucial; our past storms don't dictate our direction. By firmly grasping the helm and recognizing our command over our journey, we can steer through rough waters toward a future of brighter horizons.

The first step to overcoming self-limitations is acknowledging the learned helplessness paradox. The challenge then lies in recognizing these parasitic thoughts, confronting them with determination and mindfulness, and using techniques like gratitude journaling, positive affirmations, or reflective meditation to pivot toward positivity. *You've got this!*

As we break free from the shackles of limiting beliefs and embrace a positive mindset, our next venture leads us into emotional intelligence. Understanding our emotions is the cornerstone of steering our actions and reactions on this voyage of life.

SKILL 3:
EMOTIONAL INTELLIGENCE

"Emotional intelligence begins to develop long before any formal learning takes place."
—Daniel Goleman

I REMEMBER A TEACHER WHO PROUDLY DISPLAYED "KNOW Thyself" on his classroom door, echoing the famous inscription from the ancient Temple of Apollo at Delphi. It served as a daily reminder to self-reflect and understand our inner selves before stepping out to face the world. The great philosopher Socrates said, "The unexamined life is not worth living."[3] He viewed self-knowledge as the foundation of wisdom. This phrase, "Know Thyself," deeply resonates when we delve into Emotional Intelligence (EI). It's not merely an invitation for introspection but a compelling charge to understand our innermost selves. In EI, this translates to a keen awareness of our emotions, strengths, weaknesses, and what triggers us. Such understanding is crucial not only for personal introspection but also for navigating our interactions with others. This foundation of self-awareness is critical for developing other EI facets, like empathy, self-regulation, and effective social interactions.

Being skilled in tasks is important, but mastering self-knowledge and interpersonal skills is often even more crucial. This mastery begins with a thorough grasp of your emotions, paving the way for deeper connections and collaborations with others—a vital component of a successful life.

THE ART OF EMOTIONAL INTELLIGENCE

Expanding your emotional vocabulary will give you more nuanced insight into identifying and describing emotions in yourself and others. Generally, our feelings are much more nuanced and complex at a given time than meets the eye. Imagine you're an artist with a vast palette of emotions. Each hue and shade represents a different feeling, and just like in art, these emotions can blend and mix, creating a spectrum of experiences.

- **Core Emotions:** Consider these as your primary colors—basic but essential: happiness, sadness, anger, fear, surprise, and disgust. Simple yet powerful, they form the foundation of your emotional world.

- **Secondary Emotions:** Now, imagine blending those primary colors. You get new shades, right? That's what secondary emotions are like. Joy is a brighter shade of happiness; grief is a deeper tone of sadness. Rage is like anger but fierier; terror is fear at its most intense; and amazement is surprise in its purest form.

- **Tertiary Emotions:** *Here's where it gets fascinating!* Mix those colors further, and you get an even more diverse palette. Feelings like satisfaction and pride come from happiness. Sorrow and despair emerge from sadness. Annoyance and resentment are variations of anger, while anxiety and panic evolve from fear. Shock and astonishment are surprise's offspring, and feelings like contempt and scorn arise from disgust.

- **Complex Emotions:** Now, imagine creating a masterpiece with all these colors. Complex emotions are like that—intricate and multi-layered. Love is not just a single color but a blend of happiness, trust, anticipation, and more. Jealousy combines the deep hues of anger, sadness, and fear. Optimism is a mix of bright anticipation and cheerful happiness. Guilt is a somber mix of fear, sadness, and disgust, while embarrassment is a unique blend of surprise, shame, and sadness.

Like a skilled artist, identifying and understanding these emotional shades can bring you more in tune with yourself and others. It's not just about naming the emotion; it's about understanding its depth and nuance.

Here are several practical strategies to assess and strengthen your Emotional Intelligence:

- **Seek Feedback:** How we perceive ourselves often differs from how others see us. Engaging in honest conversations about your emotional responses and behavior with trusted friends, family, or colleagues can provide valuable insights.

- **Reflect on Your Responses:** Regularly reflect on your emotional reactions to situations. Ask yourself why you felt a certain way and what triggered those feelings. This practice can help you become more aware of your emotional patterns.

- **Empathy Exercises:** Try to put yourself in others' shoes actively. Understanding and acknowledging others' perspectives can significantly improve your interpersonal skills and emotional intelligence. This acknowledgment is challenging, especially if it is somebody you don't relate to or agree with, but this exercise is quite illuminating. For example, you could read a memoir of someone with vastly different life experiences or someone with whom you disagree strongly on important issues. Seek out opinions that are different from your own and then get to know the people behind the opinions. Read books written by people of ethnicities/cultures that are different from your own. (Skill 31 goes deeper.)

- **Journaling:** Writing down your thoughts and emotions is a potent instrument for self-discovery. It enables the recognition of emotional triggers and a deeper understanding of the roots of your reactions. (See Skill 7 for more.)

- **Set Personal Development Goals:** If you recall, at the beginning of this chapter (or level), you were asked to set one specific goal for what you hope to achieve by the end of this book. Set realistic goals and then work toward them systematically. For example, if you struggle with empathy, you might aim to ask more questions in your conversations to understand others better.

- **Continuous Learning:** Read books, attend workshops, and participate in training sessions on emotional intelligence. Improving your knowledge is a powerful tool for understanding and applying EI principles. Working with a coach can sometimes provide the structured approach you need to develop your EI. They can offer personalized strategies and support to help you navigate your emotional landscape.

Developing your Emotional Intelligence (EI) is an ongoing process, requiring patience and consistent effort. Improving your EI will lead to tremendous benefits in both personal and professional areas. Next, we'll focus on resilience and adaptability, crucial to tackling life's challenges. Resilience is often misunderstood; it is not merely about toughening up, but rather, true resilience involves facing those tough emotions, situations, and suffering, using skills to process what the experience is, and then having the self-efficacy, skills, and determination to keep going. Becoming more emotionally intelligent allows you to experience powerful emotions without being wrecked by them so that you can be more resilient.

SKILL 4:
RESILIENCE + GRIT

*"The oak fought the wind and was broken,
the willow bent when it must and survived."*
—Robert Jordan

L IFE INEVITABLY PRESENTS US WITH CHALLENGING TIMES. IT'S
not about *if* we will face difficulties but *when* they will arise.
Often, the trials we encounter are beyond our control, yet we hold the
power to choose our response.

Resilience is the ability to rebound from setbacks, challenges, or
adversity. It involves embodying the qualities of a willow tree, which
bends in strong winds but remains unbroken. This tree is a paragon of
adaptability, flexing gracefully under pressure. Resilience, similarly, is
rooted in a core of inner strength and stability. Like a tree's roots, this
inner core provides us with the foundation to be both adaptable and
steadfast, enabling us to navigate life's storms with grace and resilience.

Take, for instance, the global COVID-19 pandemic—a real test of
resilience for many. During this time, my family was living in Malawi,

one of the world's poorest countries, where only 11% of the population had access to electricity.[4] My family's experience in Malawi during this period was jarring. The pandemic brought fragile systems to their knees in an impoverished country where vital resources like ventilators were scarce. A medical doctor mentioned to me there were only about five in the entire nation at that time!

Amidst this crisis, the impact on my family was deeply personal. We lost colleagues and friends to the virus. Also, the international school where my three children studied was thrown into disarray. With the shift to online learning, the lack of reliable internet and electricity became painfully apparent. Many expatriates, including teachers and administrators, either left or resigned, leading to a rapid decline in the school's functionality. Faced with no other choice, we withdrew our boys from the school. Amy found herself balancing homeschooling with her full-time job, while Hannah started attending a school in Virginia virtually, managing a six-hour time difference. It was a period of immense strain, but through it, our family eventually found ways to adapt, and eventually, we emerged stronger.

> **Building resilience isn't just about enduring; it's about confronting hard truths and actively finding ways to cope and improve your situation.**

Here are several strategies that can help you navigate challenging times more effectively:

- **Develop a Support Network:** Surround yourself with friends, family, or colleagues who can offer support, understanding, and advice when facing challenges. This principle applied in Malawi, too. For example, when torrential rains caved in part of a mud-brick house of a poor Malawian friend, community members and friends banded together to help. Your resilience is much stronger when you have people around you who care. Also, *be* that friend who cares! (See Skill 38 – Building Relationships.)

- **Find Your Center:** Begin by anchoring yourself in the present moment through practices like mindfulness, meditation, or prayer. This initial step of grounding is crucial for achieving mental clarity and calmness. It allows you to pause and become fully aware of your mental state, setting a solid foundation for perspective shifting.

- **Shift Your Perspective:** Take a longer view and view adversity as a growth opportunity. Find the positive. Changing your perspective can change the way you experience difficult situations. (See Skill 2 – Believe in Yourself.)

- **Focus on What You Can Control:** In any adverse situation, identify the aspects you can influence and focus your energy there rather than on elements beyond your control. (See Skill 9 – Prioritization Mastery.)

- **Set Small, Achievable Goals:** Don't try to "boil the ocean." Break a large problem into smaller parts. Breaking down overwhelming situations into manageable tasks can make them seem less daunting. Small victories are empowering, and they add up to a larger triumph. (See Skill 8 – Goal Crafting.)

- **Maintain a Routine:** Keeping to a regular schedule can provide a sense of normalcy and stability during turbulent times. (See Skill 14 – Forming Better Habits).

- **Exercise Regularly and Sleep Well:** Physical activity can reduce stress and improve your mood, enhancing your ability to cope with adversity. Sleeping well detoxifies your body and mind, which is necessary for coping. (See Skills 18 and 19 – Physical Fitness and Sleep Hygiene.)

- **Journaling:** Writing down your thoughts and feelings can help you process your emotions and gain clarity about the situation. (See Skill 6 – Reflective Journaling.)

- **Practice Self-Care and Self-Compassion:** Take some personal time. Be kind to yourself during tough times. Acknowledge your feelings without judgment and give yourself the same care and understanding you would offer a good friend.

- **Limit Anxiety-Inducing Inputs:** Recognize what gives you worry or anxiety and limit your exposure. For instance, if your challenge is related to more significant events (like a pandemic), stay informed, but don't overconsume news that could add to your anxiety. We talked earlier about Garbage-In-Garbage-Out, but it's even worse sometimes if the garbage stays in. It's best to avoid garbage.

- **Engage in Healthy Hobbies or Activities:** Distracting yourself with enjoyable healthy activities can relieve stress and enhance your mood. But "healthy" is crucial because you want to avoid unhealthy coping mechanisms during tough times.

- **Seek Professional Help if Needed:** Sometimes, the best move is to talk to a counselor or therapist who can provide guidance and strategies for dealing with challenges.

TAKING IT TO THE NEXT LEVEL: FROM RESILIENCE TO GRIT

At a higher level, the developed ability to be resilient lends to the ability to persevere. Resilience and grit are on a skill spectrum. Whereas resilience is about the ability to bounce back from setbacks, that skill, once honed, translates into a powerful force for enduring challenges over a longer haul, which is what we could call perseverance. Sometimes, we use the word "grit" to describe somebody who can persevere over the long term.

Grit is a psychological trait that combines passion and perseverance for long-term goals. It's about sustaining commitment and determination to achieve something over an extended period despite obstacles, failures, or plateaus in progress. The concept of grit has been popularized by psychologist Angela Duckworth, who identified it as a key driver of success.

The US Marines epitomize both resilience and grit.

As members of the US Embassy community in Guatemala, Amy and I had the privilege of attending the celebration of the 248th birthday of the US Marine Corps. The event was spectacular, but what truly captivated me was the personal story shared by the guest speaker, Sergeant Major Dan Miller, a retired Marine who devoted thirty years to serving his country. Sgt. Major Miller's story is a remarkable testament to resilience and determination. He recounted how, as a high school student eager to join the Marines, he faced a significant setback due to a severe leg injury. Undeterred, he dedicated himself to rigorous physical therapy and eventually met the strict physical requirements for enlistment. He said that experience taught him to never give up in the face of adversity.

He shared how his mentor would remind him that there are both good and challenging days, but if you get out of bed in the morning and put your feet on the ground, you have already won the day. This mindset guided him through a distinguished career, where he served in various capacities, including as a machine gunner, and participated in multiple deployments—in Desert Storm and twice in Operation Iraqi Freedom. Despite his accomplishments, Sgt. Major Miller's challenges didn't end with his retirement. He was diagnosed with traumatic brain injury and post-traumatic stress disorder (PTSD), conditions that many veterans face.

In true spirit, he turned this personal battle into an opportunity to help others, working with the Wounded Warrior Project to support fellow veterans dealing with similar wounds. His story left a lasting impression on me, illustrating the profound impact of sustained perseverance and the power of turning personal struggles into a force for positive change. His story embodied both resilience and grit.

Feeling overwhelmed when confronted with life's challenges is a natural response. However, by embracing these strategies, you can develop resilience and grit, empowering you to navigate tough times more easily. Envision these challenges as mountains to be scaled, recognizing the importance of owning your successes and failures. Each represents a crucial feedback loop and a stepping-stone toward your next growth phase, helping you forge and refine your inner strength.

Moving forward from the resilience-building strategies we've discussed, our next step is to delve deeper into the internal world of mindfulness and find tranquility within.

SKILL 5:
MINDFUL PRESENCE

"Mindfulness isn't difficult.
We just need to remember to do it."
—Sharon Salzberg

HERE'S A REALITY CHECK: IN TODAY'S DISTRACTING WORLD,
our minds often wander away from the present moment, focusing on the past or future and neglecting the now. John Kabat-Zinn, a
mindfulness expert, humorously suggested we're more 'human doings'
than 'human beings,' highlighting our focus on action over presence.[5]
Which one are you?

Mindfulness, an ancient practice backed by modern science,
brings our attention to the present, promoting peace and grounding.
It reduces stress, boosts focus, and enhances mental health, involving
being fully present and observing our thoughts without judgment.

The challenge lies in remembering to practice mindfulness regularly, even if it's just for a few minutes each day.

Throughout my years as a student and a professional, I've used intentional, mindful breaks to help manage stress and maintain focus or composure. Also, I've experimented with different ways to get myself into different states of mind. Instrumental music has always been a powerful tool to induce a mindful state, allowing me to step away from external noise and internal chatter to be fully present in the moment. That's powerful and more real than anything described. Also, making time for meditation has helped me weather high-pressure environments or challenging situations.

Meditation, a core aspect of mindfulness, offers various approaches, from focusing on breath to engaging in movement practices like yoga or tai chi. Meditation involves focusing the mind to achieve heightened awareness and inner calm. For beginners, guided meditations can be a helpful starting point, providing structure and direction to ease into the practice.

Some people confuse mindfulness, meditation, and prayer, although each differs in approach and purpose while offering various psychological and spiritual benefits. Mindfulness typically aims at increasing awareness and acceptance of the present moment, whereas prayer involves seeking a connection with God, giving thanks, asking for guidance or help, or expressing devotion. I personally find that praying is vital to stay grounded, renewed, and connected to my higher purpose. Without that grounding, my pursuits of self-improvement might feel rudderless, lacking direction, or perhaps empty. Meditation can be viewed as a technique of mind-body awareness that may encompass practices of either mindfulness or prayer, leading to heightened awareness and inner calm.

Here are critical aspects of mindfulness and some brief exercises to get a feel for different techniques.

- **Present Moment Awareness:** Staying attuned to the current moment.
  - Exercise: 5-4-3-2-1 Technique
  - How to Do It: Pause for a moment and observe five things within your sight, touch four objects nearby, listen for three

sounds around you, detect two distinct smells, and savor the taste of one thing. This exercise is designed to center your attention on the present moment.

○ Remember that mindfulness involves intentionally focusing your attention on the present moment. Focusing on sensory experience is helpful for beginners. For example, drinking a cup of hot tea can be a mindfulness meditation exercise. Focus your attention on the warmth of the cup in your hands. How do your hands feel? Is the cup smooth? Inhale deeply and notice how the tea smells. Take a sip and focus on the warmth in your mouth and the flavors you taste. Can you feel the warmth traveling through you as you swallow the tea?

- **Non-Judgmental Observation:** Observing thoughts and emotions objectively.

  ○ Exercise: Mindful Breathing

  ○ How to Do It: Sit comfortably and focus on your breath. Observe your thoughts as they come and go, but instead of engaging with them, simply acknowledge their presence and let them pass like clouds in the sky.[6]

- **Connectedness**: Feeling in sync with one's body, environment, and the present.

  ○ Exercise: Grounding Your Senses

  ○ How to Do It: Sit or stand and focus on your current environment. Identify and acknowledge the sensations you feel—the ground beneath your feet, the air against your skin, the sounds surrounding you—to foster a sense of connection with the here and now.

- **Acceptance:** Embracing thoughts and emotions as passing experiences.

  ○ Exercise: Leaf on a Stream Visualization

○ How to Do It: Visualize sitting by a gently flowing stream. For every thought or emotion that comes to you, place it on a leaf and let it float down the stream. This visual symbolizes the acceptance and release of your thoughts and feelings.

- **Compassion:** Extending kindness to oneself and others.

  ○ Exercise: Loving-Kindness Meditation

  ○ How to Do It: Find a quiet space to sit. Close your eyes and think of someone you care about. Silently wish them happiness, health, and peace. Then, direct these wishes to yourself and gradually extend them to others, including those you find challenging.

As we find our center to soothe and focus our minds, we lay the groundwork for introspective exploration. This leads us to our next skill, reflective journaling. Here, in the quiet moments of reflection, we discover the transformative power of documenting our journey, thoughts, and aspirations.

SKILL 6:
REFLECTIVE JOURNALING

"Fill your paper with the breathings of your heart."
—William Wordsworth

R EFLECTIVE JOURNALING IS FAR MORE THAN JUST A RECOUNT-ing of daily events; it's an introspective journey into the very core of who you are. This practice opens a window into your essence, providing clarity amid life's routine chaos and helping you discover your unique voice. My personal journey with journaling began in a transformative Theory of Knowledge (TOK) class in high school, led by an inspiring teacher, Billy Miles. This class not only sparked my interest in philosophy but also introduced me to the discipline of daily journaling. Every day, we were tasked with reflecting on introspective topics, an exercise that significantly sharpened my analytical and reflective skills, allowing me to transform loosely structured ideas into more coherent thoughts.

Before this experience, my writing was primarily confined to note-taking, a passive process of recording information presented to me. However, I came to understand the profound difference between merely recording information and actively using writing as a tool for clarification and creative expression. This distinction, often emphasized by educators like my wife Amy, who holds a PhD in Education, highlights the dynamic nature of *making notes* compared to the passive act of *taking notes*. Making notes involves actively engaging with the material, observing, and reflecting, which not only cultivates higher-order thinking skills such as creativity and introspection but also improves information retention.

Reflective journaling elevates the process of making notes to a higher plane. It transcends the realms of creativity and reflection, transforming the practice into a powerful tool for self-discovery and personal growth. In reflective journaling, you're not just documenting events or thoughts; you're actively engaging with them, questioning and delving into their meanings and their impact on your life. This practice turns journaling into a profound journey of self-exploration and personal development.

The influence of reflective journaling is evident in the lives of many notable individuals. For instance, Leonardo da Vinci's journals reveal a visionary mind exploring a myriad of subjects, while Anne Frank's diary offers a poignant and deeply personal narrative of her experiences. Reflective journaling serves as a mirror to the soul, offering clarity, emotional catharsis, and a deeper understanding of oneself. Whether grappling with complex issues or observing the progression of your thoughts over time, journaling can be an incredibly insightful and therapeutic tool.

Additionally, journaling is an invaluable resource for fostering self-awareness. It provides a cathartic outlet for emotional release, which can alleviate stress, enhance mood, and offer clarity in problem-solving. It also gives you a unique perspective on the evolution of your thoughts and views over time. Engaging in consistent journaling, even if only briefly each week, can reveal fascinating patterns in your personal development that might otherwise remain hidden.

STARTING YOUR JOURNALING JOURNEY

Choosing a suitable medium for journaling can significantly influence your experience. My experience with digital platforms like DayOne and traditional paper diaries has shown that each has its merits. Digital journals are accessible and easily searchable, perfect for those on-the-go moments. On the other hand, paper journals offer a physical connection to your words, although they lack the searchability of their digital counterparts. To kickstart your reflective journey, consider using prompts like "What am I grateful for today?" or "What challenged me today, and how did I respond?"

Building a journaling habit takes commitment. Establishing a set time and space for writing can foster regularity in your practice. Equally important is ensuring the privacy of your reflections, whether through locking away your journal or password protecting your digital entries.

Journaling brings us closer to discovering our passions and going beyond self-awareness to ignite the desires that drive us. This understanding enriches our life story, adding vibrant layers to the narrative of who we are and what we aspire to achieve.

SKILL 7:
DISCOVERING YOUR PASSION

*"The only way to do great work is to love what you do.
If you haven't found it yet, keep looking. Don't settle."*
—Steve Jobs

DREAM BIG, BUT BE OPEN TO EVEN BIGGER DREAMS. Sometimes, you don't know what is possible. Or sometimes you don't know what you would like. Life is a process of self-discovery, and these things unfold in time. But be intentional about exploring and discovering what is possible and what you are passionate about so that you can take control of your journey to accomplish your dreams. It's about dreaming big and being open to the possibility that you are destined for something even more significant than you can imagine. Often, what we deem as the pinnacle of our desires is a prelude to what we can genuinely achieve or be.

Remember, discovering your passion is like embarking on a journey of exploration. The possibilities are limitless, and each step helps clarify what excites and motivates you. It's important to be open-minded and proactive in this search. Keep an eye out for what sparks deeper interest in all areas of life, as they can guide you toward your true passions. Your passion could exist in simple daily pleasures, like cooking or gardening, or in something else, such as coding or volunteering. It might emerge from creative expression in music, the fulfillment of contributing to your community, or the thrill of creating something new or innovative. With some introspection and soul-searching, you can unearth your calling in life with more clarity.

FINDING YOUR IKIGAI

An insightful approach for uncovering your calling is applying the Japanese concept of your *"ikigai"* (生き甲斐), which translates roughly to "a reason for being" or "a reason to wake up in the morning." One insightful interpretation of the *ikigai* concept represents the intersection of four elements: what you love, what you are good at, what the world needs, and what you can be paid for. When various aspects of your life are in harmony, a person can experience a deep sense of fulfillment and satisfaction in their daily life.

Four thought-provoking questions to get you started:

1. **What Do You Love?** This factor pertains to things you deeply enjoy or feel passionate about. It's about what you love doing so much that you lose track of time while engaged.

2. **What Are You Good At?** This element focuses on your skills and talents. It involves recognizing your strengths and what you excel at.

3. **What Does the World Need?** This aspect relates to how you can contribute to the world. It's about meeting the needs of others and making a meaningful impact.

4. **What Can You Be Paid For?** This component is about your livelihood, the practical aspect of earning a living, and sustaining yourself financially by doing what you love and are good at and what the world needs.

The central overlapping area in the *ikigai* diagram, where all four elements intersect, is the sweet spot where you might find your calling. Here, the idea is to find a balance that includes all these aspects, leading to satisfaction, happiness, and meaning in life.

(*) The lesser-known story about this diagram is that it's not really the Japanese version of *ikigai*. Many books have been written about the *ikigai* using the *Ikigai* Venn diagram, created by Marc Winn, who was inspired by Dan Buettner's research on Blue Zones (regions in the world where people have unusually long lifespans) and Andres Zuzunaga's diagram of "purpose."[7] While Winn admits his limited understanding of Japanese culture, this diagram has significantly popularized *ikigai* in the West. Nonetheless, it's important to recognize that the true essence of *ikigai* in Japanese culture extends beyond a Venn diagram, embodying a deeper and more holistic sense of life's purpose and fulfillment. Still, this insightful visualization, thanks originally to Zuzunaga, is a stroke of genius. It is a tremendously useful visual tool for clarifying personal purpose, which can be easily modified for individual use.

Find your inspiration from many sources, but ultimately, we are all unique, and *it is your own genius* that truly matters. Don't live somebody else's dream. Find *your* unique, passionate purpose and live your calling to its fullest.

To interpret the Ikigai diagram, you can start by reflecting on these four areas in your life. Ask yourself:

- What activities or subjects make you feel excited or deeply content?

- What are the strengths or talents that others recognize in you?

- In what ways can you contribute to society that are meaningful to you?

- How can you make a living by leveraging your passions and skills in a way that serves a greater cause?

Finding your *ikigai* is a personal journey and can be a fulfilling process of self-discovery and introspection. It's not just about making your next career choice; it's a broader perspective on finding harmony and fulfillment in various aspects of life.

Here's some advice to help you discover your life passion:

- **Reflect Often:** Regularly take stock of what excites you and what feels like a chore. Take time to think about your experiences. Which ones energize you? Which ones drain you? If you ever find yourself in a *state of flow* where engagement is so deep that everything else fades away, take note, as that's a good indication you are doing something you are passionate about. Writing down your thoughts can help you discern patterns and guide your next steps.

- **Stay Curious and Open-minded:** Let your interests guide and lead you to new interests. Read widely, try new activities, speak to people in various roles and career fields, take courses, or travel. Each new experience can help clarify what resonates with you. Make sure to branch out as you explore.

- **Challenge Yourself:** Challenging yourself is crucial in discovering your true passion. It's about stepping out of your comfort zone and embracing tests that reveal your deep-seated interests. For example, volunteering for a project can expose you to new ideas and roles, pushing you beyond familiar boundaries and possibly uncovering a hidden passion. Similarly, learning a new skill—be it a language, a craft, or a technical ability—can awaken an interest or talent you didn't know existed. These challenges are opportunities to explore and understand what truly resonates with you.

- **Talk About It:** Conversations can be enlightening. Share your search for passion with friends, mentors, and family. Their insights could open doors you hadn't considered. If you are a person of faith, pray about it.

- **Be Patient:** Finding your true passion can take time. It's a journey, not a sprint. Keep at it, and don't get discouraged if the answer isn't immediate.

I'VE DISCOVERED MY LIFE PASSION. NOW WHAT?

Be a person of action. Let's make it happen! The difference between a dream and a goal is the realism you bring to it. Remember the four P's—Passion, Possibility, Planning, and Productivity—as your roadmap to making your dreams real.

Four Steps for Making your Dreams Real

They represent the steps to the exciting process of 1) discovering your Passion, 2) exploring what's Possible, 3) making Plans to get there, and 4) being Productive along the way. This path takes vision, commitment, and discipline. As we talk about goal-setting and productivity, remember they're the practical steps to help you bring your passion to life. Be methodical, be enthusiastic, and take charge of your journey. The path to a life driven by passion starts with the steps you take today.

Remember that what is possible right now is not the limit of what is possible going forward. Building capability unlocks possibility. Proper planning and productivity will expand your limits and advance the boundary of realizing your passions and dreams.

The application of the four Ps—Passion, Possibility, Planning, and Productivity—is where the magic happens. It's where your dreams take flight on the wings of actionable steps. As we transition into the following skills of goal-setting and productivity, consider these the tools to construct the life you're passionate about. Dream big, explore relentlessly, plan wisely, and act diligently. This is your odyssey; chart your course to a life of passion fulfilled.

To recap, one way to remember key concepts in this chapter is with the acronym FOCUSED (Focusing your attention, Optimism, Comprehension of emotions in self and others, Unbreakable resilience + grit, Self-awareness through mindfulness, Exploring yourself through journaling, and Discovering your passion).

In mastering our minds, we've unlocked the power of understanding, resilience, and passion. This foundation sets us up for the next phase: transforming our aspirations into reality. Level 2 will guide us in setting and achieving meaningful goals.

LEVEL 2:
DREAM IT, THEN DO IT

D O YOU REMEMBER THAT KID WHO WANTED TO BE AN ASTRO-naut? Sometimes aspirations evolve, and other times, they never materialize. We've all encountered people who start with dreams and aspirations that slowly fade away, becoming forgotten echoes of what could have been. This narrative is far too common, yet it stops there, never seeing the light of day. Unfortunately, that's a story we often hear, but it doesn't have to be your story. To actually make your dreams into a reality, you need to set meaningful goals and produc-tively manage to achieve them. Think of goals as your personal GPS, guiding you toward excitement, purpose, and fulfillment. Whether it's nailing a career goal, chasing a wild passion, or leveling up your personal game, setting and smashing those goals feels amazing.

And guess what? Amping up your productivity is the turbo boost you need. Level 2 is about cracking the code of goal-setting, mastering the art of hitting your targets, and uncovering tools and habits that will send your productivity into the stratosphere. Let's learn how to turn your aspirations into your reality systematically!

Self-Assessment

As you get into the themes of strategic planning and productivity in Level 2, let's begin with a self-assessment to help you navigate these concepts more effectively. Reflect on these questions to connect the chapter's content with your personal and professional life. Write down the answers to these questions before starting the chapter.

1. **Vision for the Future:** What is your vision for the next five years? How do you see skills in strategic planning and productivity contributing to that vision?

2. **Current Planning Habits:** Reflect on your current planning habits. How do you prioritize and plan your daily activities? Are there areas where you feel your planning could be improved?

3. **Productivity Challenges:** What are the main challenges you face in being productive? How do you currently manage digital distractions and maintain focus?

4. **Habit Formation:** Think about a habit you've successfully formed in the past. What strategies did you use, and how might these strategies help you form the productive habits discussed in this chapter?

5. **"Good Enough" Concept:** How do you define "good enough" in your work or personal projects? Are you often striving for perfection, and how does this affect your productivity?

These questions are designed to prime your thinking and align your learning with your personal growth goals. As you explore strategic planning and productivity, use these reflections to guide your understanding and application of the skills in this chapter.

SKILL 8:
GOAL CRAFTING

---

*"The tragedy in life doesn't lie in not reaching your goal.
The tragedy lies in having no goal to reach."*
—Benjamin E. Mays

N AVIGATING LIFE WITHOUT GOALS IS LIKE VENTURING INTO A vast, dense jungle without a map or compass. You've likely heard the saying, "If you're not growing, you're dying." This holds true in life's quest for progression. Without setting meaningful goals, one can easily become mired in aimlessness and procrastination, like wandering in circles in an uncharted forest. Goals serve as our navigational tools, providing clear targets to head toward. They bridge the gap between dreaming and achieving, ensuring we don't spin our wheels in vain or, even worse, head in the wrong direction entirely. As we set and advance toward our goals, we gradually see our progress, much like a traveler moving closer to a destination, with each step marked by a compass. In the jungle of life, goals are our guide, offering us clarity and control, and steering us steadily toward where we want to be.

Effort is much more rewarding when you have a clear sense of direction and progression. Goals are not just markers of where we want to go; they activate our brain's reward system, fueling our motivation and commitment. Effective goal setting not only enhances self-confidence through clear markers of achievement but also streamlines the decision-making process. It provides a roadmap for your efforts, reducing stress by breaking down ambitious plans into manageable steps.

Setting goals goes hand-in-hand with cultivating a long-term vision, which is vital for achieving aspirations and realizing your full potential. Setting goals is pivotal in channeling your efforts efficiently and unlocking your capabilities in various areas of life.

My wife, Amy, who contended with asthma much of her life, decided to embrace long-distance running at the age of forty-four. She met her initial goal of finishing a half-marathon and then complemented her routine with strength training. Propelled by this achievement, she meticulously and quietly charted a course toward the challenge of running a marathon while I was serving in Poland and Ukraine. With steadfast dedication to enhancing her endurance, she triumphantly crossed the finish line of her first marathon months later. Tenacity and success are sometimes contagious. Inspired by her mother's tenacity, our twelve-year-old daughter Hannah joined the seventh-grade track team and began participating in races across Guatemala and El Salvador.

> **The key to effective goal setting lies in choosing goals that not only ignite your motivation to take action but, more importantly, guide you in the right direction!**

Setting your sights on a longer-term, inspirational vision is essentially the way to set a long-range goal. You want to set a vision, which is a broad, aspirational image of the future that you want to achieve. How do you set a vision? Build off your passion (see Skill 7) and spend quality time envisioning an ideal future. Some might call this vital process by different names, such as "envisioning," "dreaming up," or even "manifesting." Take an intentional and active role in essentially designing your ideal life. Doing this takes some soul searching because your goal may not be as ambitious or desirable as it could be.

It's of utmost importance that your goals inspire you. This visioning process is necessary, but it is not sufficient in itself. The point of goal setting is ultimately to clarify and get closer to where you want to be. Properly honed goals can help clarify the path to greatness, but it's crucial to break lofty goals into more manageable chunks by setting a balance of short-term and long-term goals. Short-term goals act as milestones for our larger, longer-term aspirations.

Make sure your goals are taking you in the right direction! To do this, first, make sure that your goals are in harmony with your core values or a broader cause. Also, regularly seek advice and input from knowledgeable and trusted individuals to challenge and refine your perspectives. Additionally, rigorously examine your assumptions and the data supporting them.

I'll share about a bizarre incident that once happened to me. When I was in Malawi, I took a class on wilderness navigation with some colleagues, which involved using a compass and a map to find our destination. I was certain I was using the compass correctly, but several of my colleagues were going in the opposite direction. I could have been stubborn and continued going against the grain, assuming everybody else was wrong, but I stopped to check why this was happening. It turned out that by some freak incident, my compass had suddenly flipped polarity, and my North was pointing South, and vice versa. I found out something was off by comparing my compass to others' compasses. The moral of this true story is that sometimes we might need to double-check our life navigational tools to ensure we are going in the right direction.

An excellent technique for chunking large, lofty, or long-term goals into more manageable pieces is to develop SMART Goals.

You want to establish high-quality, near-term goals. One way to do this is to make sure your goals are SMART—Specific, Measurable, Achievable, Relevant, and Time-bound—to transform vague dreams into actionable plans. Avoiding nebulous and unrealistic goals is critical to effective goal setting. For example, a non-SMART goal might be "I want to get fit," whereas a SMART goal is "I will run three times a week for thirty minutes to prepare for a 5K race in three months."

Let's break down the various aspects of a SMART goal:

- **Specific:** Clearly define what you want to accomplish, with as much detail as possible. Instead of saying, "I want to lose weight," specify, "I want to lose ten pounds."

- **Measurable:** Ensure your goal has concrete criteria for tracking progress and measuring outcomes. For weight loss, this could be tracking pounds lost or inches reduced.

- **Achievable:** Your goal should be realistic and attainable, not so lofty that it's out of reach. Losing ten pounds is more achievable than losing fifty pounds in a short time frame. Sometimes, setting incremental goals is motivating because improving something by 1% each time, for example, will lead to remarkable gains over time with focused consistency, thanks to setting achievable goals.

- **Relevant:** Ensure the goal is important to you and aligns with your other objectives. If improving health is a priority, weight loss could be a relevant goal.

- **Time-bound:** Set a deadline for reaching your goal to create a sense of urgency. For example, "I want to lose ten pounds in three months."

By applying these criteria, you create a goal that is clear, trackable, realistic, aligned with your values, and has a defined timeline, greatly enhancing the likelihood of success.

Just because a goal is SMART, doesn't automatically mean that it is wise. SMART is a handy way of smartening up your goals, but keep in mind that not all goals need to be SMART. Some of the more inspirational or longer-term ones (such as something closer to a vision statement) are unsuitable to put through the specificity of the SMART, which is okay. Bold goals are motivating! To do truly great things, your goals need to aim high. But when you want to translate your loftier into more immediate goals, you can build some SMART goals to help get you closer to your ultimate destination. So sometimes, perhaps non-SMART goals are smarter; more importantly, set goals that clarify your direction and move you forward.

Setting goals is only part of the puzzle. You can have the best map and compass in the world, but if you don't use it, then it is worthless. You must commit to goals, which requires prioritizing your time and focus to achieve them. Achieving goals takes focus and productive discipline. We will go into that in the following few skills.

SKILL 9:
PRIORITIZATION MASTERY

"Most of us spend too much time on what is urgent and not enough time on what is important."
—Stephen R. Covey

NOW THAT YOU HAVE YOUR GOALS SET, WHAT DO YOU DO first? Too many things demand our time daily, and knowing which items to focus on can be overwhelming. Ironically, an overwhelming to-do list with no focus will paralyze your progress. If you have ever heard of "analysis paralysis," that condition happens when you have too much to process, like an overloaded computer.

If *everything* is a "priority," then *nothing* is truly a priority.

It is impossible to do everything that is needed at the same time. That is why we need established priorities, which are those few items you are deciding to focus on before the other items. In my professional life, I've worked for bosses who call everything a priority. This approach is the antithesis of being strategic, which is poor leadership, as it leads to staff feeling overwhelmed and burned out. Especially when demands are overwhelming, when you prioritize something, you must deprioritize something else. Otherwise, the word "priority" loses its meaning. You need to apply principles to know what to prioritize and some tools to help make this process more efficient.

During my bustling senior year of high school, my friend Nicole handed me a thought-provoking book, *The 7 Habits of Highly Effective People* by Stephen Covey.[8] This book, arriving at a critical juncture in my life, impacted my thinking tremendously. Particularly impactful was the concept of "Put First Things First," teaching me to prioritize tasks based on importance, not urgency. This idea, rooted in Covey's Time Management Matrix, drew inspiration from former US President Dwight D. Eisenhower, who famously distinguished between the urgent and the important. Eisenhower's words, "The urgent are not important, and the important are never urgent,"[9] reshaped my perspective on decision-making and time management, guiding me toward better choices as I navigated the threshold of adulthood.

Covey's insightful Time Management Matrix is also known as the Eisenhower Box or the Eisenhower Matrix, and I've made a few modifications to modernize it:

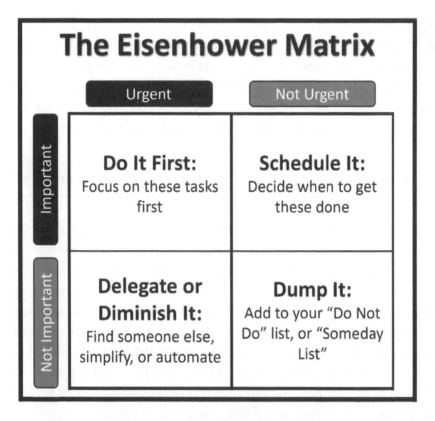

Categorize your tasks using the Eisenhower Matrix and achieve greater productivity and focus on your priorities:

- **Important and Urgent (upper-left quadrant):** These tasks are critical and require immediate attention. Examples include handling a crisis at home, school, or work, meeting a tight project deadline for an important project, or responding to an urgent family matter. Prioritize these and address them first.

- **Important but Not Urgent (upper-right quadrant):** These tasks are significant but don't require immediate action. Examples might be planning a future project, exercising for long-term health, or scheduling regular team meetings for ongoing projects. Set aside dedicated time to focus on these tasks, scheduling them into your calendar. You can also work on these projects over time.

- **Urgent but Not Important (lower-left quadrant):** These tasks demand attention but don't contribute significantly to your long-term goals or values. Examples include answering non-critical emails or phone calls or attending meetings with no direct relevance to your key responsibilities. Try to delegate these tasks whenever possible. If delegation isn't an option, see if you can streamline them by simplifying the process (e.g., decluttering or consolidating it) or using automation tools to remove your need to invest your mental energy into it.

- **Not Urgent and Not Important (lower-right quadrant):** These tasks neither require immediate action nor contribute to your goals. Examples could include mindlessly scrolling through social media or busywork with little value. Eliminate these tasks by adding them to your "Do Not Do" list, signifying a conscious decision not to engage with them, or place them on a "Someday List" if they might have future relevance. Doing so frees up more time and energy for the tasks that truly matter. Isn't that liberating?

By categorizing and addressing your tasks this way, you effectively streamline your workload, focusing on what truly matters and enhancing overall efficiency and productivity.

Be strategic with your life and your priorities. A crucial part of being strategic lies not just in the actions we take but equally in the ones we choose to leave behind. If you don't learn to draw healthy boundaries, you will be overrun. It's essential to be able to say no if you are overwhelmed with too many tasks or demands, especially those originating from others. Everybody has a limit; carrying too much and trying to do it all can be paralyzing and not good for your well-being. Learn to draw boundaries. You can still be diplomatic in how you say no (or even a "yes, but") if you must. *Don't be a doormat, or you will get walked on.*

HOW DO YOU KNOW WHICH TASKS ARE IMPORTANT?

Those tasks that either further your goals or that you have personally invested value in are important ones. Those are the ones that matter and lead to your longer-term fulfillment.

Don't forget to invest in things that add higher-level capability to do the important stuff. In other words, creating leverage is important. Rather than focusing on getting things done, building and strengthening the systems, processes, tools, and skills for improving things is important. For instance, reading this book and learning these skills is an important priority because investing in developing these skills makes you more effective in life.

Speaking of getting things done, next you will learn how to equip yourself with tools that make you more productive.

SKILL 10:
SYSTEMATIZING PRODUCTIVITY

"Productivity is never an accident. It is always the result of a commitment to excellence, intelligent planning, and focused effort."
—Paul J. Meyer

ONCE YOU HAVE FINALLY CLARIFIED YOUR GOALS AND PRI-oritized your tasks, you need to get stuff done with productivity. To work smarter, not harder, applying leverage is key. Some people refer to the 80/20 rule (or the Pareto principle), a principle of leverage to focus on the 20% of things that help you achieve 80% of results.[10]

One main way to create leverage is through systemization, *your secret weapon!* It's about building and strengthening the systems, processes, tools, and skills that improve efficiency and effectiveness. Creating leverage means investing in elements that amplify your efforts and yield greater returns.

Imagine transforming mundane, everyday tasks into a symphony of efficiency. This transformation is possible when you harness the power of automation. Digital tools that manage finances, schedule appointments, or even automate household chores like cleaning and grocery shopping become catalysts, freeing up precious time and energy. This newfound freedom opens doors to engaging in activities that truly matter, allowing you to chase personal aspirations with renewed vigor.

Another aspect of leverage is developing skills that have broad applications. For instance, improving your communication skills enhances personal relationships and boosts professional opportunities. Similarly, learning to code isn't just about writing software; it's a way of thinking logically and solving problems, which is valuable in many life areas.

Systematizing productivity is about setting up structures that support consistent and efficient output. Doing this involves creating routines, utilizing productivity tools, and regularly reviewing and adjusting your strategies to ensure they remain aligned with your goals.

Work smarter, not just harder. Leverage systems, tools, and creative resources to multiply your productivity and achieve goals faster.

If you learn to put systems in place, you can multiply your productivity many times over. These typically include software or apps that help you organize tasks, manage time, and streamline your work to increase efficiency and achieve goals faster. They're not just apps; they're your digital partners in the quest to get stuff done—efficiently and without the stress.

The speed of technology has accelerated to unbelievable paces. In today's fast-paced world, using the right tools and technology can make a difference in your productivity and quality of life. Mastering the right tools offers a competitive edge in all areas of life, be it professional or personal. I place a high value on investing in identifying and using valuable tools because they provide substantial leverage. Productivity tools liberate valuable time and mental energy by automating routine tasks or streamlining complex processes. This freedom allows me to focus on more significant pursuits requiring creativity, strategic thinking, and personal touch.

THE COPE METHOD

In response to the overwhelming demands on our time, I developed the COPE Method to systematically enhance productivity by effectively leveraging the best tools.

The COPE Method provides a systematic, four-stage way to cope with the multiple demands on your time, applying leverage to achieve higher productivity. The idea is that you need a leveraged way to

Capture what needs to get done (your time demands), then **Organize** those demands (applying prioritization and focus), and then **Produce** (getting stuff done efficiently and effectively). You use tools and systems for each step to maximize productivity. Lastly, you **Evaluate** the outcomes, learning from successes and failures, and making adjustments for future endeavors.

Let's go into more detail on the COPE Method and understand which tools can help at each stage.

Capture:

The first phase of the COPE Method focuses on capturing all tasks, ideas, and responsibilities as they come to mind. This step is crucial because ideas and to-dos often strike spontaneously and can easily be forgotten if not captured or noted down. Whether through digital apps or traditional methods like pen and paper, the key is to have a reliable system to ensure that important thoughts, needs, or ideas are captured at the right moment and not lost in the shuffle of daily activities. Getting it from your thoughts to a captured form reduces your cognitive load.

I generally carry Post-it notes and a pen with me wherever I go. If I think of something that needs to be done or have an idea I want to capture, I write it on a Post-it note. Either I'm old-fashioned that way, or perhaps it is easier for quick capture. Later, when I'm back at my computer, I transfer my Post-it notes into my digital to-do list. However, some great tools exist for digitally capturing these thoughts, such as voice memos.

A pen can be a lifesaver! Carrying a pen and something to write on goes back to my college days as a volunteer Emergency Medical Technician (EMT) at the Williamsburg Fire Department. I would never want to be without something to write with during medical emergencies, and I didn't have a smartphone back then, so I carried a pen. That way, when taking a patient's vital signs, I could write everything down in the moment. Later on, as a management consultant, I also started carrying Post-it notes because I never knew when to break out a facilitation session to brainstorm new ideas. Post-it notes are just so helpful; they can even help save lives. This method is an excellent example of creating leverage with sometimes simple tools. I have found that writing down critical thoughts at the right moment is an investment in amplifying my efforts and results in greater returns over time.

- **Note-Taking:** Digital tools like OneNote, Evernote, or Notion are handy for spontaneously jotting down ideas, lecture notes, or tasks. Handy apps like Otter also exist for recording and transcribing meetings.

- **Post-it Notes and Pen:** A classic method for immediate idea capture, especially when digital tools aren't available. Did you know the mere act of physically writing with pen and paper engages multiple sensory and cognitive processes, contributing to improved memory retention compared to typing on a keyboard?

- **Email Management:** Sometimes tasks arrive via email. There are ways to organize that better so you extract the actionable stuff from the inbox.

Organize:
After you've captured your tasks and ideas, the next crucial step is to organize them. Organizing them requires sorting, prioritizing, and scheduling each item to transform a jumble of thoughts into an actionable plan. Effective organization involves ranking tasks by importance and urgency and strategically allocating time and resources. Using the right tools can streamline this process, helping to categorize

tasks, establish deadlines, and delegate responsibility when necessary, thus forming a clear roadmap for execution.

- **Task Management Tools**: Using organizational apps like Todoist or Google Tasks will help you prioritize them effectively. For visual project planning and organization, tools like Trello can be helpful.

- **Scheduling Tools**: Ensure efficient allocation of your time with tools such as Google Calendar, which will help you manage schedules, track deadlines, and remember appointments.

- **Project Management Platforms**: For handling more complex tasks and team collaborations, team-centric platforms like Clickup, Asana, or Monday.com can help offer a comprehensive view and control over various project elements.

- **Document Management Systems**: Organize and store your files and documents systematically using platforms like Google Drive, facilitating easy access and organization.

Produce:

The third phase of the COPE Method is about production—actually getting things done (GTD). This stage is where efficiency and effectiveness come into play. Using the right tools can significantly enhance productivity by helping manage time effectively, automate repetitive tasks, and facilitate smooth communication and collaboration. The goal here is not to be merely busy but to be productive, ensuring that the time and effort invested yield meaningful results. Using leverage, you want more output using less input.

- **Time Management:** Apps like Be Focused, a Pomodoro timer, optimize time for focused work sessions. I tend to use countdown timers on my watch or smartphone.

- **Workflow Automation:** Apps like Zapier and IFTTT streamline routine tasks, freeing up time for more crucial work.

- **Communication & Collaboration:** Platforms like Discord, Slack, or Google Chat spaces can enhance team interaction and joint project work.

- **Artificial Intelligence (AI):** AI tools like ChatGPT or emerging alternative AI platforms, detailed in Level 5, can automate various tasks and quickly evolve.

Evaluate:

The final phase of the COPE Method is about learning and adapting, assessing the outcomes of your actions, learning from successes and failures, and adjusting. Evaluating could involve reflecting on the efficiency of the process and tools, the quality of the output, and the achievement of desired goals. It is important to engineer feedback loops to apply continuous learning to keep upgrading your approaches and tools.

By effectively leveraging tools in each stage, you can maximize your productivity, leading to better time management and overall success in both personal and professional settings.

As savvy as these tools are, they're just the start. And sometimes, you've got to strip it back to basics—a good old pen and paper can work wonders. The best tool is your brain! Use your brain to invest in your skills and tooling, and you will reap immense payback from that worthy investment. It is essential to systematically try out new tools and find what works for you.

The main goal is learning to implement productivity systems to leverage how you address demands on your time, prioritize, and get things done. Owning your time is owning your life. How can you make every hour count?

SKILL 11:
TIME MANAGEMENT

"Time is what we want most, but what we use worst."
—William Penn

Have you ever had a day where it felt like time flew by faster than you could blink, and then another day where the day grinds, time slows down, and it seems the day will never end? How we perceive time varies.

People are wired to think about time differently, both philosophically and practically. Time is rigid and obeyed by some; it is more fluid to others. I've been to over fifty countries, and I can tell you that time is measured, experienced, and managed quite differently in different cultures worldwide. Even in my own family, there are fundamental differences in how time is perceived and experienced. However, the one thing we all share as human beings is that our time on Earth is limited. Not just our limited lifespans, but the usable time for each of our years is limited.

Let's do some basic math. Each of us has 8,760 hours in a year (excluding leap years, of course), or 365 days with twenty-four hours a day. Then, we must subtract the hours we are asleep. Young adults typically require about seven to nine hours of sleep per night for optimal health and functioning. So, after accounting for an average of eight hours of sleep per night, we have approximately 5,840 hours available in a regular year. So, you pull some all-nighters, no problem, let's round that to 6,000 waking hours. The question of the year is, how will you spend your precious 6,000 waking hours this year?

TIME MANAGEMENT

So, you've set your priorities, but how do you execute them efficiently? What does it mean to "manage time?" Time management is not just about squeezing as many tasks as possible into your day; it's about *optimizing* your time. It involves understanding, planning, and effectively controlling the time spent on activities, ensuring that you *focus on what truly matters*.

Fresh out of college, I embarked on a management consulting career at PricewaterhouseCoopers. My first consulting project was called the Transit-time Management System (TTMS). This multi-million-dollar program was responsible for dissecting and optimizing the journey of mail within the United States Postal Service, from its origin to destination. In this environment, I transformed into an efficiency aficionado. Time, in all its fleeting and precious nature, became our team's focal obsession. This experience didn't just contribute to the project; it laid the cornerstone of my understanding of time management, a skill I quickly learned that was vital not only in the business world but also in every facet of life.

TAKING STOCK OF YOUR TIME USAGE

A solid first step in managing time is to conduct a personal time analysis. This process involves keeping logs of how you spend your time. Because we can experience time in a highly variable way, how you spend your hours is not necessarily how you perceive it. Therefore, taking stock of how you spend your time can be surprising and insightful. The insights from these logs can be eye-opening, revealing patterns and habits, both productive and unproductive.

This process requires tracking your daily activities to gain fundamental insights into how you actually spend your hours. By doing a time analysis, you get a reality check on how you're using (or misusing) your time. It's a decisive step toward becoming more productive and making time for what truly matters to you. You might consider using time-tracking tools, such as Toggl or Clockify, to make a time analysis easier.

ALIGNING TO YOUR CIRCADIAN CYCLES

Your biology can have a significant impact on your time management, for better or for worse. One of the insights you can gain from a personal time analysis is understanding your chronotype, which is part of your circadian rhythm. Your circadian rhythm is an internal clock that cycles roughly every twenty-four hours, influencing various physiological processes, including sleep-wake patterns.[11] Your chronotype refers to where you naturally fall within this cycle, determining whether you're more alert in the morning or evening. Understanding both your circadian rhythm and your chronotype is crucial for recognizing your daily energy levels and optimizing your time management accordingly.

Align your work with your body's natural rhythms. Schedule tasks when you're most alert and creative for maximum productivity.

Understanding your body's unique rhythms is vital. Everyone has times of the day when they are most alert and creative. Some people are morning people (larks), and others might be night people (night owls). For example, if I need to do creative work, I know that I'm more productive in the morning before lunch, so I try to schedule creative work earlier in the day.

Here's how it usually goes, although yours might differ: In the late morning, most people hit their peak in alertness and brainpower. That's your golden hour for tackling the tough stuff—studying for exams, writing essays, or working on complex projects. Post-lunch, you might hit a bit of a slump. Don't sweat it; it's normal. Use this time for lighter activities, like organizing your workspace or catching up on readings. Then, as the afternoon rolls on, you'll likely get a second wind—a perfect opportunity to dive back into more demanding tasks.

So, work with your body's natural rhythm instead of trying to power through when your energy's low. Schedule your day around these peaks and dips. It's about working with your body, not working against it. This way, you get more done without burning out. For instance, I generally like to focus on important tasks or decisions when my energy peak is high and do other things (including recharge) when my energy point is lower. Remember, it's not just about how long you work; it's about how smart you work with the time you have. Once you understand your rhythm better, you can use that to plan your day strategically.

PLANNING OUT YOUR DAY WITH STRATEGIC TIME-BLOCKING

Time blocking allows you to divide your day into segments, each dedicated to a specific task. You can be strategic by planning your day as much as possible around your circadian rhythms.

Here's a step-by-step guide on how to do it:

1. **List Your Tasks:** Write down everything you need to do, including work, personal errands, and breaks.

2. **Prioritize:** Determine which tasks are most important.

3. **Estimate Time:** Decide how much time each task will likely take.

4. **Divide Your Day:** Break your day into blocks of time, which can vary in length based on the task.

5. **Strategically Schedule Tasks:** Place each task into a time block, focusing on priority and your most productive times (per your circadian rhythms) for specific tasks. Matching up your energy with your task is critical; for example, you wouldn't want to schedule risky decisions or delicate conversations at a low-energy point.

6. **Group Similar Tasks:** It's generally more efficient to do similar tasks in batches than to switch tasks, as this minimizes cognitive load.

7. **Include Breaks:** Ensure you have short breaks to maintain focus.

8. **Adjust as Needed:** At the end of the day or week, review your schedule and adjust for the next day or week.

Time blocking helps create a clear plan for your day, reduces decision fatigue, and ensures essential tasks get completed.

POMODORO TECHNIQUE - TAKE YOUR TASK IN STRIDE

Do intensive work in well-timed spurts. The Pomodoro Technique, created by Francesco Cirillo in the 1980s, is a simple way to boost focus and manage time effectively. The technique gets its name from the tomato-shaped kitchen timer that Cirillo used as a university student, "pomodoro," the Italian word for tomato.[12] Here's a quick rundown:

1. **Pick a Task:** Choose what you need to work on.

2. **Set a Timer for Twenty-five Minutes:** This is your work time. Any countdown will do. I use the timer on my watch or smartphone.

3. **Work Hard, No Distractions:** Focus only on your task.

4. **Take a Five-Minute Break:** Relax, stretch, or just chill.

5. **Repeat:** After four rounds, take a longer break (fifteen to twenty minutes).

The Pomodoro Technique is effective because it matches our brain's natural attention span. It uses short, focused work intervals (usually twenty-five minutes) followed by breaks. This technique keeps your brain fresh and prevents burnout, making large tasks feel more manageable. It also helps minimize distractions, knowing a break is coming soon. Plus, completing each interval gives a sense of accomplishment, boosting motivation.

Remember, time management is a skill that can be learned and refined, but it all starts with time awareness. By taking control of your time, you take control of your life, leading to greater productivity, less stress, and more success in all your endeavors.

SKILL 12:
DIGITAL DETOX

"Almost everything will work again if you unplug it for a few minutes, including you."
—Anne Lamott

I N SKILL 1, WE DISCUSSED THE OVERWHELMING INFLUX OF IN-formation in our digital age. With the prevalence of smart devices, our attention is constantly bombarded by a stream of digital content.

Human beings are largely a device-connected species now. As of 2024, 66% of the world uses the internet and spends an average of six to seven hours daily on the internet, according to DataReportal.[13] This incredible level of internet usage isn't just about doomscrolling on social media or binging the latest series. Everything from school to work has gone digital, and internet use has become a way of life.

However, too much screen time can be "toxic" to our health. We're talking headaches, fatigue, and even serious stuff like social isolation, anxiety, and heart disease. Plus, being stuck to your screen usually means sitting down a lot, which isn't great for your physical health.

Sometimes, trying to divert my kids' attention away from their computers and games is akin to peeling superglue off a delicate glass— both tricky and fraught with potential backlash. The grumpiness that ensues when we remove their devices is a testament to how addictive digital media can be. These are real withdrawal symptoms too, like a coffee addict might feel without their morning cup. This addiction isn't age-specific; too much digital exposure can adversely affect anyone. Like any potent substance, digital consumption needs moderation. The addictive nature of digital technology affects dopamine levels, similar to the effects of certain drugs.

Even Steve Jobs, Mr. iPad himself, would agree with this one! In an eye-opening revelation, Jobs, the billionaire founder of Apple, reportedly didn't allow his teenage daughter to use an iPad when it was first released.[14] In an interview held two years after the release of the iPad, Jobs was asked about the revolutionary product. "Your kids must love the iPad?" Jobs responded, "Actually, we don't allow the iPad in the home. We think it's too dangerous for them, in effect." His decision speaks volumes about the need for mindful digital consumption.

Digital technology, while enhancing productivity in many facets, also poses the risk of information overload and unproductive distraction. The relationship we have with our digital devices requires careful balance. Overindulgence can derail us from our goals and impact our mental well-being and even our cognitive functioning.

HOW INFORMATION OVERLOAD LOWERS YOUR WORKING IQ (INTELLIGENCE QUOTIENT)

Information overload, characterized by an excessive influx of information from various sources like emails, phone calls, and instant messages, has significantly impacted cognitive functions, which we could say taxes your "working IQ."

While digital technology can boost productivity, it can also lead to information overload, affecting mental well-being and working IQ. Excessive digital information from emails, calls, and messages impairs focus and cognitive sharpness. One study revealed that constant digital exposure can lower IQ by ten points, akin to the effect of sleep deprivation.[15] This 'info-mania' is widespread, with many addicted to continual digital connectivity, adversely affecting work performance and decision-making.

The brain's limited working memory gets overwhelmed, reducing the efficiency and quality of cognitive functions. Furthermore, multitasking, often mistaken for productivity, actually decreases information intake and focus.[16]

Constant task-switching hinders the brain's performance, similar to overloading a smartphone with apps. Managing this digital overload is essential, with strategies like setting boundaries and focusing on one task at a time to maintain cognitive health in today's digital world.

HOW TO RECLAIM YOUR BRAIN
WITH A DIGITAL DETOX

Consider the human brain as a muscle that needs rest. Just as physical muscles require recovery time post-exercise, our cognitive faculties need respite from the relentless digital onslaught. Incessant digital stimuli tax our mental resources more than we often realize.

Regular digital detoxes, whether monthly or even weekly, can have profoundly positive effects on various aspects of life. These detoxes contribute to improved focus, as reduced screen time minimizes distractions and enhances concentration on tasks at hand. A significant benefit of digital detoxes is the improvement in sleep patterns, especially when screen use is limited before bedtime. This practice not only fosters better rest but also positively impacts mental health, leading to reduced anxiety and heightened overall well-being. Moreover, digital detoxes pave the way for increased in-person interactions, which are crucial for strengthening relationships.

To make the most of these detox periods, consider indulging in outdoor activities, which are excellent for stress relief and mood enhancement. Reading is another enriching alternative; it expands your knowledge, boosts brain function, and enriches emotional depth. Additionally, engaging in mindfulness practices, pursuing creative hobbies, partaking in physical exercise, and learning new skills offer a well-rounded approach to taking a break from screens. Such activities not only provide a respite from digital consumption but also contribute to personal growth and emotional balance.

A digital detox involves consciously reducing or eliminating digital device usage for a set period. Here's how to approach it:

1. **Set a Detox Duration:** Start with a manageable period, like a weekend or a certain number of daily hours.

2. **Notify Contacts:** Inform friends and colleagues to set expectations about your limited availability.

3. **Plan Alternative Activities:** Engage in non-digital activities like reading, outdoor sports, or spending time with family.

4. **Physical Distance:** Keep your devices in another room or use apps that limit your usage.

5. **Reflect:** Use this time to introspect and reconnect with your non-digital interests and passions.

Taking a break from your screens and doing a digital detox isn't just about cutting down on social media or gaming time; it's a great way to level up your brain's control center. Think of it as a workout for skills like staying focused, making smart plans, and keeping cool when things change. By stepping away from your devices, you're practicing how to resist those constant pings and notifications, which is like training your brain to wait for better rewards.

Engaging in a digital detox is potent in strengthening executive function skills. These skills, including self-control, planning, decision-making, and flexible thinking, are essential for successful self-regulation.

Not to mention, it's good to exercise your brain and not always use technology as a crutch. Planning a detox means getting creative with your time and finding new ways to relax or get stuff done without relying on tech. This practice, while perhaps initially daunting, is an opportunity for personal growth. Not only does it exercise your brain, but it also helps in finding a healthy balance between digital and real-world experiences, enhancing life beyond the digital sphere.

SKILL 13:
FINDING THE GOOD ENOUGH

"Don't let the perfect be the enemy of the good."
—often attributed to Voltaire

LEARN TO STRIKE THE RIGHT BALANCE BETWEEN QUALITY AND time. Perfectionism stems from too much emphasis on the quality of your work while disregarding or overlooking the time allocated to the task. Such an imbalance can lead to a slow and painful death of productivity. On the other hand, too much focus on speed over quality can cut corners and lead to sloppy results.

A perfectionistic friend spent hours trying to put shingles on his roof perfectly. He spent several weeks on the whole project, aiming to align each shingle perfectly. The project was nearly complete when a storm blew off the temporary covering he was using for the unfinished portion. Unfortunately, the roof got water damage. Had he gone a little faster and found a "good enough" standard for those shingles, he would have finished in half the time and not suffered the storm damage. On the other hand, had he gone too fast, he could have improperly installed the shingles, which might have required fixing later. The key is finding the optimum good enough standard that is both time-efficient and quality-sufficient.

**Learn to "satisfice" by seeking the optimum
balance of quality and time.***

---

* "Satisfice" is a decision-making strategy that aims for a good-enough result, which is also useful skill. The word is a blend of "satisfy" and "suffice," and it was coined by the American economist and cognitive psychologist Herbert A. Simon in 1956. Herbert A. Simon, "Rational Choice and the Structure of the Environment," Psychological Review 63, no. 2 (1956): 129-138, https://doi.org/10.1037/h0042769.

Finding the "good enough" doesn't mean cutting corners at all. But it is a form of prioritization. If you are getting buried in a singular task and trying to perfect it, ignoring all the other priorities, then you are at risk of losing the war to win a battle concerning your time allocations.

Especially when you have too much to do, make sure to draw a clear boundary that is good enough. When you get there, stop and move to the next priority. That will prevent you from sinking into a productivity death spiral.

Warning: one person's good enough is not another person's good enough. It's essential to hold standards that are suitable to your purpose. Don't compromise your standards, and know when to move forward. Too much perfectionism can be unhealthy, and it can backfire.

SKILL 14:
FORMING BETTER HABITS

"We are what we repeatedly do.
Excellence, then, is not an act, but a habit."
—Aristotle

I F YOU WANT TO BE EXCELLENT, DEVELOP EXCELLENT HABITS. Learning how to make, break, and re-engineer your habits is foundational to your success in life. Think about it—your habits are like your own personal code that can launch you to success or be your biggest stumbling block. But here's the good news: you have the power to shape who you want to be, thanks to neuroplasticity.

Picture your brain as this super flexible network, buzzing with neurons (your brain cells). Every time you repeat a habit, these neurons get better at talking to each other. It's like blazing a trail in the woods; the more you walk it, the more apparent it gets. This phenomenon is neuroplasticity—your brain's extraordinary skill of adapting and forming new connections throughout your life.[17]

Every new skill you learn, every fresh habit you start, even just switching up your day-to-day routine, is helping your brain build new pathways. It's like your brain's version of road construction, adding new routes and improving the old ones.

HABIT FORMATION

During my early teenage years, marked by a blend of mischief and a strong disdain for cigarette smoke—a common vice among friends and some family members—I embarked on a unique crusade against smoking. Armed with a pack of rubber bands for every pack of cigarettes they purchased, I developed a peculiar talent for shooting cigarettes right from their lips. I certainly don't recommend anybody doing this; I'm sure to the smokers, it was sometimes dangerous and really annoying (by design), and so there were moments I was sure I was going to get pummeled. Despite my best efforts, their smoking habits persisted, unaffected by my rubber band intervention. It turns out that habits, whether good ones or bad ones, are pretty hard to change. That is unless you know more about how they work.

Habits are like a loop—there's a cue (something that sets you off), a routine (what you do), and a reward (that sweet payoff that makes you want to do it again).

Your brain loves to save energy, so when you do something often, it turns it into a habit. That way, you don't have to put much thought into it. It's like how a family got healthier by slowly changing their eating habits—it wasn't an overnight thing; they tweaked their routines until healthy eating became their new normal.

Whom you associate with is also super important. You tend to become more like those you hang around. It's human nature. Therefore, associate with people who are positive, success-minded, and encouraging; these are the kinds of friends who will help inspire you to be a better version of yourself and not the other way around. Avoid spending too much time around people who are negative, fatalistic, and discouraging.

When you start a new habit, your brain starts carving out a new neural path. Sure, it's challenging at first, but it gets easier with practice. And the opposite is true, too—stop a habit, and those neural paths get used less, eventually fading away. The trick? Repetition. The more you repeat a habit, the more automatic it becomes.

TIPS FOR HABIT MASTERY

Start Small
- Choose a tiny habit you want to build. Big changes start with small beginnings.

Consistency is Key
- Do your new habit at the same time and place every day.

Patience Pays Off
- Building new habits takes time. Stick with it.

Stack Your Habits
- Piggyback new habits onto things you already do.

Stay Positive
- Your attitude matters. A positive mindset helps cement new habits.

LEARN HABIT ENGINEERING FROM THE PROS

Your habits, good or bad, shape who you are. You can improve yourself by engineering better habits. James Clear's book, *Atomic Habits*, is insightful for understanding how to form good habits and break bad ones. I recommend you add Clear's book to your reading list, or he also offers an excellent Masterclass if you prefer to listen. Clear lays out a simple, incremental approach to change. Make it obvious, attractive, easy, and satisfying—these are his critical principles for engineering your habits.

Clear fleshes out four core techniques for transforming your habits.[18]

1. Make It Obvious:

- This principle focuses on the power of cues in our environment. To form a new habit, make the cues for it blatantly obvious. For example, keep a book on your pillow if you want to start reading more. Clear suggests using the "habit stacking" formula: "After [CURRENT HABIT], I will [NEW HABIT]" to build new routines.

- Conversely, reduce exposure to the triggering cues to break a bad habit. If you're trying to minimize screen time, keep your phone in another room while you work or study.

2. Make It Attractive:

- Make the habits you want to adopt more appealing. One technique Clear suggests is "temptation bundling," which involves linking an action you want to do with an action you need to do. For instance, only listen to your favorite podcast while exercising.

- The idea is to associate the hard habits with positive experiences, making them more desirable and something you're excited to do.

3. Make It Easy:

- Simplicity is key here. The easier a habit is, the more likely you will stick to it. Reduce the friction associated with good habits. If you want to start jogging every morning, lay out your workout clothes the night before. As another example, one thing I do to make eating a healthy breakfast easier is to prepare a six-day batch of healthy seed and nut mix for my Greek yogurt in mini-containers once weekly. The pour-over packages make a healthy breakfast more convenient.

- For breaking habits, increase the friction. If you spend too much time on social media, delete the apps or log out after each use to make mindless scrolling less convenient.

4. Make It Satisfying:

- We're more likely to repeat a habit if it's satisfying. Clear advises adding an element of immediate gratification to your habits. For example, if you complete a study session, reward yourself with something enjoyable, like a piece of chocolate or a short break to do something you love.

- Use a habit tracker for visual proof of your progress. Seeing a chain of successful days can be highly motivating to keep the streak going.

OUR HABITS AND IDENTITY ARE CONNECTED

James Clear emphasizes the importance of identity in shaping our habits and goals. For instance, if you aspire to be an aerospace engineer like my son David, you must embody that identity now and develop the right habits. This journey is more than just acing your math and physics classes (though those are fundamental). It involves immersing yourself in the identity aligned with your goals. In David's case, that is the world of aerospace engineering.

David began by immersing himself in aerospace technology and industry trends. He regularly attended relevant events, followed influential aerospace figures and companies, and kept up to date with the latest research and developments. David actively thought about solving real-world engineering problems and engaged in related projects, even building models and simulations. He and a small group from school engineered a high-altitude weather balloon that successfully reached through the stratosphere in Guatemala. *Now, that's leveling up!*

This proactive approach wasn't just about gaining knowledge but about aligning his current identity with his future self as an aerospace engineer. He started thinking and acting like an engineer, focusing on design, function, and innovation. This method is about more than just preparing for a future role; it's about embodying it in the present.

MAKE SMALL, INCREMENTAL IMPROVEMENTS

Then, there's this idea of making tiny improvements—even just 1% better each time. It might not sound like much, but these little changes add up. Think of it like leveling up in a game; each small step might not seem huge, but you're suddenly way ahead of where you started as they stack up.

It's about being consistent, not trying to overhaul your life overnight. These small, steady changes can accumulate into massive growth over time, like a snowball rolling down a snowy hill. So, focus on those little wins, and watch how they transform your life in the long run!

**Small, consistent improvements lead to
transformation and excellence over time.**

Consistency matters! In 2009, a medical researcher, Phillippa Lally, conducted a study to determine how long it takes to form a new habit, and she found it takes between eighteen to 254 days (with an average of sixty-six days) to turn a new behavior into a habit.[19]

According to Dr. BJ Fogg, a leading behavior scientist and author of *Tiny Habits*, the process of forming habits is gradual, with each day of practice building on the next. He recommends breaking down the desired behavior into tiny steps to make it more manageable and easier to stick to. He also suggests rewarding yourself for taking small steps toward your goal to motivate yourself to keep going. The amount of time it takes to form a new habit is debated, but some experts suggest that the time it takes to form a new habit depends on individual motivation and commitment to the process.[20]

Fogg developed a behavior model maintaining that three factors must simultaneously be present for a behavior to occur: Motivation, Ability, and a Prompt (or a trigger or cue). When a behavior does not occur, at least one of these three factors is missing. B=MAP (Behavior = Motivation + Ability + Prompt) is a way to remember this. To develop new habits, make sure you have these three factors.[21]

Forming new habits and mastering new skills takes focus, time, and effort. Patience and persistence in your journey and celebrating even the most minor successes are essential. With each day of practice, you are building on the last and getting closer to your goals. Remember to be kind to yourself and keep going, even when progress is slow. You can form new life-changing, brain-rewiring habits with patience, persistence, and dedication.

As a recap, a way to help remember the key concepts in this chapter is ASPIRES (**A**im setting, **S**trategic prioritization, **P**roductivity tools and systems, **I**ntentional time management, **R**efresh by detoxing, **E**nough as in good enough, and **S**trategic habit formulation).

By incorporating these principles, you can more effectively shape your daily routines and habits, leading to lasting positive changes in your life. Remember, it's not just about setting goals; it's about the system you follow to achieve them. Engineering better habits is a way to be a better version of yourself.

Having learned to set and pursue our goals effectively, we now possess a clear direction for our lives. This clarity in purpose and action paves the way to Level 3, where we embrace a healthy lifestyle integral to sustaining our achievements.

LEVEL 3:
NOURISH YOUR BODY AND MIND*

E VER FEEL LIKE YOU'RE RUNNING ON EMPTY? LET'S CHANGE that. Today's choices are tomorrow's outcomes. In our fast-paced, instant-gratification world, it's easy to put health on the back burner. But what if you could unlock high-octane energy to power through your day?

Level 3 is about turbocharging your life. We're talking nutrition that fuels your adventures, exercise that makes you feel unstoppable, and sleep that supercharges your brain. This chapter takes a comprehensive or *holistic* approach, meaning you consider all aspects of your being, encompassing the importance of the whole and the interdependence of all factors, including physical, mental, social, etc. We explore the foundations of biohacking, which focuses on optimizing various aspects of your body and mind through evidence-based, incremental changes in diet, exercise, sleep, and other techniques to improve overall performance and well-being.

Plus, we'll dive into mindfulness and stress-busting techniques to keep you energized and ready for whatever comes your way. Level up to nourish your body and mind like never before and take on life's adventures with flair and unstoppable energy!

---

*   *Disclaimer:* This chapter (Level 3) has been medically reviewed by Dr. Nour Hassan, a certified and registered nutritionist and medical physician. However, it is not intended to offer direct medical advice. Individual health needs and conditions vary greatly. Therefore, always consult your physician or healthcare provider before beginning any nutritional or exercise program.

Self-Assessment

As we head into Level 3, it's time to reflect on how we nourish our body and mind. This chapter is about building a physical and mental wellness foundation that supports all other life skills. Consider these questions to align your learning with the chapter's focus. Write down the answers to these questions before starting the chapter.

1. **Physical Wellness:** Consider your diet, exercise routine, and sleep habits. Are there areas you would like to improve? How do you see your body as an integrated unit?

2. **Mental Well-being:** Reflect on your current methods for managing stress and mental health. What practices do you find most beneficial?

3. **Nutrition and Cooking:** How confident are you in your nutritional knowledge and cooking skills? Are there specific aspects you're eager to learn more about? What are ways to eat freely while maintaining healthy eating habits?

4. **Integrating Fitness:** Think about your current fitness routine. Are you looking for new strategies to integrate fitness more effectively into your life?

5. **Hydration and Sleep:** Evaluate your hydration habits and sleep quality. How might better understanding and improving these areas impact your daily energy and focus?

Use these reflections to guide your exploration of Level 3. The body is a multicellular, integrated system. By focusing on nourishing both your body and mind, you're setting a solid foundation for all other life skills. This chapter aims to provide you with practical knowledge and strategies to enhance your overall well-being.

SKILL 15:
HEALTHY EATING

"Let food be thy medicine and medicine be thy food."
—Hippocrates (a.k.a. the "Father of Medicine")

UNDERSTANDING THE IMPACT OF DIET ON YOUR PHYSICAL health, mental clarity, and overall vitality is essential to your well-being. You are what you eat, after all. This approach to health is driving more physicians toward specialties like holistic and functional medicine, emphasizing personalized, comprehensive care.

In Skill 1, we talked about GIGO (Garbage In, Garbage Out) for your brain, but it's also true for your body. However, eating right isn't just about avoiding junk food; it's about striking a balance. For optimal functioning, your body requires a mix of macronutrients, such as proteins, fats, and carbohydrates, as well as micronutrients, like vitamins and minerals. Imagine your body as a high-performance engine; it needs the right fuel to run smoothly.

Unhealthy food is a silent global emergency that is disarming the unaware and slowly killing people. Take a stand for your health!

I've worked in a lot of developing countries with significant amounts of stunting, a condition of impaired growth and development in children due to chronic malnutrition. Stunting is a serious public health concern, particularly in low and middle-income countries where malnutrition and food insecurity are prevalent. In some of the most impoverished regions in Guatemala, for instance, seven out of ten children under the age of ten suffer from stunting, resulting from chronic undernutrition.[22] Stunting has profound and lasting effects, impairing cognitive development and reducing educational attainment, ultimately leading to economic disadvantages. It also raises the risk of chronic diseases. It weakens the immune system, making people more susceptible to illnesses, and for women, it can complicate childbirth. Stunting's effects are mostly irreversible, highlighting its lifelong impact on physical, mental, and economic well-being.

However, richer countries also have widespread dietary issues. For example, in America, we are seeing an obesity epidemic. Nearly 42% of American adults and about one-fifth of children are either overweight or obese.[23] On a grand scale, the prevalence of junk food in well-marketed packaging is silently poisoning the average American diet.* Unfortunately, our "food" often contains toxic chemicals designed to maximize corporate profits at the expense of individual nutrition. Consumption of ultra-processed food is linked to damaging effects on your body, brain, and even mental health.[24]

In confronting America's obesity crisis, we must also scrutinize the seductive siren call of flavors in our food. The Dorito Effect, coined by author Mark Schatzker, spotlights the insidious way artificial flavors seduce us into eating nutritionally void, calorie-laden foods.[25] These flavors are more than just taste—they're a sophisticated lure, drawing us away from the wholesome sustenance our bodies crave.

Imagine biting into a chip and being overwhelmed by a burst of cheese and spice—except there's no real cheese or spice in sight, just cleverly crafted chemicals that mimic them. This issue is at the heart of the Dorito Effect: It's the food industry's magic trick—flavor without substance, leading us to eat more yet receive less. Our bodies get tricked, and our taste buds get hijacked, all while nutrition takes a backseat to profit.

---

* It's not only the "food" that is toxic with chemicals, but also the packaging itself sometimes. There are a lot of harmful microplastics that make it into our bloodstream, which have long-term consequences to our health. Consumer Reports put out an issue entitled "How to Eat Less Plastic" in February 2024 where they investigated how plastics are very much getting into our food. They found that bisphenols and phthalates in food and food packaging are widespread in American food with growing evidence of potential health threats. Studies have linked them to insulin resistance, high blood pressure, reproductive issues, early menopause, and other concerns (pages 26-28).

To truly tackle obesity, it's not enough to count calories—we need to make every calorie count. That means fostering a taste for real food, where flavors aren't conjured in a lab but grown in the soil. By understanding and resisting the Dorito Effect, we empower ourselves to make choices that nourish not just our bodies but also the world we inhabit.

Looking at the deadliest health issues worldwide, including heart disease, cancer, obesity, strokes, type 2 diabetes, and many others, it's clear they all share a connection to something we can change: OUR FOOD CHOICES.[26]

This epidemic has significantly increased the risk of heart disease, type 2 diabetes, various types of cancer, and orthopedic conditions. Factors contributing to this include a lack of physical activity, unhealthy dietary choices, alcohol use, smoking, vaping, and a family history of chronic diseases.

MAKING INFORMED DIETARY CHOICES

Let's not sugarcoat the importance of this matter. Convenience is a sweet path to a slow death. Taking the easy path—whether grabbing that fast food or driving rather than walking somewhere—these choices will weaken you one decision at a time, and when it becomes a habit, that weakens your willpower to change for the better. Concerning food, it's easy to fall into unhealthy eating patterns, especially with the convenience of processed foods.

The key to not eating well-marketed garbage is to become a savvy, health-conscious consumer. When grocery shopping, focus on fresh produce and whole foods. Learn to read food labels—generally, the more natural the ingredients, the better. It's about making choices that nourish your body without toxifying your bloodstream with harmful chemicals. Additionally, studies have found that eating fast food, loaded with sugar and calories, increases endorphin release, which is why you might feel a sense of happiness when eating fast food, a precursor to addiction.[27] Therefore, you might feel intense cravings for these kinds of foods.

My son Zack achieved a high fitness level by age sixteen through mastering his nutrition and fitness. He learned abs are made in the kitchen, not just in the gym. He started eating balanced meals containing ample proteins, healthy fats, complex carbohydrates, and vegetables. He cut down on sugars and processed foods and saw significant changes in his body composition. The key is that healthy eating is a choice; it takes a combination of awareness, knowledge, and discipline to maintain a healthy diet.

MY POWER BREAKFAST BREAKTHROUGH

I have taken the convenient path for my breakfast routine for most of my life. My go-to breakfast was Cinnamon Toast Crunch cereal with milk and a coffee. Midway through the day, my stomach would growl, and my energy level would wane. In response, I would snack and drink more coffee. It took years to connect the dots that how I felt in the morning was due to my breakfast routine. My energy level started to get very low at work by 10 a.m., which was too early. By mid-afternoon, I experienced brain fog. So, I started experimenting with ways to maintain my energy and stamina. For starters, I revamped my breakfast routine, which was a game-changer for me.

Swapping out my typical sugary cereals for better options like protein-rich eggs and Greek yogurt with some nuts, seeds, and low glycemic index fruit (like some blueberries) gave me more energy throughout the day and significantly reduced my morning brain fog. It's incredible how a simple change in your first meal can impact your entire day's flow. My upgraded breakfast habit was a breakthrough, but I didn't stop trying new things. For example, I started taking a fifteen-minute walk before lunchtime, giving me the mental refresh to stay focused. These are all little adjustments that can make a world of difference, but it takes awareness and a bit of trial and error.

OVERCOMING TEMPTATIONS AND SETBACKS

Cravings and temptations are a part of life, but how you deal with them matters. Sometimes, it's okay to indulge, but it's about not making it a habit. Create a supportive environment—surround yourself with healthy options and friends who share your health goals. Don't purchase unhealthy food, because it will be tempting if it is in your home.

Meals are often social experiences; if your friends eat unhealthily, you will be more likely to eat unhealthy food. By all means, be social, but don't get dragged down by other people's bad habits. Or even better, hang out with people who have healthy habits. Alternatively, make sure not to go out with them while you are hungry; instead, maybe drink a protein shake, for example, before going out. This advice goes beyond food; beware of absorbing any unhealthy habits from others, whether unhealthy food, alcohol, drugs, or any other poor habits. One poor decision can have lasting consequences. Regardless of your age, the desire to fit in with others is really influential, but in this case, it's better to stand out and be the healthy one.

Remember, healthy eating isn't about strict diets or deprivation; it's about feeding your body the nutrients it needs to thrive. Small, consistent changes in your dietary habits can substantially improve your health, energy, and overall quality of life.

SKILL 16:
NUTRITION ESSENTIALS

"You don't have to eat less. You just have to eat right."
—Anonymous

SO, YOU'VE DECIDED YOU WANT TO EAT A HEALTHIER DIET. Now, what should you eat? Navigating the world of nutrition can seem like decoding a complex puzzle, but it doesn't have to be. Understanding the basics can empower you to make healthier choices that benefit your body and mind.

Nutrition is all about vitamins, minerals, antioxidants, proteins, and more. Each plays a unique role in keeping you healthy. For example, vitamins support your immune system, minerals are essential for bone health, and antioxidants fight against cellular damage. Proteins not only build muscles, which help your body's metabolism and energy regulation, but also provide amino acids that are vital for forming immunity antibodies, repairing cells, and other essential bodily functions.[28]

Consider the impact of vitamin-fortified foods globally. In regions facing malnutrition, adding essential vitamins to staple foods has dramatically improved public health, showcasing the power of proper nutrition.

Sifting through nutrition advice can sometimes feel like trying to find your way through a maze of misinformation. From age-old diet myths to the latest superfood fads, it's easy to get lost in a sea of nutrition advice that might not be entirely accurate.

COMMON NUTRITION MYTHS

Myth	Reality
Certain "Superfoods" are a cure-all	While so-called superfoods can be nutrient-rich, they are not magical cures. A balanced diet is more important than any single food.
Carbs are bad for you	Carbohydrates are a vital energy source. It's about choosing the right kind of carbs, like whole grains, over processed ones.
Fat makes you fat	Healthy fats, like those in avocados, nuts, and olive oil, are essential to your body and can actually help in weight management.
High-protein diets are the best for weight loss	While protein is important, balance is key. Excess protein can also be stored as fat. Generally, it's advised to consume 15-30 grams of protein per meal. Going beyond this, especially over 40 grams, may not provide additional benefits and could lead to inefficiencies such as excess being stored as fat or increased uric acid levels.

Be careful with measurements. Just keep in mind there is a difference between the weight of the food with protein on the scale and the protein it provides to your body. For example, 85 grams of chicken might actually provide around 24 grams of protein to our body.

It's all about balance!

ESSENTIAL BASICS FOR IMPROVING YOUR NUTRITION

Understanding nutrition involves recognizing how nutrients impact various systems like heart health and acknowledging that it's a personal journey. What benefits one might not suit another. Explore what works for you best using reliable research and, if needed, a nutritionist's guidance. Below is a concise guide to essential nutrients and foods for ten major health areas, summarizing what research has to say:

Cardiovascular Health: Essential for maintaining heart function and overall circulatory efficiency.

- Omega-3 Fatty Acids (salmon, flaxseeds): Reduce inflammation and heart disease risk.[29]

- Potassium (bananas, spinach): Regulates blood pressure and is important for cardiac muscle integrity.[30]

- Fiber (oats, legumes, kale, asparagus, and spinach): Lowers harmful cholesterol levels. It slows the absorption of sugar, helping stabilize blood sugar levels—acts as a prebiotic, providing fuel for beneficial gut bacteria.[31]

- Nitrates (beets, beet juice): Dietary nitrates get converted into nitric oxide in the body, which helps to improve blood flow and lower blood pressure by dilating blood vessels.[32]

- Limit saturated and trans fats (found in fried foods, baked goods, and processed snacks).[33]

- Reduce sodium intake (avoid high-salt processed foods and fast food or canned food).[34]

- Cut down on red meat, pork, and full-fat dairy products. Replace red meat with less inflammatory protein sources such as chicken, turkey, and salmon. Also, consider replacing dairy products with coconut milk or yogurt, almond milk or yogurt, or cashew milk.[35]

Digestive System Health: Crucial for nutrient absorption and waste elimination.

- Probiotics (yogurt, kefir): Enhance gut health (flora and digestion).[36]

- Dietary Fiber (whole grains, vegetables, seeds): Supports bowel health and regularity. Creates a stronger gut microbiome; healthy gut bacteria are needed for good digestion with less bloating, GERD, or maldigestion reaction.[37]

- Avoid overly processed and high-sugar foods: can disrupt gut health. Sugars feed unhealthy gut bacteria, which kills off the healthy bacteria.[38]

- Limit artificial sweeteners: some can cause digestive discomfort.[39]

- Limit intake of acidic foods (e.g., red meat, coffee, dairy): if they cause discomfort, as they can lower the body's pH. Consider balancing with alkaline foods like fruits and vegetables to regulate pH levels.[40]

Weight and Metabolic Health: Impacts overall health, energy levels, and risk of chronic diseases.

- Protein (chicken, turkey, salmon, shrimp, lentils): Aids in satiety and muscle maintenance.[41]

- Complex Carbohydrates (quinoa, sweet potatoes, black or brown rice, potato, tapioca, cassava): Provide energy and help regulate blood sugar.[42]

- Swap processed foods for whole foods: can significantly impact weight management.[43]

- Cut back on sugary beverages and high-calorie, nutrient-poor snacks.[44]

- Limit refined carbohydrates (like white bread and pastries).[45]

- Avoid or reduce alcohol consumption: it can contribute to weight gain.[46]

Mental and Cognitive Health: Influences brain function, mood, and cognitive abilities.

- B Vitamins (leafy greens, whole grains, chicken, turkey, salmon, eggs, legumes): Essential for brain function.[47]

- Antioxidants (berries, nuts, coconut oil, avocado, avocado oil, herbs such as turmeric, cinnamon, and ginger): Combat oxidative stress and may improve mood.[48]

- Limit foods high in added sugars and refined carbs.[49]

- Reduce caffeine (limit caffeine to 2 or fewer cups per day, and timing is crucial; not through the first hour after you wake up, and not after 3 p.m.) and alcohol intake, as they can affect sleep and mood.[50]

- Avoid trans fats and saturated fats, which are linked to an increased risk of cognitive decline.[51]

Musculoskeletal Health: Fundamental for mobility, strength, and structural support.

- Calcium (dairy products, fortified plant milks): Crucial for bone health.[52]

- Vitamin D (fatty fish, sunlight exposure): Enhances calcium absorption.[53]

- Magnesium (almonds, black beans): Important for muscle and nerve function.[54]

- Reduce consumption of soft drinks, which may be linked to lower bone mineral density.[55]

- Avoid excessive alcohol, which can interfere with calcium absorption and bone health.[56]

- Proteins and their sources are essential.

Immune System and Disease Prevention: Key to fighting infections and reducing disease risk.

- Vitamin C (citrus fruits, bell peppers): Supports immune function.[57]

- Zinc (pumpkin seeds, seafood): Vital for immune cell function.[58]

- Cut down on added sugars and refined carbs, which can weaken the immune response.[59]

- Reduce intake of fried and charred foods, which contain harmful compounds.[60]

- Proteins and their sources are essential.[61]

- Ensure sufficient water intake (actually, this is relevant for all areas).

Energy and Hormonal Balance: Affects energy levels, metabolism, and overall hormonal health.

- Vitamin D, especially in the form of cholecalciferol.[62]

- Vitamin B complex its sources mentioned above.[63]

- Two Brazil nuts daily for their selenium content.[64]

- Iron (red meat, spinach): Important for energy production. [65]

- Pair plant-based iron sources with Vitamin C-rich foods for better absorption.[66]

- Healthy Fats (avocados, olive oil, coconut oil, avocado, avocado oil, seeds, nuts except peanuts): Important for hormone production.[67]

- Electrolytes (coconut water, bananas): Support hydration and physical activity.[68]

- Avoid crash diets or extremely low-calorie intake, which can disrupt hormonal balance.[69]

- Limit caffeine, especially in the afternoon, as it can affect sleep and energy levels.

- Reduce consumption of processed foods high in added sugars and unhealthy fats.

Environmental and Lifestyle Factors: Helps the body adapt to and manage external and lifestyle stressors.

- Antioxidants (green tea, cocoa nibs, coconut oil, avocado, avocado oil, herbs such as turmeric, cinnamon, ginger, and dark chocolate): Protect against environmental stressors.[70]

- Adaptogens (ashwagandha, Rhodiola rosea, ginseng, holy basil, reishi mushroom, cordyceps, Schisandra berry, licorice root): This particular class of plants and herbs have unique abilities to help the body resist and adapt to stress, whether physical, chemical, or biological.[71]

- Avoid or limit exposure to foods with high pesticide residues or pollutants.[72]

- Limit processed and fast foods, which are often high in unhealthy additives.[73]

- Reduce plastic use in food storage and cooking to limit exposure to harmful chemicals.[74]

Skin, Hair, and Nail Health: Reflects overall health and can impact self-esteem and social interactions.

- Biotin (eggs, nuts): Supports hair and nail growth.[75]

- Omega-3s and Vitamin E (walnuts, sunflower seeds): Promote skin health.[76]

- Hydration is essential; choose water over sugary drinks for skin health.[77]

- Limit dairy and high-glycemic foods if they exacerbate skin issues.[78]

- Avoid excessive alcohol and tobacco, as they can age the skin.[79]

- Cut back on deep-fried and greasy foods, which can negatively impact skin health.[80]

- Use sunscreen to protect against harmful ultraviolet rays, which will age your skin.

- Zinc and Iron - support against hair loss, skin health, and much more.[81]

General Wellness and Vitality: Encompasses overall physical and mental well-being.

- Make your meals colorful with a variety of fruits and vegetables. Half of your plates should be at least vegetables.[82]

- Water: Vital for overall body function.[83]

- Vitamin A (sweet potatoes, carrots): Essential for eye health.[84]

- Selenium (Brazil nuts, seafood): Supports respiratory health.[85]

- Avoid or limit highly processed and sugary foods.[86]

- Limit foods high in additives and preservatives.[87]

Each nutrient significantly impacts various health aspects. Omega-3 fatty acids, for example, reduce inflammation for better cardiovascular health, while probiotics enhance gut health. A diverse, balanced diet is crucial for adequate nutrient intake. Remember, dietary needs are personal and sometimes require professional guidance.

Moderation is key; it's about balance, not deprivation. Attune to your body's responses to different foods, as it often indicates what you need for optimal health. This approach to nutrition isn't just about sustenance; it's an explorative journey in cooking and connecting with your food, turning simple ingredients into nourishing, delightful meals. Speaking of preparing meals, that's the next skill.

SKILL 17:
PREPARING MEALS

"Cooking is at once child's play and adult joy."
—Craig Claiborne

EMBARKING ON THE ADVENTURE OF COOKING IS NOT JUST about feeding yourself; it's about exploring a world of flavors, textures, and aromas. It's a journey that's as rewarding as it is delicious.

Cooking is essential because it gives you extraordinary freedom to ensure what food you put into your body. You also have more control over ensuring the right mix of nutrients is a part of your meals. Also, cooking at home brings a multitude of benefits. It's healthier and more economical, but preparing meals is also profoundly satisfying and therapeutic. Not only that, but you have a say in what goes into your food!

Tastes are very personal. I love branching out and trying diverse foods from around the world. On several occasions, I've taken cooking lessons to bring delicious dishes back home—such as learning to make plov (an aromatic rice pilaf) in Uzbekistan. I also learned how to make delicious potato-filled pierogies (dumplings) in Poland. These are simple joys that bring warmth to the heart and the stomach.

Remember, a healthy diet starts with healthy food ingredients and cooking styles.

THE FIVE PRIMARY TASTES

Taste	Description
Sweet	Typically associated with sugars and sweeteners, it provides a pleasant, sugary sensation.
Sour	Often linked to acidic ingredients like citrus fruits or vinegar, it delivers a tart and tangy flavor.
Salty	Associated with salt and salty seasonings, it enhances and intensifies the taste of dishes.
Bitter	Commonly found in foods like dark leafy greens and coffee, it imparts a sharp and sometimes astringent taste.
Umami	Known as the savory or "meaty" taste, it is found in ingredients like mushrooms, soy sauce, and aged cheeses, adding depth and richness to dishes.

Good cooking involves balancing and harmonizing these five tastes and paying attention to texture, aroma, and presentation. Achieving a well-rounded and enjoyable meal means understanding how to combine these tastes effectively. This balance can vary depending on the cuisine and personal preferences. Still, the key is to create a pleasing combination of sweet, sour, salty, bitter, and umami flavors to satisfy the palate.

Additionally, using fresh, high-quality ingredients, proper cooking techniques, and experimentation with various seasonings and herbs can elevate your dishes to the next level. Successful cooking involves creativity, attention to detail, and a passion for crafting delicious and satisfying meals.

STARTING SIMPLE:
BASIC RECIPES FOR BEGINNERS

If you're new to cooking, start with the basics. Simple techniques like boiling, sautéing, and baking can open doors to various dishes. Try easy, nutritious recipes that require minimal ingredients but deliver maximum flavor. Remember, every great chef starts with the basics.

For instance, an initial venture into cooking might begin with something as simple as a pasta dish or a basic stir-fry. These early experiences can spark a lifelong passion for culinary exploration.

Here are five simple, fast, healthy recipes to kickstart your cooking journey. These dishes are simple to prepare and packed with nutrients, making them perfect for anyone looking to eat healthily without spending too much time in the kitchen.

1. Classic Veggie Omelet

- Ingredients: 2 eggs, ½ cup chopped vegetables (like bell peppers, onions, spinach), salt, pepper, 1 tsp olive oil.

- Instructions:

  - Beat the eggs, salt, and pepper in a bowl.

  - Heat olive oil in a pan, sauté the vegetables briefly, then pour the eggs over them.

  - Tip: Make sure not to use high heat when cooking with olive oil. Always cook on medium heat with olive oil because it has a low smoking point.

  - Cook until the eggs are set, fold the omelet, and serve!

2. Simple Avocado Toast

- Ingredients: 1 ripe avocado, two slices of whole grain bread (or even better to use gluten-free bread, almond bread, or cassava bread), lemon juice, salt, pepper, and red pepper flakes (optional).

- Instructions:
    - Mash the avocado with lemon juice, salt, and pepper.
    - Toast the bread and spread the avocado mixture on top.
    - Sprinkle with red pepper flakes for an extra kick.

3. Quick Stir-Fry Vegetables with Quinoa

- Ingredients: 1 cup quinoa, assorted vegetables (like carrots, broccoli, bell peppers), 2 tbsp soy sauce, 1 tbsp olive oil, garlic (optional).
- Instructions:
    - Cook quinoa as per package instructions.
    - Heat olive oil in a pan, add garlic (if using), then stir-fry the vegetables.
    - Add cooked quinoa and soy sauce, stir well, and serve.

4. Easy Greek Salad

- Ingredients: Cucumber, tomatoes, red onion, olives, feta cheese, olive oil, lemon juice, salt, dried oregano.
- Instructions:
    - Chop the cucumber, tomatoes, and red onion. Mix in a bowl.
    - Add olives and crumbled feta cheese.
    - Dress with olive oil, lemon juice, salt, and oregano.

5. Banana and Peanut Butter Smoothie

- Ingredients: 1 banana, 2 tbsp peanut butter (or a healthy alternative such as almond butter or coconut butter), 1 cup almond milk (or regular milk), a dash of cinnamon, ice cubes (optional).

- Instructions:
  - Blend the banana, peanut butter, milk, cinnamon, and ice until smooth.
  - Pour into a glass and enjoy!

These recipes are not only delicious but also versatile. Feel free to substitute ingredients based on your dietary preferences and what you have on hand. Expand your cooking repertoire with new recipes to further develop this skill, preferably focusing on healthier options. Happy cooking!

SKILL 18:
PHYSICAL FITNESS

"The last three or four reps is what makes the muscle grow.
This area of pain is where a true champion is made, setting them apart
from the rest. It's about having the courage to endure and push through
the pain, no matter what."
—Arnold Schwarzenegger

THIS POWERFUL QUOTE BY ARNOLD SCHWARZENEGGER, a legend in bodybuilding, highlights a crucial aspect of physical fitness—the blend of mental resilience and physical strength. Being physically fit isn't just a matter of routine exercise; it takes mental fortitude and dedication.

Regular exercise does wonders for both your body and mind. It's not just about building muscles or losing weight; it's about improving your heart health, boosting your mood, and even sharpening your mind. Plus, staying active can significantly reduce the risk of chronic diseases.

The best workout is the one that you enjoy and stick to.

There's a whole world of exercises, from yoga and swimming to weightlifting and cycling. Also, sports are great for keeping fit as well.

BUILD YOUR PERSONAL FITNESS PLAN

- **Assess Your Fitness Level:** Before jumping into a fitness routine, it's essential to understand your current fitness level, including evaluating your cardiovascular fitness, muscular strength, flexibility, and body composition.

- **Define Your Fitness Goals:** Be specific about what you want to achieve. Whether it's gaining strength, improving cardiovascular health, losing weight, or increasing flexibility, your goals will dictate the type of exercises you include in your plan.

- **Create a Balanced Routine:** A well-rounded fitness plan should include various types of exercises:

  o Cardiovascular exercises like running, cycling, or swimming for heart health and endurance.

  o Strength training with weights or bodyweight exercises to build muscle and bone density.

  o Flexibility exercises like yoga or stretching to improve joint range of motion.

  o Balance and coordination exercises are crucial to prevent injuries.

- **Start Slowly and Gradually Increase Intensity:** If you're new to exercising, start with shorter, less intense workouts and gradually increase the duration and intensity as your fitness improves. Also, it's important not to get injured!

- **Incorporate Variety and Fun:** Keep your routine interesting by trying new activities, sports, or fitness classes. Choosing activities that you enjoy increases the likelihood of sticking with your plan.

- **Plan Your Workout Schedule:** Consistency is critical. Schedule your workouts like any other important activity. The Department of Health and Human Services recommends at least two and a half hours of moderate aerobic activity or seventy-five minutes of vigorous activity every week, in addition to strength training exercises at least twice a week.[88]

- **Listen to Your Body:** Pay attention to your body's signals. Rest is crucial for recovery and performance. Overtraining can lead to injuries.

- **Track Your Progress:** Keep a fitness journal or use an app to track your workouts, set goals, and note your progress. Doing this can be motivating and help you adjust your plan as needed.

- **Nutrition and Hydration:** A balanced diet and proper hydration are essential to your fitness journey. Ensure you're fueling your body with the proper nutrients and drinking plenty of water.[89]

- **Seek Professional Advice When Needed:** If you're unsure how to start or reach specific goals, consider hiring a personal trainer or consulting a fitness expert. There are a multitude of great fitness programs available.

A fundamental concept in physical fitness is developing critical motor skills like coordination, strength, endurance, and agility. Interestingly, these skills are interconnected, meaning improving one can boost the others, which is why cross-training can be helpful. Take strength training, for example. Lifting weights doesn't just build muscle; it can enhance your stamina too.

When planning your workouts, focus on activities you enjoy that challenge these motor skills. Create a balanced approach to physical wellness where each aspect supports and enhances the others. A more holistic approach to fitness will make your workout routine more enjoyable and ensure a well-rounded development of your physical capabilities.

Enhancing your motor skills can be as simple and enjoyable as incorporating mobility workouts into your routine. These workouts are about embracing basic yet essential movements—squatting, twisting, pressing, and pulling in different directions. These simple actions play a significant role in improving your overall wellness. They are not just exercises; they're a way to fine-tune your body's ability to move more freely and effectively. Regularly engaging in mobility workouts boosts your physical health and equips your body with the flexibility and strength to tackle everyday tasks quickly and confidently. Be sure to rest between workouts so that your body can recover.

Post-workout, it's essential to consume enough protein for muscle repair and to meet your general needs. According to the Mayo Clinic, protein should constitute 10-35% of your daily calories. So, on a 2,000-calorie diet, that would imply aiming for 50-175 grams of protein. The amount varies based on your lifestyle: sedentary adults should have about 0.36 grams per pound (for instance, a 140-pound person needs roughly 50 grams daily), while active people and weight trainers require about 0.50-0.68 grams per pound. Intense trainers may need more, but try not to exceed 0.91 grams per pound.[90] For tailored advice, consider consulting a dietitian.

MAINTAINING MOTIVATION AND BREAKING THROUGH BARRIERS IN FITNESS

The cornerstone of a successful fitness journey is setting achievable goals. It could be running a distance, lifting a specific weight, or committing to regular weekly physical activity. Clear, attainable objectives keep your eyes on the prize and help you stay the course.

It also helps when you surround yourself with encouraging people, or even better if you can exercise with others. Being part of a supportive fitness group can significantly amplify your motivation.

Celebrating your progress, no matter how small, is equally important. Each step forward, whether adding an extra mile to your run or an extra pound to your weights, is a victory in its own right. Recognize and appreciate these milestones; they're the stepping-stones to your fitness goals.

SKILL 19:
SLEEP HYGIENE

"Sleep is the best meditation."
—Dalai Lama

W HEN YOU SLEEP, YOUR MIND AND BODY ENTER A STATE OF deep rest and rejuvenation, much like the mental and physical relaxation achieved through meditation. In this state, the body repairs itself while the mind sorts and processes the day's experiences, consolidating memories and resetting emotional balance. Just as meditation brings clarity and calmness, a good night's sleep refreshes and prepares you to face the challenges of a new day with a clear, focused mind and a revitalized body.

Life often feels like a whirlwind of responsibilities, deadlines, and constant hustle. In this fast-paced world, it's easy to overlook one of the most critical aspects of maintaining a healthy, sharp, and energetic lifestyle: sleep.

WHAT HAPPENS IF YOU DON'T GET GOOD SLEEP?

The impact of insufficient sleep can be far-reaching, including even altering gene expression in human blood cells![91] Physically, it's not just about feeling tired; good sleep is essential for maintaining heart health, repairing muscles after a long day, and keeping your immune system robust—crucial in a fast-paced professional environment. Sleep serves your mental functions by replenishing your cognitive abilities. For instance, for healthy adults, getting consistent, stable sleep of at least seven hours per night improves working memory and response inhibition (i.e., a critical component of executive functions, which are higher-level cognitive processes that enable us to plan, focus attention, remember instructions, and juggle multiple tasks successfully).[92] Think of it as an investment in your memory, problem-solving skills, and decision-making abilities, all critical assets in your professional toolkit. Emotionally, quality sleep is like a regulator, helping you manage stress and maintain emotional stability, thus guarding against mood swings and mental health challenges, such as depression and anxiety. It even plays a role in managing your weight, as lack of sleep can disrupt hunger hormones.

Moreover, sleep deprivation can be a safety hazard in a world where alertness and quick reflexes are often required. In the long term, the stakes get even higher, with chronic sleep deprivation linked to severe health issues like heart disease and type 2 diabetes. Remember, these aren't just general guidelines but the building blocks for a successful professional life. Prioritizing sleep is more than just avoiding the negatives; it's an active step toward thriving in all spheres of life.

For over a year, my son, Zack, struggled to sleep well with chronic migraines, which really affected his ability to focus and keep up with school. He switched to homeschooling, which gave him the flexibility he needed to manage his health better. By seeking advice from a sleep specialist, focusing on his health, and making gradual changes in his daily routines, Zack managed to get back on track. It's a real example of how tackling sleep issues with persistence and incremental lifestyle adjustments can make a big difference in our lives.

TIPS FOR GETTING BETTER SLEEP

Sleep is far more complex than just closing your eyes and drifting into dreamland. It comprises multiple cycles, each with different stages, and getting enough of each stage is essential to feeling fully rested. Lack of sleep can wreak havoc on everything from your mood to your ability to think clearly and make sound decisions.

- **Get enough sleep.** As for the average hours of sleep recommended for different age groups, these are the general guidelines according to the experts:[93]

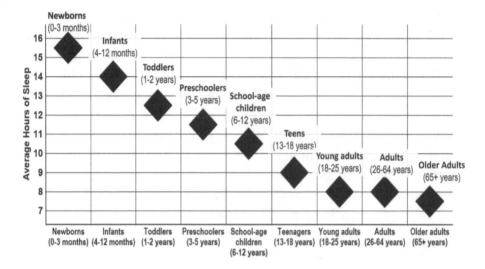

- **Regularize your sleep routines.** Maintaining a regular sleep schedule is paramount to achieving quality rest. Going to bed and waking up consistently daily helps regulate your body's internal clock, promoting better sleep quality. Also, create a pre-sleep routine. Establishing a relaxing bedtime routine signals your body that it's time to wind down. This routine could include reading a book, taking a warm bath, or practicing relaxation exercises.

- **Improve day habits that affect your sleep.** However, it's not just about when you sleep; what you do during the day can significantly impact your nightly rest. Factors like consuming caffeine late in the day (after 3 p.m.), indulging in lengthy naps (more than twenty minutes), and experiencing high stress can disrupt sleep patterns. Be cautious about what you consume, especially in the hours leading up to bedtime. Avoid heavy meals; take a light snack if you're slightly hungry.

- **Manage stress.** Stress and sleep are closely related. Managing stress through effective time management, organization, and relaxation techniques can significantly improve sleep quality. Incorporate relaxation techniques, especially if you often have a racing mind due to stress. Techniques like meditation, deep breathing exercises, or gentle yoga can help calm the mind, making it easier to fall asleep.

- **Exercise regularly.** Engaging in consistent physical activity can greatly enhance your sleep quality. Aim for exercising five days per week, allowing time for muscle recovery, and ideally, you can alternate focus on different muscle groups each day. However, avoid exercising too close to bedtime to prevent overstimulation, which can make falling asleep more challenging.

- **Design a comfortable sleep environment.** Your bedroom should be a sanctuary designed for restful slumber. For instance, invest in comfortable bedding, maintain a cool room temperature, and minimize noise and light. Surprisingly, even the color of your bedroom walls can influence your sleep quality! Ensure your mattress and pillows are comfortable and sufficiently supportive. The proper sleep setup can make a significant difference in your sleep quality. Another thing I like to do is turn on a fan to help drown out other noises.

- **Dim the lights, including the digital lights.** One of the most significant sleep disruptors in the modern age is technology, particularly screens. The blue light emitted by phones and laptops can deceive your brain into believing it's still daytime, disrupting your natural sleep cycle. Light affects your circadian rhythms. Exposure to natural light during the day, especially in the morning, helps maintain a healthy sleep-wake cycle, which is essential for those who spend most of their day indoors.

- **Keep a sleep diary.** Track your sleep patterns and habits to identify factors affecting your sleep. This data can be beneficial if you seek professional help for sleep issues. There are technologies such as Fitbits, Apple watches, or Oura rings that track your sleep patterns and provide valuable insights.

- **Supplements can help.** For example, ensure adequate magnesium intake, particularly in the bisglycinate form, for better relaxation and sleep quality.[94]

- *Pro tip:* **Learn to lucid dream purposefully.** During nightly sleep cycles, your prefrontal cortex, key in decision-making and personality, undergoes crucial rest. This rest period is vital for memory consolidation, learning, and emotional regulation. Train your brain to intentionally incorporate lucid dreaming into your daily life, where you can revise and learn new skills and even solve problems in your sleep. Start by noting your lucid dreaming goals in a journal before bed. This process can guide your subconscious toward these objectives in your dreams, blending rest with personal development. You can sleep productively! However, more research is needed to determine how lucid dreaming affects your overall sleep hygiene.[95]

Enhancing your sleep quality can profoundly enrich your waking life. Better sleep leads to improved focus, energy, and overall well-being.

SKILL 20:
HYDRATION

HYDRATION IS VITAL FOR ALMOST EVERY FUNCTION IN OUR body, yet it's so easy to overlook. Let's dive into why staying hydrated is crucial and how to keep up with your water game.

Do you know how you feel after a long day without enough water? That's dehydration, and it's not just about feeling thirsty. Water is like the oil in a car's engine for your body—it keeps everything running smoothly. But when you're not drinking enough, things can start to go a bit haywire.

WHY YOU NEED TO SIP MORE OFTEN

- **Your Body is a Water Park:** About 50-70% is water. Every cell, tissue, and organ needs to function correctly. It helps eliminate waste, maintain normal temperature, lubricate joints, and protect sensitive tissues.

- **Are You Feeling Drained?** Not consuming enough water can lead to dehydration, which can drain energy and cause tiredness, even if mild.[96] It's like trying to run your phone on a 5% battery.

- **Thirst Isn't Always the Signal:** Especially as we get older, our thirst alarm isn't as sharp. So, waiting until you're thirsty might mean you're already dehydrated.

RISKS OF NOT DRINKING ENOUGH

- **Workout woes:** Exercising without enough water can lead to heat injuries. Imagine trying to run a marathon in the desert without a water bottle.

- **Kidney issues:** Your kidneys are the body's filtration system, but without enough water, they can't do their job, leading to kidney stones and infections. Ouch!

- **Headaches:** Dehydration can cause headaches and even make your brain feel like it's shrinking. Have you ever tried studying or gaming with a pounding headache? Not fun.

- **Digestive problems:** Your gut needs water to keep things moving. Without it, you might end up with constipation, which is as uncomfortable as it sounds.

- **A range of other issues:** Dehydration can lead to severe health issues, such as strokes, heat strokes, fatigue, decreased concentration, and syncope (fainting).

HOW MUCH LIQUID DO YOU NEED?

For years, a general rule of thumb has been that you should drink eight glasses of water daily. However, this is not necessarily accurate for everybody since a glass is not a standard measurement, people are of different weights, and we have different needs based on activity level, climate, etc. Also, it's not just your water that counts.[97] Your morning smoothie and that juicy apple you snack on? They count, too!

Stay well-hydrated by drinking water regularly: with meals, between meals, around exercise sessions, and whenever you're thirsty.

It's important not to overconsume large amounts at once, as the body will simply expel excess water. Most of your water intake should be from morning to afternoon, when your body is most active and needs more hydration. *A key sign of adequate hydration is infrequent thirst and having colorless or light-yellow urine.*

So, how much water should you drink daily? There is not a one-size-fits-all answer since it depends on many individual factors.[98] However, you can estimate your baseline water needs starting with your body weight. Applying guidance from the US News & World Report and The American College of Sports Medicine, this rule-of-thumb calculation adjusts for additional fluid needed for minutes of exercise since exercise increases water loss through sweat.

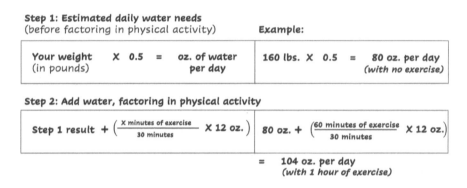

Step 1: Estimated daily water needs (before factoring in physical activity)   **Example:**

| Your weight (in pounds) | X 0.5 | = | oz. of water per day | 160 lbs. X 0.5 | = | 80 oz. per day (with no exercise) |

Step 2: Add water, factoring in physical activity

$$\text{Step 1 result} + \left(\frac{\text{X minutes of exercise}}{\text{30 minutes}} \times 12 \text{ oz.}\right) \quad 80 \text{ oz.} + \left(\frac{\text{60 minutes of exercise}}{\text{30 minutes}} \times 12 \text{ oz.}\right)$$

$$= \quad 104 \text{ oz. per day} \text{ (with 1 hour of exercise)}$$

Go ahead, calculate yours now!

Keep in mind that these are general guidelines. Individual needs may vary due to climate, activity level, health conditions, and diet. Also, remember that other beverages and foods, particularly fruits and vegetables, contribute to your total water intake. However, also be aware that overhydration can sometimes be a problem.

But let's get real—most of us aren't drinking enough water, and it's messing with our mojo. Here's a quick guide to standard container sizes to help you out:

- **Small glass size:** 8 ounces (237 mL), like those little water bottles or your standard coffee cup.

- **Mugs:** 12 ounces (355 mL), perfect for those oversized mugs you love.

- **Standard Issue:** 16.9 ounces (500 mL), your go-to bottled water size.

- **Sports bottles:** 20 ounces (591 mL), great for those gym or biking sessions.

- **Big Gulp:** 33.8 ounces (1 liter) for when you're serious about hydration.

Keeping well-hydrated boosts your health, revitalizes your energy levels, and even gives your skin a radiant glow. So, keep sipping that water throughout the day and observe the positive difference it makes in how you feel and look!

One tip for staying hydrated is to create water-drinking routines. For example, drink eight ounces before bed and sixteen ounces upon waking, adding twenty-four ounces to your daily intake. Consuming sixteen ounces of water before each meal can aid in weight management and reduce food intake while contributing an additional forty-eight ounces daily.[99] Also, carry a water bottle with you! Preferably, use a water bottle that marks the amount of water you consume.

Remember, keeping hydrated is vital to keeping your body and mind in shape. Water, fruits, vegetables, and beverages like milk, juice, and herbal teas contribute to hydration. Pay attention to your thirst!

What you drink matters, too. Beverages like coffee and alcohol might be tempting, but they can dehydrate you in excess.[100] It's important to moderate the consumption of sugar-sweetened drinks due to their high-calorie content. Remember, it's all about balance.

SKILL 21:
MENTAL HEALTH AWARENESS*

"There is hope, even when your brain tells you there isn't."
—John Green

M ANY INDIVIDUALS BEAR HEAVY BURDENS SILENTLY, WITH
their struggles often unnoticed or unseen. Regrettably, the
stigma associated with mental health issues has long been a barrier,
deterring numerous people from openly discussing their experiences
or seeking necessary help. This stigma has contributed to a culture of
silence and isolation around mental health, making it crucial for us to
foster a more understanding and supportive environment.

In the wake of the COVID-19 pandemic, the world witnessed a
dramatic escalation in mental health challenges, profoundly affecting
the lives of all ages. According to Mental Health America, mental
health anxiety screenings worldwide surged by nearly double, revealing
a staggering increase in anxiety and depression during the pandemic's
first year.[101] The crisis impacted the mental health of diverse demo-
graphics across ages and regions. These alarming statistics underscore
a critical and growing need to understand, address, and prioritize
mental health in our daily lives. In today's fast-paced world, taking
care of your mental health is as important as your physical health.
Understanding mental health, recognizing disorders, and knowing
how to seek help are vital skills for everyone, especially young adults.

Just like other aspects of your health, there are things you can
do to help your mental health, many of which relate to several skills
throughout this book. One can develop a comprehensive approach

---

* *This section (Skill 21) was professionally reviewed by Kathryn Wilson, PhD in clinical psychology.*

to maintaining and enhancing mental health by focusing on critical areas.

Physical Health and Wellness

- **Regular Exercise:** Improves mood and cognitive function. Not to mention, it also improves sleep quality!

- **Balanced Diet:** Affects mood and energy levels positively.

- **Adequate Sleep:** Essential for mood regulation and mental clarity.

Mind and Emotion Management

- **Mindfulness, Meditation, and Prayer:** Helps in staying grounded and reducing stress.

- **Learning Stress Management Techniques:** Includes deep breathing and progressive muscle relaxation.

- **Practicing Gratitude:** Enhances mood and overall outlook.

- **Setting Realistic Goals:** Provides a sense of accomplishment and purpose.

- **Reflective Practices:** Activities such as journaling, prayer, or spending time in nature can be spiritually fulfilling and contribute to mental peace and clarity.

- **Aligning Personal Values and Beliefs:** Understanding and aligning with one's core values and beliefs can provide a strong foundation for mental resilience and purpose in life. It is also critical to identify and move beyond limiting beliefs.

Social and Lifestyle Adjustments

- **Social Connections:** Crucial for mental health; helps combat loneliness.

- **Community Involvement:** Engaging in community or faith-based activities can provide a sense of belonging and purpose.

- **Hobbies and Interests:** Engaging in enjoyable activities reduces stress.

- **Digital Detox:** Improves mental health by reducing screen time.

- **Continuous Learning:** Keeps the brain active and improves mental fitness.

Self-Care and Professional Support

- **Professional Help When Needed:** Seeking therapy or counseling might be helpful for giving you new perspectives and tools.

- **Self-Care and Compassion:** Treating yourself kindly reduces stress and enhances well-being.

- **Limiting Alcohol and Avoiding Drugs:** Crucial for maintaining mental health.

WHEN THINGS START TO GO WRONG

Sometimes, things may go south. All human beings have low points, and some more than others. In an increasingly complex world, being vigilant about the early signs of mental health issues, like depression and anxiety, is essential. These signs can be subtle—shifts in mood, energy, sleep patterns, or a loss of interest in things you once enjoyed. It's important to remember that only a professional can accurately diagnose these conditions, so if you notice these changes in yourself or someone close to you, seeking help is crucial. Talking openly about your feelings is integral to maintaining good mental health. Building a solid support network of friends, family, or professionals can offer the understanding and assistance needed during challenging times.

Moreover, knowing when and where to seek professional help is important. Many educational institutions provide on-campus mental health services, and numerous local or online therapists and counselors are available. Engaging in conversations about mental health can break down barriers and create safe spaces for expression. Remember, reaching out for support reflects strength and a commitment to your well-being. Additionally, exploring online resources, community groups, and various therapy options can provide additional support layers.

In emergency situations, be aware of your area's hotlines and crisis intervention services. These resources can be lifesavers in critical moments—whether for you or others. Mental health, like physical health, requires ongoing attention. Regular consultations with mental health professionals, even without acute symptoms, can form a part of a proactive mental wellness strategy. By creating a personalized mental health plan with a professional, you can equip yourself with coping mechanisms, self-care routines, and an understanding of potential triggers. Remember, taking care of your mental health is a brave and necessary step toward a healthier, more balanced life.

SKILL 22:
STRESS MANAGEMENT*

"It's not stress that kills us. It is our reaction to it."
—Hans Selye

I F UNMANAGED, STRESS CAN WREAK HAVOC ON YOUR LIFE. Given the swift tempo of contemporary life, it's no surprise that stress is a shared experience, especially for young adults navigating through life's numerous challenges. The impacts of stress are far-reaching, affecting not only our mental health, often leading to anxiety and depression, but also our physical well-being, manifesting in heart problems, weakened immune responses, and digestive issues. It disrupts sleep, changes our eating habits, and even clouds our thinking.

Everyday stress triggers include school or work pressures, financial worries, relationship troubles, health concerns, significant life changes, and the relentless pace of daily responsibilities. In an era where we're constantly bombarded with negative global news, managing stress becomes crucial. Developing coping strategies, like finding time for relaxation, staying active, and reaching out for support, isn't just wise; it's essential for maintaining balance and well-being in our dynamic lives.

It's important to distinguish good stress from bad stress.

Stress isn't all bad; it comes in two forms: eustress, the positive kind that motivates and energizes us, and distress, which can be harmful and draining. Being aware of stress symptoms, whether physical,

---

* *This section (Skill 22) was professionally reviewed by Kathryn Wilson, PhD in clinical psychology.*

like headaches, or emotional, like feeling swamped, is key to managing it. Remember, everyone experiences stress, but it's how we deal with it that shapes its impact on our lives. Let's explore how to understand stress better, manage it effectively, and strengthen our resilience against it, turning a potential setback into a powerful stepping-stone.

TECHNIQUES TO MANAGE AND REDUCE STRESS

Effective stress management often involves techniques similar to those used in mental health awareness, as the two are related:

- **Mind and Emotion Management** (Mindfulness and Meditation, Stress Management Techniques, Practicing Gratitude, Setting Realistic Goals, Reflective Practices, Aligning Personal Values and Beliefs)

- **Social and Lifestyle Adjustments** (Social Connections, Community Involvement, Hobbies and Interests, Digital Detox, Continuous Learning)

- **Self-Care and Professional Support** (Professional Help When Needed, Self-Care and Compassion, Limiting Harmful Substances)

- **Physical Health and Wellness** (Regular Exercise, Balanced Diet, Adequate Sleep)

Relaxation techniques like deep breathing, meditation, and visualization are key in calming the mind and body. These may involve adjusting thoughts, breathing patterns, or sensory experiences. It's important to find stress-relief methods that work for you and are healthy for both body and mind. Try various strategies and keep a journal so you can note which are particularly effective for you. Incorporate them into your daily routine. Don't wait for moments of stress to begin trying these techniques. Practice them when you are calm so you can do them properly and without much thought when you feel overwhelmed.

21 WAYS TO UNWIND AND DE-STRESS

1. **Mindset reset:** If your stress is rooted in worry, you might need to recalibrate your mindset or adjust your perspective. Fill your mind with positive content such as uplifting thoughts, gratitude, faith, and determination—leaving no room for negative thought patterns to fester. Sometimes the stress of the moment sucks you in, and it helps to pause and focus on the bigger picture.

2. **4-7-8 Breathing Technique**: Inhale quietly through the nose for four seconds, hold the breath for seven seconds, and exhale forcefully through the mouth for eight seconds. Repeat four times. In addition to the 4-7-8 breathing technique, there are various other breathing exercises, such as box breathing (equal-length inhales, holds, exhales), diaphragmatic breathing, or alternate nostril breathing, which can help calm the mind and reduce stress.[102]

3. **Progressive Muscle Relaxation**: Tense each muscle group during inhalation and relax them during exhalation. Start from the toes and work up to the head. Taking it further, combine progressive muscle relaxation with guided imagery by envisioning each muscle group relaxing as you move through your body. This technique can create a deeper sense of relaxation.[103] While doing progressive muscle relaxation, focus your mind on the sensations in your muscles as you flex and then relax. Notice how muscle tension feels different than relaxation. Pay particular attention to the unwinding, unfolding sensations that occur during relaxation. Visualize the relaxing sensations as a warmth spreading through your body, bringing relaxation as it travels.

4. **Mindfulness Meditation:** Sit in a comfortable position, focus on your breathing, and keep your attention on the present moment, avoiding distractions from past or future concerns. *See Skill 5 for more.*

5. **Guided Imagery:** Guided imagery involves using your imagination to create relaxing mental images or scenarios. You can do

this on your own or with the help of a guided audio recording. Visualization can be a powerful tool for relaxation.

6. **Music Therapy:** Music is a powerful tool.[104] Listen to calming music, like classical or acoustic. Playing a musical instrument can also be effective in reducing stress. When I am stressed, the right music brings me immediately into a more relaxed state.

7. **Herbal Teas:** Consuming calming herbal teas like chamomile, peppermint, or lavender can provide a soothing effect, aiding relaxation and sleep.

8. **Aromatherapy:** Using essential oils such as lavender, bergamot, or ylang-ylang in a diffuser or as part of a massage oil can reduce stress and promote well-being.

9. **Light Therapy:** Exposure to a light therapy box can be beneficial, especially in combating seasonal affective disorder (SAD) and improving mood and sleep patterns.[105]

10. **Physical Activity:** Engage in daily walks, particularly in natural settings, or brief stretching exercises to lower stress levels. *See Skill 18 for more.*

11. **Tai Chi and Qi Gong:** These ancient Chinese practices involve slow, flowing movements, deep breathing, and mindfulness. They can help reduce stress, improve balance, and enhance physical and mental health.[106]

12. **Yoga:** Yoga combines physical postures, breathing exercises, and meditation to promote relaxation and flexibility. It's an excellent practice for both physical and mental well-being.

13. **Biofeedback:** Biofeedback techniques use monitoring devices to provide real-time information about your body's physiological responses, such as heart rate or muscle tension. You can then learn to control and reduce stress responses through practice.

14. **Journaling:** Writing down your thoughts and feelings in a journal can be a therapeutic way to process emotions, gain insight, and reduce stress. Journaling can help you identify sources of

stress and develop strategies for managing them. *See Skill 6 for more.*

15. **Progressive Relaxation Apps:** There are several Smartphone apps that guide you through progressive muscle relaxation exercises, making it easy to practice anytime, anywhere.

16. **Art and Creativity:** Engaging in creative activities like drawing, painting, coloring, or crafting can be a form of relaxation and self-expression. It allows you to focus your mind on a creative task and temporarily shift your attention away from stressors.

17. **Warm Baths or Showers:** A warm bath or shower can help relax tense muscles and provide a soothing sensation. Adding Epsom salts or essential oils to your bath can enhance the experience.

18. **Laughter and Humor:** Watching a funny movie, reading jokes, or spending time with people who make you laugh can release endorphins and alleviate stress.

19. **Social Connection:** Spending quality time with friends and loved ones, whether through conversation, activities, or support groups, can provide emotional support and reduce stress. *See Skill 38 for more.*

20. **Nature Therapy:** Spending time in natural settings, such as parks or forests, can calm the mind and reduce stress. This is often referred to as "forest bathing" or *shinrin-yoku.*[107]

21. **De-clutter:** Clutter and disorganization stress out many people. Remove junk from your life and embrace simplicity. Decluttering—whether your space or your calendar—leads to less stress. This tip addresses a root cause of stress, which might make it the most important tip of the list. More importantly, the underlying principle here is to address the root cause of your stress if you can.

Additionally, incorporating strategies such as countering negative thoughts with positive affirmations, focusing on solutions, establishing a robust support network, and engaging in self-care is crucial for stress management and resilience building. These approaches help cultivate a positive outlook and help with navigating life's stress-inducing challenges more effectively.

After you improve your stress-coping skills, you will start building resilience, boosting your tolerance to stress. With practice, you will develop preferred strategies to handle stress more effectively and maintain a positive perspective.

In summary, to recap the key concepts of this chapter, remember WELLNESS (Wholesome eating, Essential nutrients, Learning to cook, Lifestyle fitness, Nurturing sleep, Ensuring hydration, Supporting mental health awareness, and Stress handling).

Through understanding the essentials of physical and mental health, we've laid the groundwork for a life of strength and resilience. Our next step, in Level 4, is to channel this well-being into enhancing our brain's potential for learning and creativity.

LEVEL 4:
BOOST YOUR BRAINPOWER

WHAT WOULD YOU DO WITHOUT YOUR BRAIN? THINK ABOUT IT: your brain is arguably your most important tool. Believe it or not, much of what we already covered helps boost your brainpower. Let's quickly review some of those skills before expanding on some new ones:

- Mindfulness and focus involve practices that enhance concentration and attention, which are essential for mental efficiency and allow for sharper focus and more adequate cognitive processing. (Skills 1, 5, and 9)

- The importance of taking a digital detox to give your brain a break from information and stimulus overload protects your working IQ. (Skill 12)

- Forming better habits is central to cognitive enhancement. Adopting lifestyle habits that support brain health is integral to maintaining and improving cognitive abilities. (Skill 14)

- The impact of a healthy lifestyle (e.g., diet, sleep, and exercise) on the brain is profound. (Level 3, and Skill 23)

This chapter introduces techniques to boost key aspects of your brainpower by cultivating higher-order skills such as critical thinking, memory and recall, and creativity. We also delve into biohacking approaches, including the use of nootropics, to improve brainpower and overall health. Incorporating these practices into your daily routine can significantly improve cognitive capabilities and mental wellness, taking your brainpower to the next level.

Self-Assessment

As we enter Level 4, which is dedicated to unlocking and maximizing your brain's capabilities, let's embark on a self-assessment that aligns with the unique focus of this chapter. Reflect on these questions to connect more deeply with the upcoming content. Write down the answers to these five questions before starting the chapter.

1. **Learning and Memory:** Reflect on your current learning habits. How do you usually absorb new information, and how effectively do you retain it?

2. **Nutrition for the Brain:** Consider your current diet. Are there changes you can make to better support brain health and cognitive function?

3. **Critical Thinking Application:** Think of a recent situation where you used critical thinking. How did you approach it, and what was the outcome?

4. **Memory in Daily Life:** Identify a practical scenario where enhanced memory skills would be beneficial. How could improving your memory impact this situation?

5. **Creative Solutions:** Recall a problem or challenge you faced recently. How might creative thinking or a different learning approach have led to a better solution?

As you proceed through Level 4, use these reflections to guide your understanding and application of the skills related to brain optimization, critical thinking, and effective learning strategies.

SKILL 23:
BRAIN NUTRITION*

"Most people probably don't equate a healthy diet with a good mood or better memory. But, like an expensive car, our brains require premium fuel to function at its best."
—Kristine Carlson[108]

FEELING UNFOCUSED OR MENTALLY FOGGY CAN BE A COMMON challenge, especially when juggling life's demands. However, including brain foods in your diet can be a game-changer, helping you to sharpen focus, boost productivity, and enhance overall cognitive performance.[109] A plate of brain food a day keeps mental fog at bay.

BRAIN FOODS: YOUR COGNITIVE SUPERCHARGERS

---

* *This section (Skill 23) was professionally reviewed by Kathryn Wilson, PhD in clinical psychology.*

The best brain foods to incorporate into your diet for enhanced brain health include:

- **Oily Fish:** They are a rich source of Omega-3 fatty acids, crucial for brain health. Omega-3s help build membranes around each cell in the body, including brain cells, thus improving the structure of neurons.

- **Green, Leafy Vegetables:** Foods like kale, spinach, collards, and broccoli contain brain-healthy nutrients such as Vitamin K, lutein, folate, and beta-carotene. These nutrients may help slow cognitive decline. They help protect your brain from oxidative stress and cell damage caused by free radicals in the body and support overall brain health.

- **Fruits and Whole Foods:** A diet rich in fruits, vegetables, whole grains, legumes, and healthier fats can enhance the brain's memory functioning. These foods provide a variety of essential nutrients that support brain health.

- **Blueberries:** Blueberries are among the top brain foods. They are known for their antioxidant properties, which can positively affect the brain, potentially improving brain function and delaying age-related decline.

- **Nuts and Seeds:** They're not just for snacking, especially walnuts and flaxseeds. These little nutritional powerhouses are rich in Omega-3s and antioxidants, supporting brain health and cognitive function.

- **Eggs:** Eggs are beneficial for the brain, mainly because of their high choline content. Choline is a micronutrient used by the brain to create acetylcholine, a neurotransmitter that helps regulate mood and memory.

- **Healthy Fats:** Healthy fats like olive oil and avocados can provide similar brain benefits for vegetarians or those who prefer not to eat fish. These fats are essential for overall brain health and cognitive function.

- **Dark chocolate:** Dark chocolate is lauded for its brain-boosting potential, thanks to high concentrations of flavonoids that improve blood flow to the brain and stimulants that enhance focus and energy. Its mood-enhancing properties further make it a delicious and beneficial choice for cognitive health.

Including these foods in your diet can contribute significantly to maintaining and improving brain health. Remember, no single food can ensure a sharp mind, but a balanced diet combining these elements can offer brain-boosting benefits.

A diet that fuels your brain isn't just about these specific foods; it's about overall balance and nutrition.[110] Incorporating diverse fruits, vegetables, whole grains, lean proteins, and healthy fats creates a diet that supports your brain and entire body. Also, reducing your processed foods and sugar intake can significantly improve your concentration and cognitive function.

BRAIN-HEALTHY SUPPLEMENTS AND NOOTROPICS

Taking supplements can be beneficial when they address specific dietary deficiencies, health conditions, age-related needs, or lifestyle factors.

Some of these brain-healthy supplements are nootropics, which are dynamic compounds that powerfully affect the central nervous system. Some are naturally occurring compounds, like ginseng, while others are synthetic compounds. Nootropics are often referred to as "smart drugs" and are available in various combinations. As with any supplement, check with your healthcare provider before beginning a regime of supplements or nootropics, as some can interact with medications or certain health conditions. Also, supplements are best for complementing a healthy diet, not replacing it.[111] Some examples:

- **Omega-3 Fatty Acids:** Crucial for brain health and functioning, including healthy aging. These essential long-chain fats, which our bodies cannot produce independently, are found in foods like flaxseed oil, wild salmon, mackerel, walnuts, and sardines, as well as in fish oil supplements. Studies have also suggested that Omega-3 supplements can be used to treat symptoms of depression.[112]

- **B Vitamins:** Essential for brain function. B vitamins, including B complex supplements, significantly support cognitive health and brain function.

- **Antioxidants:** Help protect the brain from oxidative stress and improve cellular health. They are vital for combating free radical damage in the brain.

- **Ginkgo Biloba:** This is one of the oldest living tree species, and its leaf extracts are found in various supplements. Ginkgo biloba can enhance blood circulation and act as an antioxidant. These properties can improve brain function, particularly regarding memory and concentration.

- **Bacopa Monnieri:** Also known as Brahmi, this herb has a long history of use in Ayurvedic medicine. It has been traditionally used to enhance memory, learning rates, and cognitive processing.[113]

- **Citicoline:** A naturally occurring psychostimulant derived mainly from animal tissue. Studies have shown that citicoline increases the energy available to neurons and enhances neurotransmitter activity, leading to improvements in memory, attention, and concentration.[114]

- **Ginseng:** Triggers the production of nerve growth factor, which leads to the growth of new neurons and facilitates neuroplasticity. Numerous studies have shown that ginseng enhances learning and memory.[115]

- **Rhodiola rosea:** Adaptogen herb that increases the resiliency of neurons during times of stress and enhances overall brain function. It has been shown to improve memory, focus, and learning.[116]

Biohackers can attest to the benefits of experimenting with new approaches to discover personal breakthroughs. I have experimented with multiple foods and supplement combinations to make incremental improvements in my focus and performance throughout demanding workdays. When I started taking daily mushroom supplements along with Vitamin B complex, I noticed I had remarkably higher energy levels and better concentration and memory. Mushroom supplements have been gaining popularity as a natural means to support brain health, with several vital types bringing potential cognitive benefits.[117] Here's an overview of some notable mushroom supplements and why they might be beneficial:

- **Lion's Mane (*Hericium erinaceus*):** Perhaps the most well-known mushroom for brain health, Lion's Mane is reputed for its ability to support nerve growth factor (NGF) production.[118] NGF is essential for the growth, maintenance, and survival of neurons. Research suggests that Lion's Mane may enhance cognitive function, boost concentration, and potentially aid in the recovery of nervous system injuries. It's also being studied for its potential in treating neurodegenerative diseases like Alzheimer's and Parkinson's.

- **Reishi (*Ganoderma lucidum*):** Known for its calming properties, Reishi may help reduce stress and promote better sleep, which are crucial for cognitive health.[119] It's also recognized for its immune-boosting and antioxidant effects.[120]

- **Cordyceps (*Cordyceps sinensis*):** Often used by athletes for its energy-boosting properties, Cordyceps may also support brain health by improving oxygen utilization and enhancing circulation.[121] This benefit can lead to better brain function and overall vitality.

- **Chaga (*Inonotus obliquus*):** Rich in antioxidants, Chaga mushrooms can help protect the brain from oxidative stress, which is implicated in cognitive decline and neurodegenerative diseases.[122]

While the potential benefits of mushroom supplements for brain health are promising, it's important to use supplements cautiously. Supplements are not regulated as much as pharmaceuticals, so their quality can vary. Always choose high-quality products from reputable sources. Additionally, consult with a healthcare provider before starting any new supplement, especially if you have existing health conditions or are taking other medications, as there could be interactions or side effects to consider.

EXERCISE: THE BRAIN'S PHYSICAL WORKOUT

Regular exercise, particularly aerobic activities like jogging, swimming, or biking, is a critical factor in enhancing both physical and mental health, significantly impacting memory improvement.[123] It enhances neurogenesis, or the growth of new brain cells, particularly in the hippocampus, which is the center of memory. Exercise increases blood flow to the brain, delivering vital oxygen and nutrients for optimal function and enhancing neural connectivity for improved brain cell communication. This physical activity not only sculpts a healthier body but also sharpens the mind, reducing stress and anxiety leading to clearer thinking and stronger memory retention. In essence, routine aerobic exercise offers a comprehensive benefits package for your brain's health and performance.

Nurturing your brain through proper nutrition and regular exercise is essential for enhancing your mental performance and overall well-being. By adopting these habits, you're setting yourself up for a sharper, more focused, and creatively rich life.

SKILL 24:
CRITICAL THINKING

"It is the mark of an educated mind to be able to entertain a thought without accepting it."
—Aristotle

CRITICAL THINKING ACTS LIKE A FILTER THAT KEEPS JUNK reasoning from entering your mind. Just as brain nutrition is crucial for optimal function, critical thinking involves nourishing the mind with higher-quality reasoning.

Recognizing bad reasoning is essential; it empowers you in all aspects of life. Without this skill, you risk being swayed by more persuasive individuals, essentially living as a sheep to be herded by more persuasive people. In an age where information is overly abundant and opinions are more than plentiful, the ability to think critically is crucial.

Critical thinking involves analyzing information and arguments, separating fact from opinion, and distinguishing rational thought from emotional reaction. It's about being open-minded yet skeptical, questioning assumptions, and considering various viewpoints. This skill empowers you to make well-informed decisions, solve problems effectively, and understand the world more deeply. Whether deciphering a news article, engaging in a debate, or planning your future—honing your critical thinking skills will provide a foundation for success in both your personal and professional life.

STEPS TO IMPROVING YOUR CRITICAL THINKING

Step 1: Identify the argument being made
Let's be clear about what we are talking about when we refer to "argument." There is a difference between *having an argument* versus *making*

an argument. The former refers to heated debates or fights. When we talk about arguments in logic and **reasoning**, or *making an argument,* it's more about presenting a point of view backed by evidence and reason.

An argument is a collection of statements, with one or more premises providing data and reasoning to support a conclusion. Think of it like assembling puzzle pieces to grasp the full picture. Understanding this concept is foundational to logical reasoning. It's important to recognize that not all premises are explicitly stated; some are implied.

It's also essential to understand the content of what is being claimed or said in the stated context. The same statement can mean different things to different people in different situations, which is how misunderstanding can happen.

Step 2: Learn to spot fallacies

I sometimes pick up a newspaper or an opinion article and dissect the arguments. Often, there are several fallacies. A fallacy is an error or weakness in an argument or thought process. Fallacies are like the junk food of reasoning; they sell cheap, unhealthy reasoning in abundance. Fallacies make you buy the wrong conclusions, usually to push somebody else's agenda, but sometimes, fallacies are purely unintentional.

Fallacies happen when something is wrong with the data, the reasoning, the language used, or the strategic or psychological basis of the argument.[124] Spotting fallacies takes some analytical work. You need to examine the premises and see if they support the conclusion. Are the premises true? Do they logically lead to the conclusion? Spotting fallacies is a crucial skill. It helps you separate fact from fiction and make sound judgments and better decisions.

Here are some common types of fallacies to be on the lookout for:

- **Misuse of Authority or Tradition:**
  - *Appeal to Authority:* Using an authority figure's opinion as proof of an argument without providing evidence. Example: "This famous person thinks X, so X must be true."

  - *Appeal to Tradition:* Arguing something is right because it has always been done that way. Example: "This practice is best because it's been our tradition for centuries."

- **Appeals to Emotion or Popularity:**
  - *Appeal to Emotion:* Attempting to manipulate an emotional response in place of a valid argument. Example: Using dramatic but irrelevant imagery to sway opinions.
  - *Appeal to Fear:* Attempting to manipulate someone's fear to gain support for an argument. Example: "If we don't follow this policy, terrible things will happen!"
  - *Ad Populum (Bandwagon):* Assuming something is true or popular because many people believe it. Example: "Most people agree with X; therefore, X must be correct."

- **Attacks on the Person or Source:**
  - *Ad Hominem:* Attacking an individual's character or personal traits to discredit their argument. Example: "John's project idea is bad because he's lazy."
  - *Tu Quoque:* Dismissing someone's argument by asserting their failure to act consistently. Example: "You say smoking is bad, but you eat junk food."

- **False Comparisons and Generalizations:**
  - *False Dilemma:* Presenting only two options when more exist. Example: "You're either with us or against us."
  - *False Equivalence:* Comparing two unrelated or incomparable things. Example: "Not exercising is as bad as smoking."
  - *Hasty Generalization:* Drawing a conclusion about a group based on a small sample. Example: "I met two aggressive dogs, so all dogs must be aggressive."
  - *Straw Man:* Misrepresenting an argument to make it easier to attack. Example: "He wants to improve healthcare, so he must want to abolish private medicine entirely."

- **Flawed Reasoning Patterns:**

  - *Begging the Question (Circular Reasoning):* Restating a claim in different words to prove it. Example: "The new curriculum is effective because it's the best one, and it's the best one because it's been proven to be effective."

  - *Non Sequitur:* Making a conclusion that doesn't logically follow from the premises. Example: "She's wearing red shoes. She must be fun."

  - *Post Hoc (False Cause):* Mistakenly attributing causation to sequential events. Example: "My team wins every time I wear this hat."

  - *Red Herring:* Introducing a distracting topic to divert attention from the main issue. Example: "We can't worry about the environment when there are people who are unemployed."

  - *Slippery Slope:* Assuming a small action will lead to extreme outcomes. Example: "If we allow A to happen, then Z will eventually happen too."

  - *Loaded Question:* Asking a question that has a presumption built into it. Example: "Have you stopped cheating on your exams?"

  - *Equivocation:* Using ambiguous language to mislead. Example: "I have the right to watch what I want, which means it's right to watch anything."

  - *No True Scotsman:* Dismissing a counterexample by redefining the group. Example: "No true patriot would agree."

Step 3: Take fallacy-spotting skills to the next level through logic

Most fallacies are just bad logic. As a philosophy major at the College of William and Mary, I took two formal logic classes, which in many ways felt like a math class because we did exhaustive numbers of proofs. We learned how to reduce arguments to symbols and apply logical rules to test the validity of arguments. These classes helped my critical thinking because fallacies start melting away after improving logical reasoning skills.

There are different types of logic, like deductive and inductive logic. Deductive logic is about certainty—if the premises are true, the conclusion must be true. In contrast, inductive logic deals more with probability—the premises support the conclusion but don't guarantee it. Each type has its place, and learning to recognize and use them appropriately can supercharge your reasoning skills.

Logic benefits everyone, not just philosophers or computer scientists. At its core, logic is the study of reasoning. It's about understanding the principles that determine whether an argument is valid or invalid, sound or unsound. Logic helps you structure your thinking, making your arguments more robust and your conclusions more reliable.

Step 4: Be mindful of biases and keep them in check

It's crucial to understand the concepts of bias and fallacy. They may seem similar but play different roles in processing information and forming opinions.

Whereas fallacies are essentially errors or weaknesses in logical reasoning, biases are typically more subjective. Bias refers to a predisposition or inclination, often an unconscious one, that shapes your perspective, actions, or decisions. It's like having a pair of tinted glasses that color how you see the world. This inclination can draw from personal experiences, beliefs, or emotions, often resulting in a subjective viewpoint.

For example, confirmation bias makes you seek information that aligns with your existing beliefs while ignoring anything that contradicts it. Then there's in-group bias, where you favor people from your own group. Biases can be innate or learned, influencing how you process information while leading you away from objective reasoning.

Here are some examples of major forms of biases with some examples:

Cognitive Biases: These biases impact how we process information and make decisions. They often stem from our brain's tendency to simplify information processing.

- **Confirmation Bias:** This is when we favor information that confirms our preexisting beliefs. For example, if you believe online learning is ineffective, you're more likely to notice and remember articles supporting this view, ignoring evidence to the contrary.

- **Anchoring Bias:** This happens when we rely too heavily on the first information we receive. If the first car you see at a dealership has a price of $20,000, you might use this as an anchor, making all other prices seem reasonable or expensive in comparison.

Social Biases: These biases affect how we perceive and interact with other people.

- **In-group Bias:** The tendency to favor people who belong to the same group as us. For instance, a gamer might instinctively trust fellow gamers' opinions over non-gamers.

- **Stereotyping:** Assuming that everyone in a particular group behaves the same way. For example, believing all older people are bad at technology is a common stereotype.

Memory Biases: These biases influence how we remember events and information.

- **Hindsight Bias:** When we believe, after an event has occurred, that we predicted or expected the outcome. For instance, after a football game, you might claim you knew your team would win, even if you had doubts.

- **Self-serving Bias:** This is the tendency to attribute positive events to our own character but attribute negative events to external factors. For example, if you get a good grade, you think it's due to your hard work, but a bad grade is due to an unfair exam.

Decision-Making Biases: These biases affect our choices and judgments.

- **Overconfidence Bias:** Believing our abilities or insights are better than they indeed are. It's like thinking you can finish a massive project in a week, underestimating the time and effort required.

- **Status Quo Bias:** The preference to keep things the same rather than change. For instance, perhaps you are sticking to your current phone model even though a newer version offers significant improvements.

Belief Biases: These biases shape our beliefs and uphold our existing worldviews.

- **Optimism/Pessimism Bias:** This is when we expect the best or the worst outcome, respectively. If you're optimistic, you might underestimate the risks in a situation, like not studying enough for a test because you think it'll be easy.

- **Just-world Hypothesis:** The belief that good things happen to good people and bad things happen to bad people. For example, thinking someone is wealthy because they worked hard and deserve it, ignoring factors like inheritance or privilege.

Step 5: Understand Other Perspectives

Understanding other perspectives is like putting on new glasses—the world looks different. It's about recognizing and appreciating viewpoints that differ from our own. Typically, doing this does not come naturally, but this skill is crucial in a world where diverse thoughts and ideas intersect. It fosters empathy, helps resolve conflicts, and leads to more inclusive dialogue and decision-making.

Analyzing different perspectives broadens your understanding and sharpens your critical thinking. It's a mental workout that builds your ability to analyze, question, and develop more nuanced opinions. Plus, it equips you with the tools to navigate complex social and cultural landscapes.

Wrapping up our exploration of critical thinking, we've untangled the web of logical fallacies and biases. These aren't just theoretical concepts but tools for sharper, real-world reasoning. We challenge our assumptions and rethink our views by spotting these thinking traps and biases. Being able to analyze better is a path to understanding the world more deeply.

SKILL 25:
MEMORY ENHANCEMENT

"Men [and women] have become the tools of their tools."
—Henry David Thoreau

W E ALL HAVE THOSE MOMENTS WHEN OUR MEMORY FAL-
ters, like forgetting names or misplacing keys. But here's some
good news: boosting your memory is possible. Imagine effortlessly recalling faces, names, and numbers, or rapidly learning new languages.

Memory is a crucial mental function, but it is often underutilized
in our tech-dominated world. Think of memory as a muscle; exercising it makes it stronger. A sharp memory is key for effective planning,
reasoning, and action. It also enhances overall brain health. We'll
explore why we forget and introduce ways to 'hack' our memory for
better retention.

Ancient civilizations, without today's digital tools, developed
techniques to dramatically improve memory. These skills, leading to
astounding memory feats, are accessible for anyone to learn and use
today.

Sometimes, we hear of exceptional cases like Marilu Henner, an
actress with Highly Superior Autobiographical Memory (HSAM), and
Stephen Wiltshire, an artist known for his detailed cityscapes drawn
from memory. However, you don't have to be a prodigy to enhance
your memory. There are established methods to train your brain for
remarkable memory achievements. For example, learning to construct
memory palaces can offer you a game-changing memory tool.

CONSTRUCTING A MEMORY PALACE

Imagine boosting your memory to extraordinary levels, where you can
recall vast amounts of information more easily. That's where a memory

palace, or the Method of Loci, comes in. It's an ancient mnemonic technique that involves visualizing a familiar space and placing vivid, memorable images to recall information easily. It's like turning your mind into a virtual mansion of memories. Once you learn it, it's a convenient tool; for example, I have used memory palaces to memorize speeches or presentations without notes.

The memory palace has a long history of effectiveness, dating back to ancient times. Its origin is often attributed to the Greek poet Simonides of Ceos, who famously used this method after a tragic incident at a banquet. When the hall collapsed, killing everyone inside, Simonides was able to recall where each guest had been seated, thus helping identify the victims. This historical account highlights the method's effectiveness and longstanding use, with phrases like "in the first place" that are remnants of this ancient Greek practice.[125]

The memory palace technique, rooted in using spatial memory, leverages our brain's innate strength in remembering locations and spatial relationships. Your recall abilities strengthen significantly by associating the information you need to remember with specific locations within a mentally constructed space. The success of a memory palace hinges on the use of vivid and creative imagery. Employing bold, unusual, and emotionally engaging images as mnemonic devices makes the information more memorable. The more outlandish and unique the imagery, the more likely it will cement itself in your memory.

This useful technique can assist you with remembering lots of things. For example, as a study aid, it proves invaluable for memorizing diverse material, ranging from complex biology concepts to extensive historical timelines. It also serves as a practical tool for everyday tasks. For instance, you can use a memory palace to remember shopping lists or daily to-dos, transforming mundane memorization into an engaging mental exercise.

STEPS FOR BUILDING A MEMORY PALACE

There are four main steps to building a memory palace you can use to store memories:

- **Step 1: Choose a place you know well.** Start by selecting a location you know well, preferably one with a lot of detail and variation. This could be a home, school, a building, or even a street.

- **Step 2: Visualize the place in detail.** Draw a detailed mental picture of your chosen place. Designate some salient places to serve as memory stations (also called "loci"). For example, that could include corners, furniture, fixtures, and other details you can remember. The place can be inside, outside, or both.

- **Step 3: Create a path.** Starting from a logical place, such as an entrance, move through the different rooms or sections. This place will be your "memory palace." Creating a logical path that you remember is essential.

- **Step 4: Associate items with each memory station.** Technically, Steps 1 to 3 constructed your empty memory palace, and this step is about filling it with things you want to remember. As you journey through your memory palace, forge strong associations between the items you want to remember and each memory station. These items could be objects, people, or anything else you can think of in a visual way. The wackier and more memorable your associations, the better it will stick!

After you construct it, in order to use it, do a mental walkthrough; just imagine walking through it, recalling your stored items. To make the most of your memory palace, regularly imagine yourself walking through it, recalling each item. It's important to keep this mental space uncluttered—overloading it with information or reusing it too much can lead to confusion. Instead, separate memory palaces for different topics should be created. As you improve at this technique, you can expand existing ones or develop new palaces for various subjects.

MY MEMORY PALACE JOURNEY

One of the first memory palaces I constructed was my house when I lived and worked in Malawi. I created a memory journey that traced my regular morning routine from waking up, going to the bathroom, getting dressed, checking on the kids, getting breakfast, etc. Each room was a station. I would practice recalling things each day as I walked the path. It was handy. Initially, I started with ten stations, or one per room.

Later, I expanded it to forty stations by converting each room corner into a station of its own. I remembered which corner was which by thinking of the northeastern corner and moving clockwise from A to D. I used this memory palace to remember up to forty things by putting imaginary images into the corners.*

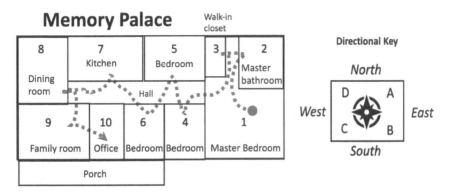

Building and using a memory palace can be a fun and creative way to enhance your memory. With practice, you'll find it an invaluable tool for study, work, and everyday life, turning memory into an art form.[126] Memory palaces are just the tip of the iceberg of memory techniques. There are so many different memory skills that could fill many books, but I hope I have piqued your interest so you can explore it further.

---

*   Since I lived in the house, the furniture would keep moving around, so I didn't want to anchor any memories to my furniture in this case. I made sure to orient myself in each room so that I would face North and start storing or recalling things from the upper right corner, Corner A, then moving clockwise, ending with Corner D in each room.

SKILL 26:
LEARNING ACCELERATION

"The more that you read, the more things you will know.
The more that you learn, the more places you'll go."
—Dr. Seuss

IN A WORLD INUNDATED WITH INFORMATION, IT PAYS TO TAKE in information faster and retain it better. Mastering the art of speed reading plus better learning retention can accelerate your learning efficiency, especially for those of us who consume vast quantities of information daily.

SPEED READING:
TECHNIQUES FOR ENHANCED COMPREHENSION

Just like being able to run faster, you can learn to read faster.[127] Speed reading isn't just zipping through text at super speed. It's all about finding that sweet spot where you're reading quickly but still really getting what the text is all about. Here are some techniques:

- **Minimize Your Distractions:** Get in a place where you can read without being distracted. One way I like doing this is using noise-canceling headphones with focus-conducive music without words. Others might prefer reading in silence.

- **Preview Before Reading:** It's essential to get in tune with the context of what you are reading before you dive in. Spend a minute skimming through the text to get a gist of the content. Doing this primes your brain for what's to come and helps you comprehend faster as you read.

- **Minimize Subvocalization:** Subvocalization, the habit of silently pronouncing each word as you read, can slow you down. Try to reduce this internal speech. One method is consciously visualizing the concepts rather than "hearing" the words.

- **Use a Pointer:** Your finger, a pen, or even a moving cursor can guide your eyes more swiftly across the page, reducing the chance of skipping back to previous words (regression).

- **Expand Your Peripheral Vision:** Train your eyes to capture more words in a single glance. This technique reduces the number of eye movements per line and increases your reading speed. Practice focusing on the center of a line and trying to perceive the beginning and end of the line in your peripheral vision.

A key to boosting your learning efficiency is actively engaging with the material, such as through questioning and summarizing, or using a tool such as mind mapping for visual organization. Teaching the material to others can solidify your understanding, while spaced repetition helps in long-term retention. Embrace multimodal learning, combining reading with audiovisual resources, and focus on deep understanding over rote memorization. These strategies enhance both memory and application of knowledge.

USE SPACED REPETITION TO BETTER RETAIN WHAT YOU LEARN

Spaced repetition might sound like a fancy term, but it's a practical technique that can boost learning and remembering. Think about it like a workout plan for your brain, where you're gradually increasing the intensity to build stronger memory muscles.

Here's the lowdown: when you learn something new, instead of cramming it all in one go, you revisit it at specific intervals over time. Say you learn a bunch of new Spanish words today. Instead of trying to memorize them all at once, you'd review them tomorrow, then maybe in two days, then a week later, and so on. When you revisit these words, they get more firmly planted in your brain.

Why does this work? It's all about giving your brain just the right amount of challenge. Review too soon, and it's boring because you just saw it. Wait too long, and you might forget it. Spaced repetition finds that sweet spot where your brain has to work a bit to recall, strengthening your memory in the process.

THE FORGETTING CURVE

The forgetting curve, introduced by psychologist Hermann Ebbinghaus, shows how information is lost over time if we don't make an effort to retain it. It's like a downward slope in remembering, starting right after you learn something new. Ebbinghaus found that without any review or reinforcement, people tend to forget an astonishing amount—around 50% of the new information within an hour and an overwhelming 70% or so within twenty-four hours.[128] Essentially, the curve tells us that our memories fade quickly, but regularly revisiting the material can significantly slow down this process of forgetting.

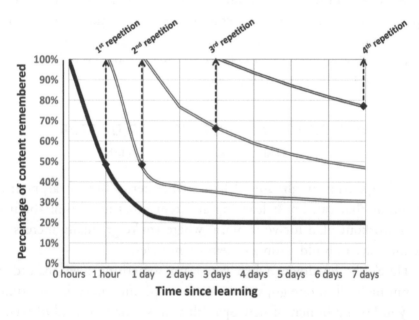

Spaced repetition is a versatile technique. It's not just for language learning; you can use it for almost anything—history dates, math formulas, science concepts, you name it. Also, you don't need any fancy tools to get started. You could use simple index cards with the Leitner System,[129] a learning technique where you sort flashcards into a series of boxes based on how well you know the material. Cards answered correctly progress to the next box and are reviewed less frequently, while incorrect ones return to the first box for more frequent review.

We're living in the digital age, right? Apps like Quizlet and Anki take this to the next level by applying algorithms for spaced repetition to improve your learning and recall.[130] They keep track of what you know and schedule reviews at the perfect time, so you're constantly challenging your brain just enough.

Spaced repetition can be a game-changer for your learning in general. It makes studying more efficient (so you spend less time hitting the books) and helps you remember stuff way longer (which is excellent when exams roll around). Plus, it's a skill that'll come in handy throughout life, whether you're picking up a new hobby, learning a skill for a job, or anything else.

By combining speed reading techniques with better retention methods like spaced repetition, you can consume information rapidly and retain and apply it effectively. This skill set is crucial for anyone aiming to thrive in the modern information-rich environment, ensuring they stay ahead in their academic and professional pursuits.

SKILL 27:
CREATIVE THINKING

*"We can't solve problems by using the same kind of thinking
we used when we created them."*
—Albert Einstein

C REATIVE THINKING OPENS DOORS TO A BETTER WORLD. IT'S a skill anyone can cultivate; it's not just for 'creatives.' Let's learn some ways to think outside the box. Divergent thinking is about generating multiple ideas, answers to problems, and discoveries. There are a ton of ways to foster divergent and creative thinking.

THE ART OF CREATIVE THINKING

A key way to unlock creative thinking is to frame the right questions. Questions are powerful tools for unlocking creative solutions, driving innovation, and uncovering new insights. By becoming skilled at asking the right questions, especially unconventional ones, you can break through barriers holding you back and open up a world of possibilities.

**Asking powerful questions can help you
uncover hidden opportunities and develop
new perspectives on existing problems.**

It can also help you to better understand yourself and the people around you, enabling you to make more informed decisions and develop meaningful relationships. By becoming more aware of the questions you ask and the quality of those questions, you can unlock the doors to a more successful and satisfying life, personally and professionally. Innovation often starts with a question.

Here are some tips for asking questions that spark creativity:

- **Open-Ended Questions:** "How could we revolutionize this process?"

- **Challenge Assumptions:** "Why does it have to be done this way? What if we changed our approach?"

- **Foster Curiosity:** "What haven't we considered? What's the wildest solution possible?"

- **Encourage Bold Ideas:** Make it safe to share any idea, no matter how 'out there' it seems. Also, "What if?" is a powerful question.

- **Focus on User Experience:** "How will this affect our users? How can we enhance their experience?"

THE SCAMPER TECHNIQUE

As a former management consultant, I was paid to develop creative ideas to improve organizations. One day, somebody handed me a brilliant book called *Thinker Toys,* and that is where I learned about SCAMPER, a handy acronym used to help stimulate creative thinking and problem-solving. It stands for Substitute, Combine, Adapt, Modify, Put to Other Uses, Eliminate, and Reverse/Rearrange. SCAMPER is particularly useful for designing something new.

- **Substitute:** What alternative elements can you use? E.g., designing a chair? Consider different seating materials.

- **Combine:** Merge different concepts. A chair and a rocker, perhaps?

- **Adapt:** Tailor solutions to new scenarios. How can a chair design fit into a minimalist space?

- **Modify:** What changes can enhance your design? Think of shape, size, and material.

- **Put to Other Uses:** Can your chair double as a coat rack or side table?

- **Eliminate:** What's unnecessary? Simplify for elegance and efficiency.

- **Reverse/Rearrange:** Reimagine the layout. Swap chair arms and legs, for instance.

Using SCAMPER can help unlock new ideas and ways of looking at a problem. It can be an effective tool for problem-solving and creative thinking.

A FAMOUS SUBTRACTION EXAMPLE

The history of doughnuts is a bit of a mystery, as it is unclear who first created the delicious treat. Some believe that native Americans invented doughnuts as early as the 19th century, while others believe that Dutch settlers brought the recipe to America in the 18th century. One of the earliest known recipes for doughnuts dates back to 1803 when an American cookbook included a recipe for "dough nuts." This recipe called for cutting the dough into small pieces, frying them in hot lard, and then rolling them in sugar.

However, the modern doughnut, as we know it today, was likely invented in the mid-19th century. An American baker named Hanson Gregory claimed to have invented the ring-shaped doughnut in 1847 when he was only sixteen. According to Gregory's story, he punched a hole in the center of the doughnuts to make them cook more evenly. Gregory's subtraction of the hole has forever changed and characterized the modern doughnut for generations.[131]

LATERAL THINKING:
ENHANCING CREATIVITY AND PROBLEM-SOLVING

Lateral thinking, pioneered by Edward De Bono in 1967, is a method of creative problem-solving that encourages looking at issues from fresh and unconventional perspectives. De Bono said, "Creativity involves breaking out of established patterns in order to look at things in a different way."[132] Here's an enhanced list of strategies with some thought-provoking questions to prompt deeper thinking. These types of questions not only foster creativity but also broaden the scope of problem-solving, leading to more innovative and effective solutions.

- **Understanding the Problem:**

    o **Reverse Assumptions:** "What if our initial assumptions are completely wrong?"

    o **Interconnections:** "How are different elements of this problem interconnected?"

    o **Root Cause Analysis:** "What is the fundamental root cause of this problem?"

    o **Probing the Unknown:** "What critical aspects of the problem might we be overlooking?"

- **Learning from Experience:**

    o **Past Successes:** "What strategies have worked for similar issues?"

    o **Use of Analogies:** "Can we draw parallels with similar situations or problems?"

- **Resource and Risk Management:**

    o **Resource Identification:** "What resources are readily available for solving this problem?"

    o **Risk Assessment:** "What are the potential risks associated with our options?"

- **Creative and Unconventional Thinking:**

    o **Unconventional Solutions:** "Can we think of a solution that's completely out of the box?" (You could use a technique like SCAMPER, creative brainstorming, mind maps, and other methods for expanding your thinking.)

- ○ **Outside Perspectives:** "How would someone without prior knowledge of this issue approach it?"

- **Broader Impact and Stakeholder Consideration:**

  - ○ **Potential Consequences:** "What unintended consequences might arise from our chosen approach?"

  - ○ **Stakeholder Inclusion:** "Who else should be involved in the problem-solving process?"

  - ○ **External Influences:** "Are there external factors that could impact our solution?"

- **Reflection and Collaborative Feedback:**

  - ○ **Reflective Breaks:** "Can stepping back from the problem provide new insights?"

  - ○ **Defining Success:** "How will we define success in resolving this problem?"

  - ○ **Collaborative Feedback:** "What fresh ideas can others contribute to this problem?"

  - ○ **Broad Exploration:** "What other factors or solutions might we be missing?"

Remember, creativity isn't an innate talent but a skill to develop with practice. Put on your creative thinking hat and try out some of these techniques to tackle your next challenge or invention. By regularly practicing these techniques and exercises, you can enhance your creative thinking and ability to innovate. Whether through mind mapping, the SCAMPER technique, or simply asking the right questions, each step is a leap toward becoming a more innovative thinker. Your creative journey might just lead to the next big breakthrough. So, go ahead, think differently, and see where your imagination takes you.

SKILL 28:
LANGUAGE LEARNING

*"One language sets you in a corridor for life.
Two languages open every door along the way."*
—Frank Smith

EARNING A NEW LANGUAGE DOES MORE THAN JUST ALLOW you to communicate with a broader range of people; it profoundly benefits your brain. Research has shown that bilingualism or multilingualism can improve cognitive skills unrelated to language. For starters, it enhances your ability to do task-switching.[133] When switching between languages, your brain becomes more adept at juggling multiple tasks simultaneously. My multilingual colleagues are some of the best jugglers I know.

Moreover, being multilingual has been linked to better memory, improved problem-solving skills, and greater mental flexibility. It also delays the onset of age-related cognitive decline and dementia. Speaking multiple languages keeps your brain sharp and agile, giving it a rigorous mental workout that can pay off in many aspects of life.

TECHNIQUES FOR EFFECTIVE LANGUAGE LEARNING

Effective language learning involves a blend of different techniques, each catering to various aspects of the process. Taking formal classes, like those available on websites like Preply, provides a structured approach, especially beneficial for grammar.

Immersive learning (e.g., watching movies, listening to music, or reading in the target language) helps in understanding the language's rhythm and flow. Regular practice is crucial; even a few minutes daily is more effective than lengthy, infrequent sessions.

Interactive language learning apps like Duolingo are excellent for building vocabulary and basic grammar. Engaging in language exchanges with native speakers on platforms like Tandem allows for practical application and mutual learning. Incorporating memory techniques, such as spaced repetition, enhances retention.

Combining a range of language-learning methods leads to a comprehensive approach to language learning. While they may not guarantee fluency, they significantly enhance the ability to engage with and navigate different cultures.

A LESS TEDIOUS WAY TO LEARN NEW VOCABULARY

Let's dive deeper into the fascinating world of memorizing languages and vocabulary. A shortcut to learning languages, or anything else, faster is to link what you are learning with something you already know.

Technique 1: Identify the shared patterns of similar words
Some languages share roots, and when you understand those patterns, you can shortcut learning a significant amount of vocabulary. For example, Spanish, French, Portuguese, and Italian are descendants of Latin, or we call these Romance languages. Even though English descended from Germanic languages, it borrowed a significant portion of its vocabulary from Romance languages.[134] So, if you are learning a Romance language like Spanish, from English or vice versa, you can learn to identify these vocabulary similarities.

Using this principle, we are going to learn thirty Spanish words quickly. Here are some example patterns to shortcut learning Spanish vocabulary:

English → Spanish for words ending in -al:
Hospital → Hospital (a main difference is the "h" is silence in Spanish pronunciation)

Manual → Manual

Personal → Personal (In Spanish, "personal" can also serve as a noun meaning "staff," similar to English "personnel")

Animal → Animal

Cultural → Cultural

Professional → Profesional (slight spelling differences)

National → Nacional (slight spelling differences)

Capital → Capital

Global → Global

Original → Original

English → Spanish for nouns ending in -tion

Information → Información

Education → Educación

Population → Población

Communication → Comunicación

Organization → Organización

Operation → Operación

Situation → Situación

Transformation → Transformación

Generation → Generación

Celebration → Celebración

We can even convert these words to their verb equivalents. To convert these nouns ending in "-tion" to their verb equivalents, we can generally make the following changes:

Information: Inform → Información: Informar

Education: Educate → Educación: Educar

Population: Populate $\rightarrow$ Población: Poblar

Communication: Communicate $\rightarrow$ Comunicación: Comunicar

Organization: Organize $\rightarrow$ Organización: Organizar

Operation: Operate $\rightarrow$ Operación: Operar

Situation: Situate $\rightarrow$ Situación: Situar

Transformation: Transform $\rightarrow$ Transformación: Transformar

Generation: Generate $\rightarrow$ Generación: Generar

Celebration: Celebrate $\rightarrow$ Celebración: Celebrar

That's thirty Spanish words in total, based on English words we already know. Pretty quick, wasn't it? We could use this principle and rapidly expand it to thousands of Spanish words. We would need to learn how to pronounce them in Spanish, practice hearing and saying them, and understand where there are any notable differences in spellings or meaning.

It's important to be aware of false cognates, which are words that seem like they should mean the same thing in different languages but actually have different meanings. These can lead to amusing misunderstandings. For example, I once inquired about the well-being of a Guatemalan colleague, who responded, "Actualmente, estoy constipado." At first glance, this might sound like, "Actually, I'm constipated." However, this sentence contains two false cognates. "Actualmente" translates to "currently" or "nowadays," not "actually," and "constipado" in this context means "having a cold" or "stuffy" in terms of a blocked nose rather than "constipated." It certainly made for a humorous mix-up.

Technique 2: If there is not an obvious linkage to something you already know, invent one using imaginative associations
The principle is associating new, unknown things you are trying to learn with things you already know. For example, take the Spanish **"Cómo estás?"** Pronounced "CO mow es TAHS," which means: How

are you? (informal). I might imagine the beautiful mountain range in Colorado called Estes. You could imagine somebody falling into a **Coma** at **Estes,** and you might ask that person, "Como estas?" Obviously, they wouldn't answer.

This technique works better when you develop your own linkages because they need to relate to something YOU are familiar with. The mnemonic linkages serve as a memory crutch. After you start using the foreign words in actual sentences, the need for mnemonic encoding goes away, and the words start sticking to your memory themselves.

Imagination is a powerful tool for learning and memory if you learn to apply it as a tool. A less tedious way to remember new vocabulary is to make funny, memorable connections with new words to familiar things. The wackier, the more memorable.

So there you have it: a range of different tools and techniques can make language learning a more memorable and enjoyable journey.

SKILL 29:
AI FLUENCY

"Artificial Intelligence is the new electricity."
—Andrew Ng [135]

SOME PEOPLE MIGHT WONDER WHY I HAVE INCLUDED A SKILL
for Artificial Intelligence (AI)* under a chapter about unlocking
your brain's superpower. At the time of this writing, the world has
changed overnight as AI went from being an academic subject to a
mainstream tool after the debut of ChatGPT and a host of other AI
systems. Now, industry experts are heralding the advent of AI as the
next Industrial Revolution.[136] If you don't understand it, you will be
left behind. AI is now a superpower, and if used properly, AI can be
used as an amazing tool to enhance what you can do with your talents.
It can save time and make you more productive.

When I worked at IBM, I remember how research colleagues
pioneered AI advances that started making the headlines. Watson was
an IBM AI supercomputer that stepped into the spotlight in 2011
when it beat two champions on the TV quiz show Jeopardy! Watson's

---

*   Artificial Intelligence (AI) is a branch of computer science focused on creating
intelligent machines capable of performing tasks that typically require human
intelligence. These tasks include learning, problem-solving, decision-making, and
understanding language.

AI works by analyzing loads of information and learning from it, just like how you
learn from reading books or listening to teachers. The more data AI has, the better
it gets at making predictions or decisions. For example, when you use a language
learning app, AI looks at how you answer questions, figures out what you're good at
and what you need more practice with, and then customizes your lessons accordingly.
AI isn't just one thing; it comes in many forms. Some AI can do specific tasks, like
recognizing your face to unlock your phone, while others, like those used by scientists
and engineers, are way more complex and can help solve big problems like climate
change or develop new medicines.

extraordinary power was understanding natural language, which is challenging for computers. It could read clues, understand nuances, and come up with answers just like a human contestant.

Then we started seeing AI go mainstream, such as in Amazon's Alexa or Microsoft's Siri on devices where you could ask simple instructions using natural language. The floodgates to AI opened after the public release of ChatGPT, developed by OpenAI, in late 2022. ChatGPT quickly gained attention for its ability to generate human-like text responses, significantly advancing natural language processing and AI-driven conversation models. Within a year, there were thousands of emerging uses of AI powered by ChatGPT and other rivals, such as Google's version of AI. AI seems to be evolving extremely quickly, but it's changing everything.

SOME OF THE MANY PRACTICAL USES OF AI FOR YOU TO TRY OUT

AI technology offers a variety of practical applications that can enhance different aspects of your life:

- As a **Homework Assistant**, AI helps with complex academic problems and essay brainstorming, acting more like a tutor than a solution provider. It's important to use AI ethically, ensuring it aids learning rather than replaces it.

- AI can be a **Creative Collaborator** in fields like music, writing, or visual arts. Tools like DALL-E generate unique visuals, while AI programs like OpenAI's Jukebox assist in composing music.

- For coding enthusiasts, AI serves as a **Programming Assistant**, aiding in writing code and creating formulas for spreadsheets, thereby streamlining the coding process.

- In language learning, AI acts as a **Companion**, adapting to individual learning styles and offering exercises in reading, writing, listening, and speaking, like Duolingo or Rosetta Stone's TruAccent® for better pronunciation.[137]

- As a **Health and Fitness Guide**, AI tailors workout plans and nutrition advice, with apps like Fitbod personalizing exercise routines and Lifesum analyzing eating habits for healthier choices.[138]

AI's diverse applications, from academic assistance to creative collaboration, programming, language learning, and health guidance, demonstrate its role as a powerful ally. The key is to use AI to augment abilities and enrich the learning process.

LEARNING TO USE AI RESPONSIBLY

The cool thing about AI is that you don't have to be a tech whiz to use it. Plenty of online courses, apps, and videos make learning about AI fun and easy. AI offers incredible opportunities for efficiency and creativity, but it's crucial to use it with awareness and caution. It's like a powerful tool that amplifies your capabilities, but with great power comes great responsibility.

Understanding and responsibly using AI involves recognizing its limitations and ethical implications. AI is a valuable tool that can enhance task efficiency, but it should not replace human judgment and creativity. Always verify AI-generated information and use it as a starting point, not as a definitive answer.

Be cautious of AI's immense potential to spread disinformation, and practice diligent fact-checking. Be mindful of privacy concerns, as AI could store or use your inputs; understand how your information is used.

Avoid overreliance on AI; it should complement, not replace, your skills and knowledge. Stay informed about AI's rapid evolution and its ethical considerations to ensure your use aligns with societal values. Lastly, critical thinking should be applied to AI outputs, as these tools may not fully grasp context or human emotions.

Take a lesson from Wall-E, who was an AI robot himself. If you remember the movie *Wall-E*, you might recall all those fat, lazy, posthuman people lying around sipping smoothies on some space cruise ship. The ship was run by AI, who wanted to keep the people lazy, fat, and complacent. That funny, classic movie is an excellent warning that we should never grow complacent or too comfortable, or we will become weaker by that complacency.

THE TECHNOLOGY VS. BRAIN DILEMMA

As we grow more reliant on technology, we must be careful not to use it as a crutch. With smartphones storing phone numbers and AI creating art on demand, one might question the need to improve brain functions like memory or learn skills like painting, music, or writing. Why bother when technology can do it for us?

While these advancements can undoubtedly improve lives, we must use them wisely. In January 2024, Elon Musk's brain-chip company Neuralink successfully implanted a chip in Noland Arbaugh, a quadriplegic. This breakthrough allowed him to control computer cursors with his mind, significantly enhancing his quality of life.[139] This is a testament to the empowering potential of technology, and as it continues to advance, we can look forward to more such life-changing innovations.

However, we must tread carefully. The technology we use should make us stronger, not weaker. As a technology lover and former IBMer, I firmly believe that technology should complement, *but not replace* our basic skills, relationships, and humanity.

> **Technology should always be a tool that serves human beings, not the other way around.**

Maintaining skills like memory is essential for our independence from technology. Imagine being captive to a company's neurological implant that requires a lifetime subscription. While some emergent technologies sound like science fiction, science fiction often precedes real science. One day, AI will undoubtedly progress into general superintelligence. Let us hope it will be benevolent.

Remember, your brain is your most essential tool. Don't outsource your brain, lest you surrender your intellectual abilities and freedom to somebody or something else to control. The idea is to unlock your brain, not lock it up.

In a nutshell, AI is a new superpower, but we must use it responsibly. It's exciting and can do awesome stuff, but remember, it's most potent when used alongside your own talents and skills. Dive into AI, explore its possibilities, and see how it can add a zing to your life and studies, but responsibly. Welcome to the future—it's going to be amazing with AI in your toolkit!

To recap, as a handy way to remember key concepts in this chapter, let's put on our BRIGHTS (**B**rain nutrition for cognitive function, **R**easoning for clearer thinking, **I**mproving memory, **G**reater learning speed, **H**at for creative thinking, **T**actical language learning, and **S**avvy with AI).

Now that we've equipped ourselves with techniques to boost our learning and critical thinking, it's time to turn these enhanced mental tools toward something equally important: our interactions with others. In Level 5, we dive into the art of interpersonal skills and learn to embrace the rich tapestry of diversity. Let's explore how our sharpened minds can help us connect more deeply and effectively with the people around us.

LEVEL 5:
BUILD BRIDGES, BREAK BARRIERS

A T THIS POINT, WE SHIFT GEARS FROM HONING INDIVIDUAL
skills to mastering the art of relationships. Here, we'll explore
the essential people skills that transform casual connections into
meaningful, lifelong relationships.

These skills extend far beyond just making friends or impressing
others in interviews. They're about forging lasting bonds and overcoming social challenges with confidence.

Level 5 builds on the emotional intelligence skills discussed earlier
(Skill 3). It will guide you through navigating various social landscapes, from chilling with friends to collaborating on projects, and
making your mark professionally. Get ready to level up your relationship skills and break through those social barriers!

Self-Assessment

As we explore interpersonal skills and appreciating diversity, let's start with a self-assessment to understand your current capabilities and aspirations in these areas. Consider these questions. Write down the answers to these questions before starting the chapter.

1. **Current Interpersonal Skills:** Reflect on your current interpersonal skills. How would you rate your abilities in listening, empathy, and assertiveness?

2. **Diversity Awareness:** Think about your exposure to diverse cultures and perspectives. How comfortable are you in diverse settings, and what do you hope to learn about embracing diversity?

3. **Public Speaking and Conflict Resolution:** Assess your comfort level with public speaking and handling conflicts. What are your strengths and areas for improvement?

4. **Networking and Teamwork:** How effective are you at networking and working in teams? Identify a recent experience that highlights your skills or challenges in these areas.

5. **Personal and Professional Goals:** What personal or professional goals do you have that relate to improving interpersonal skills and understanding diversity?

As you proceed through Level 5, use these reflections to guide your understanding and application of the skills.

SKILL 30:
TRULY LISTENING

"Most people do not listen with the intent to understand;
they listen with the intent to reply."
—Stephen R. Covey

THINK BACK TO THE BEGINNING OF THIS BOOK—DO YOU recall what Skill 1 was? It was Pay Attention! Truly listening means tuning in not just to what people say but also to what they're not saying—if you're really paying attention. This skill is the foundation for all other people skills. Truly listening to people will make you a better human being.

The world has too many talkers and not enough listeners. People like to hear themselves talk, but if not enough people listen, all the talkers just emit a lot of noise. The act of truly listening is much more than just hearing somebody. It's about investing your full attention into somebody else and comprehending and connecting to their message. This skill is of utmost importance in all spheres of life where there are personal, academic, or professional relationships.

One of the deepest desires of any other human being is to be truly understood.

Communicating with others is sometimes like stepping into a field of landmines with a blindfold. Listening with intent removes that blindfold.

Before Amy and I married in 2000, our good friend Graybill Brubaker, the pastor who married us, would explain how good communication makes or breaks a relationship. Also, he would warn us how communication is nearly a miracle. Brubaker explained how there are so many possible points of failure from the moment a thought gets conceptualized and a message is formulated, then something is communicated clearly, heard well, received fully, and still possibly misunderstood depending on the receiver. It's no wonder a lot of marriages don't last. Communication can break down so easily between people.

I LOVE SUNNY DAYS   I LOVE SUNDAES

We must try our best to get out of our way to truly listen. Specifically, two principal things often get in our way: distractions and prejudices. Whether it's our phones, thoughts, or preconceived notions, these barriers can prevent us from fully engaging with another person. Overcoming personal biases is another particularly challenging barrier.

Making an effort to listen without bias can be transformational. Removing distractions and keeping our prejudices in check require awareness and extra effort at any given moment. Start by telling yourself, "I am going to truly listen to this person, and I want to understand their perspective without passing judgment."

STRATEGIES TO BECOME A BETTER LISTENER

- **Give Full Attention:** Eliminate distractions. Put away your phone, turn off the TV, or move to a quieter place. Focus entirely on the other person (the speaker).

- **Maintain Eye Contact:** This shows the speaker that you are fully engaged and interested in what they are saying.

- **Use Open Body Language:** Nod occasionally, lean slightly forward, and maintain an open posture to convey your engagement and openness.

- **Don't Interrupt:** Allow the speaker to finish their thoughts without interruption, which shows respect for their perspective.

- **Listen Without Judging:** Keep an open mind and avoid jumping to conclusions or making judgments about what the speaker is saying.

- **Empathize:** Try to understand the speaker's feelings and viewpoints. Empathy helps to create a deeper connection and understanding.

- **Reflect Back:** Paraphrase or summarize the speaker's words to ensure you've understood correctly. Doing this demonstrates that you are actively listening.

- **Ask Clarifying Questions:** If something isn't clear, ask open-ended questions to encourage the speaker to elaborate or explain further.

- **Avoid Planning Your Response:** Rather than thinking about what to say next, focus on understanding the speaker's message. Apply patience.

- **Acknowledge and Validate:** Acknowledge the speaker's feelings and opinions, even if you disagree. Validation can be as simple as saying, "I see how that could be frustrating."

- **Read Between the Lines:** Pay attention to non-verbal cues like tone of voice and body language to grasp the meaning of what's being said.

- **Offer Feedback:** If appropriate, provide feedback or advice only after you're sure you've fully understood the speaker's perspective.

Ultimately, truly listening is a skill that demands practice and mindfulness. It's about tuning in completely, not just to the words but to the emotions and intentions and the broader context behind them. To understand a person more fully is not just to hear the message but to understand where the person is coming from. Mastering this art can enhance relationships, foster better understanding, and create a more empathetic and connected world. Sometimes, the most profound way to connect is simply by listening. Listen fully and truly. It will change your world.

SKILL 31:
EMPATHY

"Empathy is seeing with the eyes of another, listening with the ears of another and feeling with the heart of another."
—Alfred Adler

EMPATHY IS OFTEN CONFUSED WITH SYMPATHY, BUT THEY differ. Empathy is something much more profound than sympathy. It involves experiencing and understanding what another person is feeling. Empathy is a potent skill that allows you to connect with others on a much deeper level.

During my high school years, I had the opportunity to serve as a trained teen counselor for Teen Line, a hotline dedicated to actively listening to and supporting other teens. This experience was back before the internet was popular and hotlines were more common. They trained us to use active listening and empathy to really hear out a struggling teen, and we had a large book of resources and protocols for helping out in certain situations. That experience taught me how to deepen my empathy skills. Volunteering is an invaluable way to develop better people skills, especially in roles that require social interaction and support.

PEOPLE HAVE DIFFERENT LEVELS OF EMPATHY FOR VARIOUS REASONS

People exhibit varying levels of empathy due to genetics, brain structure, upbringing, emotional regulation, and cultural influences. Some studies suggest genetic factors, like those affecting the production of oxytocin ("the love hormone"), can influence empathy.[140] Brain imaging reveals that people with higher empathy have more active areas in their brain, such as the mirror neuron system, which helps in mirroring others' feelings. These neurons fire when you do something and see someone else doing it, helping you "mirror" their feelings.[141]

A person's environment and upbringing also play crucial roles. Typically, children who receive empathy from their caregivers develop greater empathic abilities. On the other hand, those from less nurturing environments may struggle with empathy.[142] Additionally, one's capacity for emotional regulation and diverse life experiences can enhance empathic understanding. Cultural background can also affect empathy levels, as some cultures promote stronger empathetic bonds than others.[143] For instance, some cultures are more collectivist, encouraging empathetic, solid connections within the community, while others are more individualistic.

However, regardless of natural inclination or your upbringing, you have the potential to enhance your empathy skills. Your level of empathy is not fixed. Instead, it's more like a muscle; the more you work it out, the stronger it gets. It can be developed and strengthened through practices like engaging with varied perspectives, active listening, and empathy-building exercises. Life experiences, including meaningful interactions with diverse groups of people, can enhance empathy. It's like broadening your horizon—the more you see and experience, the more you can understand others. So, even if you're not the most empathetic person naturally, there's always room to grow and improve!

HOW TO CULTIVATE MORE EMPATHY

Developing empathy effectively can be achieved through a structured approach, focusing on expanding understanding, communication, and reflection. Here are five strategies for developing higher empathy skills:

- **Truly Listening and Perspective-Taking:** Go beyond merely hearing words; fully engage in listening to understand the emotions, intentions, and context behind what others are saying. Put yourself in someone else's shoes, imagining their situation and understanding their feelings and reactions.

- **Curiosity and Open-Mindedness**: Foster genuine curiosity about other people, including people who are different from you. Explore their perspectives, lives, and experiences. Challenge your own prejudices and biases, and seek out common ground with others, recognizing the uniqueness of each individual's story.

- **Expanding Empathy Through Engagement:** Actively connect with a diverse range of people, including those outside your immediate social circle. Engage in meaningful conversations, focusing on empathetic understanding rather than just waiting to reply. Use open-ended questions and reflective listening to deepen these interactions.

- **Creative Empathy and Self-Reflection:** Utilize books, movies, and art to experience and understand various lives and emotions. Reflect on your feelings and experiences to better relate to others. This principle emphasizes the importance of understanding oneself and using imaginative empathy to connect with others' experiences. Seek feedback on your interactions from trusted individuals to improve your empathetic responses and deepen your understanding of others.

- **Empathy in Action:** Apply your empathetic understanding in practical ways. Act on your empathetic feelings to support and help others and use empathy during challenging conversations or disagreements. Participating in community service can expose you to diverse experiences and challenges others face.

By practicing these principles in your daily life, you can develop a more nuanced and effective approach to empathy, enhancing your ability to connect with and understand others. For instance, try actively listening and reflecting on what others say next time you're in a group. Or maybe pick a book or a movie that's totally out of your usual genre to see the world from a new angle. Remember, it's all about practice, practice, practice—the more you do it, the better you'll get at understanding and connecting with others around you. Keep it up, and you'll become a more empathetic and awesome human!

A WORD ABOUT MAINTAINING
HEALTHY BOUNDARIES

While empathy is a valuable trait, maintaining emotional boundaries is equally important. Without these boundaries, empathetic individuals risk emotional burnout, especially those working in counseling and healthcare. We must find a balance between understanding others' emotions and maintaining enough detachment to protect one's mental health.

Empathy is more than a soft skill; it's a bridge that connects individuals, fostering understanding and compassion in a world that often seems divided. By learning to walk in others' shoes, actively listen, and maintain healthy emotional boundaries, we can harness the power of empathy to create more meaningful relationships and a more empathetic society. Remember, the ability to understand and share the feelings of another isn't just about them; it's about enriching your own human experience.

SKILL 32:
ASSERTIVENESS

*"Clear is kind. Unclear is unkind. It's not mean, it's clear. Speaking truth
in a respectful way is not only the kind thing to do,
but it also builds trust and connection."*
—Brené Brown

A SSERTIVENESS IS FREQUENTLY MISTAKEN FOR AGGRESSION, but they are distinct. Assertiveness is a crucial skill that enables clear, direct communication of your needs and opinions while maintaining respect for others. It boosts confidence, reduces misunderstandings and conflicts, and promotes healthier relationships. By striking a balance between expressing oneself and respecting others, assertiveness contributes to personal growth, self-esteem, and improved relationships in both personal and professional spheres. Assertiveness is an essential skill for effective communication and overall well-being.

When culminated as a skill, assertiveness can be a powerful force for change, not just for your own needs but for that of others as well. It is an essential leadership skill. Malala Yousafzai's story is an inspiring example of assertiveness transforming into a powerful force for change. As a young girl in Pakistan, she boldly wrote under a pseudonym about her life under the Taliban, advocating for girls' education. Her courage made her a target, and she survived a brutal attack that only fueled her determination. Malala emerged as a global advocate. Her unwavering voice resounded at the United Nations and beyond, earning her the distinction of being the youngest Nobel Prize laureate. Her journey is a testament to the power of assertiveness, showing how one voice, regardless of age, can challenge injustices and inspire global movements for equality and education.[144]

**At the root of assertiveness is the right
attitude about yourself and others.**

If you lack assertiveness, you might lack respect for yourself or others. Let that one sink in! Assertiveness is about expressing your thoughts, feelings, beliefs, and needs in a clear, honest, and respectful way without violating the rights of others. It's a communication style that is neither passive nor aggressive; it's the middle ground where you respect both your rights and those of others.

Communication style matrix

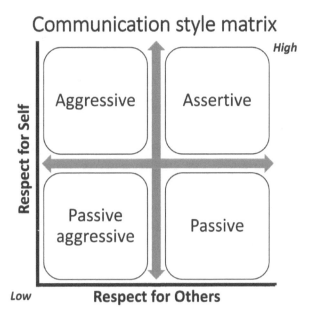

- **Assertive (High Self-Respect, High Respect for Others):** Located in the top right quadrant, assertive behavior is characterized by clear, direct communication that respects both one's own needs and the needs of others.[145]

- **Aggressive (Low Respect for Others, High Self-Respect):** In the bottom right quadrant, aggressive behavior involves standing up for oneself in a way that violates the rights of others. It's often confrontational and disrespectful to others. Nobody likes a bully.

- **Passive (High Respect for Others, Low Self-Respect):** In the top left quadrant, passive behavior shows a high regard for others' needs but at the expense of one's own. It involves avoiding conflict, not expressing one's own needs or feelings, and letting others have their way. Don't be a doormat; doormats get walked on.

- **Passive-Aggressive (Low Respect for Others, Low Self-Respect):** This falls in the bottom left quadrant. It's a non-confrontational method of expressing anger or resentment indirectly. It involves a facade of compliance or politeness while actually resisting, obstructing, or undermining others. It's about exhibiting aggression in a passive way. It is aggressive in intent or feelings but passive in the overt expression of these feelings, often resorting to indirect methods to express anger or frustration.

As we can see from the chart above, being authentically assertive requires both respect for yourself and respect for others. You need to check your respect levels if you are too passive, aggressive, or, even worse, passive-aggressive. Practicing assertive communication will foster better relationships, clearer communication, and increased mutual respect among you and others.

Because assertiveness is rooted in having the right underlying attitude about yourself and others, the most critical work in improving your assertiveness is learning to respect yourself and others. On top of that, here are five strategies that you can use to enhance your comfort and skill with assertiveness:

- **Respectful Communication:** Cultivate a balanced approach that respects both your needs and those of others. Use "I" statements to express yourself clearly and respectfully.

- **Setting and Enforcing Boundaries:** Know your limits and communicate them confidently. Practice saying no when necessary and maintain your boundaries firmly yet respectfully.

- **Body Language and Non-Verbal Cues:** Adopt confident body language with steady eye contact and open posture to reinforce your verbal messages.

- **Preparation and Reflection:** Prepare for potential assertive situations by rehearsing your approach and reflecting on your interactions.

- **Openness to Feedback:** Be receptive to how others perceive your assertiveness, adjusting your approach as needed for clearer and more effective communication.

Context matters as well. While being assertive is generally beneficial, it can sometimes be misunderstood, especially across cultural and social backgrounds. It's important to be clear and straightforward in your communication yet sensitive to how your words might be perceived in different contexts.

In summary, assertiveness is a critical skill that empowers you to communicate effectively and respectfully. It's about honoring your self-worth while acknowledging the rights of others. By mastering assertiveness, you pave the way for healthier interactions and a more positive self-image. Remember, it's not just about what you say but how you say it—with respect, clarity, and confidence.

SKILL 33:
PUBLIC SPEAKING

"All great speakers were bad speakers at first."
—Ralph Waldo Emerson

THE FEAR OF PUBLIC SPEAKING (GLOSSOPHOBIA) IS ONE OF the most common top fears. According to a Gallup Poll, an estimated 40% of Americans experience some level of anxiety or nervousness when speaking in front of a crowd, only surpassed by the percentage of Americans with the fear of snakes.[146] The other 60% either have probably developed their public speaking skills or may just have no fear. I can assure you I have been part of the 40%.

In 2018, mere weeks into my new role as the USAID Mission Economist in Malawi, fate decided to fast-track my introduction to the country. With the Mission Director unable to attend a significant national census launch event, I was nominated to go and represent the US Government. Little did I know, this was only the beginning of the day's surprises. Upon arrival, the event chair informed me that a panel speaker had canceled at the last minute and, in a twist of events, asked if I could fill in.

There I was, freshly arrived, unexpectedly catapulted onto the speaker panel, with a scant ten minutes to prepare a speech. The audience was a mosaic of over 300 census enumerators, alongside diplomats, government officials, and the added pressure of media presence, all under the watchful eye of the nation on live television.

With little time and much at stake, my Malawian colleague John offered a lifeline, passing me a pen to scribble key points on the back of a Post-it note. With this makeshift cheat sheet in hand, I approached the podium. My heart might have been pounding, and my nerves frayed, but my focus was razor-sharp. Standing before the diverse and prominent audience, I improvised a speech on Malawi's first electronic census—an entirely new subject. Admittedly, this was not my finest moment. I felt like a nervous wreck.

Yet, when words met the audience, something remarkable happened. My impromptu speech, delivered with a mixture of fervor and conviction, unexpectedly struck a chord. The room erupted into a standing ovation. What unfolded was not just an unforgettable day in my career but a pivotal learning moment. This experience underscored the profound value of being able to swiftly construct and convey a message, a skill as critical in a high-stakes international setting as it is in personal milestones like delivering a wedding toast. It was a potent reminder of the impact and necessity of mastering the art of public speaking, especially when life surprises you with its unscripted moments.

STRUCTURING A SPEECH FOR SUCCESS

Remember this quick recipe for a rudimentary three-part speech structure if you are in a fix like I was. 1) Say what you are going to say; 2) Say it; then 3) Say what you said. I also like another recipe that I like to call a "PPF sandwich" for creating a speech that is helpful in a pinch—Past, Present, Future (PPF). Or you could use another rendition of PPF, such as Past: how we got here; Present: how we are doing; Future: where we are going and how we get there. So, a PPF sandwich alone, plus packaging it between some niceties at the front and back of the speech, is how I structured my Post-it note speech at Malawi's national census, and it worked out. There are more speech recipes, of course, and as you practice speaking more, you can build quite a cookbook.

However, if you are in less of a rush, a well-planned, well-structured speech is pivotal for effective public speaking. This structure often includes a compelling introduction, an informative body, and a memorable conclusion. A great speech should be designed. Designing and structuring a speech effectively involves combining strategic planning and solid speech-making principles.

To craft a speech that resonates and persuades, consider the following steps:

1. **Invention: Pre-planning your speech**

    ○ **Goal Setting:** Determine the purpose of your speech (e.g., inform, inspire, entertain, persuade), which shapes the overall tone and approach.

    ○ **Audience Analysis:** Understand your audience, their characteristics, and any potential biases that might influence how they receive your message.

    ○ **Topic and Thesis:** Clearly define your topic and establish a central thesis or core message.

    ○ **Key Points:** Develop a few main points that support your thesis. Consider backing these up with evidence like statistics, personal experiences, or historical examples.

    ○ **Engaging Introduction:** Plan a compelling opening to capture attention. This intro could be a provocative question, a startling fact, or a personal story.

○ **Credibility and Qualification:** Reflect on why you are a credible source on the topic. Share relevant personal experiences or qualifications to build trust with your audience.

2. **Arrangement: Structuring your speech using a compelling outline**

   ○ **Set the Stage (Grab their attention):**

     » **Hook:** Start with a compelling hook to capture attention. Your hook could be an intriguing question, a startling fact, or an engaging story.

     » **Connect:** Establish a connection with your audience. Show understanding or empathy toward the audience's perspectives or challenges.

     » **Context:** Provide background or context, like outlining your problem or issue.

     » **Preview:** Briefly state what you'll be covering, which helps set audience expectations.

   ○ **Division (Say what you are going to say):** Give an overview of your speech's structure. Mention the main points you will discuss, providing a roadmap for your audience.

   ○ **The Main Content (Say it):**

     » **Articulate Each Point:** Clearly state each main point you intend to discuss.

     » **Support and Elaboration:** Support each point with facts, data, or rationale. Use evidence that is relevant and persuasive.

     » **Personal Touch:** Enhance your points with personal stories or anecdotes. These bring your speech to life and make it relatable.

     » **Additional Reinforcement:** Use quotes, references, or examples to strengthen your points.

- ○ **Summarize Key Messages (Say what you said):**

  - » **Recap:** Summarize the main points you've made, which reinforces your key messages and ensures they stay with your audience.

  - » **Concluding Thoughts:** End with a memorable conclusion that ties back to your central thesis or objective.

- ○ **Bring It Home (Make it matter):**

  - » **Relevance:** Relate your points back to the audience. Why should they care? How does it impact them? Appeal to the audience's emotions.

  - » **Call to Action:** If appropriate, conclude with a call to action. What do you want your audience to think, feel, or do after your speech?

Remember, a well-structured speech is more than just presenting information; it's about creating a journey for your audience, from the initial hook to the final call to action. Each part of your outline should contribute to this journey, making your message clear, engaging, and memorable.

Two final words of advice: First, I recommend you listen to diverse speeches. For example, listen to TED talks or famous speeches of previous presidents. Whatever interests you. Then, notice the elements that made it masterful or not. Analyzing others' speeches helps develop your repertoire. Then, practice public speaking (even if the audience is small at first), examine how it went, and keep refining. You'll not only get better, but it will get easier.

Remember, every great speaker starts somewhere, and with practice and perseverance, anyone can become an effective public speaker.

SKILL 34:
CONFLICT RESOLUTION*

"Man must evolve for all human conflict a method which rejects revenge, aggression and retaliation. The foundation of such a method is love."
—Martin Luther King, Jr.

UNDERSTANDING THE NATURE OF CONFLICT

ONFLICTS HAPPEN FOR A MULTITUDE OF REASONS. FOR EXample, sometimes conflicts arise because we're all wired differently, with our unique quirks, beliefs, and ways of expressing ourselves. Other times, there might be competing interests. Learning to understand conflict better is the first step to getting better at handling it more skillfully.

It may come as a surprise to some, but not all conflicts are bad. Jerry B. Harvey was an influential American organizational theorist known for developing the concept of the Abilene Paradox, which illustrates the counterproductive nature of group decision-making processes when people are trying to avoid conflict.[147] Harvey explained the concept from his personal account one summer in the sweltering heat of Coleman, Texas. An unexpected proposition from his father-in-law upended the family's quiet afternoon of lemonade and dominoes: "Let's get in the car and go to Abilene and have dinner at the cafeteria." Despite inner reservations about the heat, dust, and a long, 106-mile drive in an unairconditioned car across that dusty desert,

---

*   This section (Skill 34) has been reviewed by Natalia Barry, an educator, translator, and interpreter who has been an active Nonviolent Communication (NVC) practitioner since 2019. She is involved in various national and international communities, including NVC Global Rising.

each member reluctantly agreed, masking their doubts with feigned enthusiasm.

Upon returning from their arduous journey, a revelation emerged through tired exchanges. "Well, to tell the truth, I really didn't enjoy it much and would rather have stayed here," admitted the mother-in-law, sparking a cascade of confessions. Each member revealed they had only agreed to the trip, believing it was the collective will, not their own desire. Even the father-in-law hadn't really wanted to go, confessing: "Listen, I never wanted to go to Abilene. I just thought you might be bored. You visit so seldom I wanted to be sure you enjoyed it. I would have preferred to play another game of dominoes and eat the leftovers in the icebox."

This eye-opening experience revealed the absurdity of their situation, realizing they had all participated in a decision against their wishes. Jerry Harvey recognized this as the Abilene Paradox. In this phenomenon, groups take actions contrary to the individual preferences of their members, driven by miscommunication and a reluctance to voice dissent. The paradox's core lesson is the critical need for clear communication and authentic consensus in decision-making to avoid the pitfalls of unmanaged agreement.

The Abilene Paradox story highlights how group dynamics attempting to avoid conflict can sometimes lead to poor decision-making. Voicing real interests and needs is what was missing in this case. There's a type called cognitive conflict, which is when ideas clash. It's the brainy kind of conflict, where different viewpoints duke it out, and in the end, the best ideas win. Think of it like a debate club where arguing can lead to something constructive. We need an honest exchange with a clash of ideas for the best ideas to be defended and for well-considered decisions to emerge. For instance, this is the underlying principle of civil debate and dialogue. If a family member had expressed their disagreement in the Abilene tale, perhaps they would have identified a better alternative idea.

However, some types of conflict are unhealthy. There's the other kind—affective conflict, the emotional rollercoaster. It gets personal, feelings get hurt, and things can get nasty. It's what happens when a debate turns into a shouting match, where it's less about the ideas and more about who wins the argument. Usually, with this sort of unfortunate conflict, somebody is offended, offensive, or both, which fuels the fire.

The real challenge is when these two types of conflict mix—like when a healthy debate starts to feel like a personal attack. That's when judgments and misunderstandings arise.

So, how do we become more skilled at dealing with conflict? Start by spotting what's really going on. What is the underlying spirit of the conflict? Is it genuinely about trying to meet needs, or is it more about standing ground and trying to "be right?" Understanding the heart of the conflict is critical. There are also strategies for improving your communication so that conflict remains well-intentioned and constructive rather than unhealthy and destructive. Let's look at ways to help work through conflict so it results in a productive exchange or resolution.

PRACTICAL, EVERYDAY STRATEGIES FOR EFFECTIVE CONFLICT RESOLUTION

Conflict resolution is crucial, especially as you navigate relationships, academics, and the professional arena. Here are some tips to effectively resolve conflicts.

- **Stay Calm:** Before addressing the conflict, take a deep breath. Keeping your cool is key. If you're upset, take a moment to calm down before engaging in a conversation. Depending on the nature of the conflict, sometimes this might take more than a mere moment; finding the calm mindset may take days, weeks, months, or maybe more! The important thing is to find a way to regulate your own mindset and intention before engaging further so you don't contribute to a heated escalation. Staying calm does not come naturally for many of us but can be cultivated with practice. It is important to be aware of your own state in the heat of the moment so that you can regulate it more intentionally.

- **Truly Listen (Skill 30):** Give the other person your full attention. Listen to understand, not just to reply. Sometimes, just feeling heard can de-escalate a situation. For example, think: "I'm here to listen to everything you have to say. Your feelings and thoughts matter to me, and I want to understand your perspective fully."

- **Apply Empathy (Skill 31):** Acknowledge Their Feelings: Let the other person know you understand how they feel. This doesn't necessarily mean you agree with them, but it shows respect for their perspective. For example, you might say, "I can see how that situation upset you. It sounds like it was really challenging for you."

- **Choose your words carefully:** For example, use "I" Statements: Instead of saying "You always…" or "You never…" use phrases like "I feel…" or "I think…" This framing helps you express your side without sounding accusatory. Keep an eye out for the frequency of words like "always," "never," "all the time," "constantly," etc. It might surprise you how often they come up and just how much they can fuel the fire. For instance, instead of saying, "You never listen to me," you could express it as, "I've noticed that sometimes I don't feel heard when I'm speaking. It makes me feel frustrated because I value our communication. Can we find a way to ensure we both feel heard?"

- **Seek Common Ground:** Look for areas where you agree and build on those ideas that can serve as a foundation for a mutually acceptable solution. For example, you could say, "It seems we both value honesty in our discussions. Let's find a way to ensure we're both being heard and respected."

- **Be Clear and Specific:** Be specific about what is bothering you or what you need. Vague complaints are hard to resolve. Miscommunication is the root of many conflicts, so clarity and specificity help reduce miscommunications. For example, a clear need for agreement might be, "When meetings start late, I feel anxious because I have commitments afterward. Can we agree on starting on time?"

- **Focus on the Problem, Not the Person:** Keep the conversation focused on the issue and avoid personal attacks or bringing up past conflicts. Depersonalizing the discussion is instrumental for keeping the conflict cognitive (and healthy) vs affective (and unhealthy). Also, one of the worst things you can do is label somebody, which comes across as judgmental. For example, instead of saying, "You're so lazy; you never do your share of the chores," you could focus on the problem by saying, "I've noticed that the household chores aren't getting done evenly. Can we discuss how we can better divide the tasks so it's fair for both of us?"

- **Find a Win-Win Solution:** Aim for a solution that benefits both parties. Compromise might mean you won't get everything you want, but both sides should feel their needs have been considered. I highly recommend a classic book on how to do this called *Getting to Yes.*[148]

- **Agree to Disagree:** Sometimes, you won't reach an agreement, and that's okay. It can be healthy to accept differences in opinions. Learning to come to peace with those differences sometimes takes some time.

- **Seek Mediation if Needed:** If you can't resolve the conflict between you and another, involving a neutral third party (whether a common friend, neighbor, teacher, parent, counselor, or legal advisor) might be helpful depending on the specific situation.

**Conflict is a normal part of human interactions.
What matters is how you handle it.**

Effective conflict resolution skills can lead to more meaningful and satisfying personal and professional relationships.

LEARNING ADVANCED CONFLICT
RESOLUTION FROM THE EXPERTS

In the book *Nonviolent Communication: A Language of Life*, Marshall Rosenberg crafted a powerful approach to communication that encourages compassionate connection and understanding, called Nonviolent Communication (NVC).[149] This method focuses on empathy, authentic connection, and understanding in interactions. The core of NVC is about expressing our needs clearly and empathetically and listening to others' needs without judgment or aggression.

The book breaks down the NVC process into four key components:

- **Observation**: Observing what happens in a situation without attaching interpretation or judgment. For example, "When I see you kick the dog."

- **Feelings:** Identifying and expressing one's feelings concerning what has been observed. For example, "I feel worried and scared."

- **Needs:** Acknowledging the underlying needs, values, or desires affected by the situation. Doing so helps to clarify the reasons behind the feelings and observations. For example, "Because I value respect for all beings."

- **Requests:** Making explicit requests for actions that address the underlying need or concern. For example, "Would you be willing to sit with the dog for a minute to make sure she's okay?"

NVC is more than a communication technique; it's a way of perceiving and relating to the world rooted in empathy and compassion.*

---

* NVC has gained a considerable following. Some NVC Practitioners might describe NVC as not only an approach but a philosophy for better connecting with others more harmoniously. On the NVC Rising learning community (NVCRising. org) NVC is described as "a theory and practice which via a focus on communication, aims to bring any human being closer to himself and to others around him/her/them. With simple yet effective tools patterns of communication are transformed to bring more clarity, joy, meaning, awareness, and deepening connection in any type of relationship."

Rosenberg's approach draws on profound insights from decades of experience in mediation, therapy, and conflict resolution. He illustrates how shifting from a language of criticism and demand to empathy and understanding can lead to more harmonious and meaningful relationships.

CONFLICT AT THE EXTREME NEEDS A DIFFERENT SORT OF RESOLUTION

Conflict, when it reaches extreme levels, calls for a different resolution strategy. It's crucial to prevent conflicts from spiraling out of control, like a small flame that can turn into a devastating wildfire. Unfortunately, not all disputes can be resolved through communication and diplomacy. As I write this chapter, at least two major wars are going on in Ukraine and Gaza/Israel. My heart goes out to those who have been directly impacted by war. The situation is deeply saddening.

During the relentless invasion of Ukraine by Russia, I found myself amidst the turmoil, engaging with Ukrainian colleagues at the US Embassy. They shared heart-wrenching tales of their homes reduced to rubble and the unbearable loss of loved ones. Our world is no stranger to conflicts we could characterize as driven by greed, the urge to disrupt, or sheer destructiveness. Yet, often, the roots of conflict are tangled in complexities. The global landscape is frequently marked by conflicts with an array of underlying motives, including economic interests, power dynamics, or other factors, often rendering these situations complex with multifaceted perspectives to consider.

Encountering adversity, whether through individual acts or broader societal issues, underscores the importance of striving for understanding and resolution through peaceful means. Civility, dialogue, and diplomacy stand as foundational principles in seeking resolution. However, in scenarios where these approaches meet limitations, it becomes necessary to explore additional avenues that ensure the safety and rights of individuals, advocating for protection, defense, and justice within the framework of just laws and mutual respect. For example, Rosa Parks, an African American civil rights activist, became famous for refusing to give up her bus seat to a white passenger in Montgomery, Alabama, in 1955. This act of defiance led to the Montgomery Bus Boycott, a pivotal event in the US civil rights movement that culminated in the Supreme Court's decision against bus segregation based on race. Parks' refusal was a strategic act rooted in her fight for civil rights, marking a significant moment that highlighted the power of nonviolent protest and legal action in challenging racial injustice.

Strive to embody peace in your daily life by enhancing your conflict resolution skills, mindful that a more peaceful and productive world begins with our individual decisions and actions. Conflict resolution is an essential skill in all walks of life. It's about understanding the underlying causes of conflicts, actively listening to different perspectives, finding common ground, and using emotional intelligence to manage and resolve disputes. By mastering these skills, you can navigate conflicts more effectively, fostering peace and understanding in various situations.

SKILL 35:
NETWORKING

NETWORKING INVOLVES MUCH MORE THAN MERELY EXCHANGing business cards or connecting on social media platforms. Think of it as a sophisticated process of building a web of connections, where each individual represents a valuable opportunity that could lead to unanticipated and beneficial doors opening. Being strategic about who you meet can open up new friendships and opportunities that help you achieve your goals.

Consider the story of Oprah Winfrey, often called the "Queen of All Media." Overcoming her impoverished upbringing, Oprah became the wealthiest African-American of the 20th century and, at one point, the world's sole black billionaire. By 2007, her far-reaching influence was widely recognized, often earning her the title of the most influential woman in the world. Her journey is a testament to resilience, determination, and the power of transcending barriers.[150] She wasn't just lucky; she was enterprising and knew how to network like a boss. Starting young in the media industry, she used her charm and smarts to connect with anyone and everyone—from big celebrities to key players in the business. Her talk show expanded her networking platform. Fast forward, and she's a media mogul and legend. That's in large part due to Oprah Winfrey's exceptional networking skills.

So, how do you network with skill? First, know what you're after—a job, advice, mentorship, you name it. Be real, be you, and think about what you can bring to the table, not just what you can take. And hey, mingling at events doesn't have to be a strain. Here's a pro tip: Walk in thinking, "I totally belong here." Confidence is key. Keep it chill, smile, and start conversations that feel natural. Compliments work great but don't lay them on too thick.

Remember names when you talk to people—it's like adding a personal touch that says, "Hey, you matter." (Skill 36 goes into depth on remembering names better). If you see someone standing alone, be the extraordinary person who includes them. And when you've chatted enough, exit the conversation with class, leaving them thinking, "Wow, that person's awesome!" Making authentic connections makes impressions. People might forget what you say, but they will never forget how you made them feel.

But building your network is just the start. Keeping those connections warm takes some strategy. Relationships decay if they are not maintained. Check in with your contacts, keep them in the loop, and who knows? Today's acquaintance could be tomorrow's business partner. Connections are valuable assets.

LEVERAGING SOCIAL MEDIA FOR NETWORKING

In the digital age, social media is a powerful tool for networking. Social media platforms like LinkedIn, X (formerly Twitter), and Instagram offer unique opportunities to connect with professionals across various fields, each having different ideal uses. However, the key is to engage authentically. Share your insights, comment thoughtfully on others' posts, and offer genuine value in your interactions. Remember, your online presence is an extension of your personal brand, so curate it with intention. Also, remember it is a lasting impression, so be mindful of how your personal brand is strengthened or weakened based on what you post. Some platforms are like an online resume; you better believe companies look at your social media profiles.

Here are some tips for making more authentic connections and generally being more likable:

- **Be Genuine:** Authenticity resonates. Approach each interaction sincerely, showing interest in the other person's experiences and viewpoints.

- **Actively Listen**: Show that you value the conversation by actively listening, asking thoughtful questions, and engaging with the responses.

- **Add Value:** Consider what you can offer in a conversation or relationship, whether knowledge, resources, or even a different perspective.

- **Balance** Confidence with Humility: Carry yourself with confidence, but balance it with humility. Acknowledge others' achievements and contributions.

- **Be Inclusive**: Be the person who includes others, especially those who might be left out. This kindness often leaves a lasting impression.

- **Follow-Up:** Post-meeting, a quick message acknowledging the conversation can go a long way in building a lasting connection.

Lastly, remember that networking is a two-way street. It's about building mutual relationships, not just advancing your own agenda. Each connection you make, nurtured with respect and genuine interest, can become valuable to your personal and professional journey.

Networking is a super skill that can seriously level up your career and life. It's not just about who you know; it's about who knows you and who has good impressions of you. Next up, we're diving into the art of remembering names and faces because, let's face it, that's how you make every connection count.

SKILL 36:
REMEMBERING FACES
AND NAMES

"A person's name is to that person, the sweetest,
most important sound in any language."
—Dale Carnegie

I KNOW SOMEBODY WHO NEVER FORGETS A FACE AND NAME, AND that is an extraordinary gift, but for the rest of us, we can use techniques to better remember people we meet. Mastering the art of remembering names and faces isn't just a party trick; it's a vital skill for thriving in today's interconnected world. Have you ever been in that awkward spot where someone waves at you, and you draw a blank on their name? Yeah, we've all been there. *(Well, except that friend of mine with a rare gift!)*

Sometimes, it's because we're not sufficiently tuned in during introductions. Other times, it's about not committing the name to memory or not focusing enough on the person's face. And quite often, it's about not linking the name to the face effectively.

But imagine being that person who always remembers. Take Franklin D. Roosevelt (FDR), the thirty-second President of the United States. His uncanny knack for recalling names was legendary and played a huge role in his political journey.

BASIC TECHNIQUES FOR BETTER NAME RECALL WHEN MEETING NEW PEOPLE

- **Be Genuinely Interested** in People: Foster a genuine curiosity about the person you're meeting. This mindset makes it easier to remember their name because you're genuinely engaged with who they are.

- **Focus Your Attention:** One of the main reasons we don't always remember names is that we don't always hear them clearly and pay attention to them the first time. When someone introduces themselves, give them your full attention. Be intentional about remembering. Think to yourself, "I would like to remember this name." Then, avoid distractions and listen to their name.

- **Use Repetition**: Repeat the name back to them during your introduction. For example, "It's nice to meet you, Victoria." This act reinforces the memory. It also confirms you heard it correctly.

- **Use the Name in Conversation**: Use their name in the conversation and when saying goodbye. This repetition helps cement the name in your memory. Also, use the name when you say goodbye.

- **Review and Reinforce**: Recall their names and the associations you created after your interaction. Repeating the name to yourself at different intervals, such as after one minute, five minutes, and the next day can enhance your recall ability.

TAKE IT TO THE NEXT LEVEL WITH ADVANCED FACE/NAME MEMORY TECHNIQUES

I'm going to share with you steps for a fantastic memory technique to remember faces and names. I used to be terrible at remembering names. They would go in one ear and out the other. It was embarrassing always to forget people's names. Later, I learned this technique from studying the work of memory champions Luis Angel and Ron White, and then I started applying it, and it worked very well. If you master these techniques, you should be able to easily remember dozens of names of people you meet with sufficient practice.

The Baker-baker paradox is an insightful way to understand how our brains remember things. Imagine you meet two people: one tells you they're a baker (they're a bread maker), and the other says their last name is Baker.[151] Weirdly, you're more likely to remember the person who bakes bread. Why? Because when you think of a baker, you might picture dough, bread, a chef hat, and a kitchen—all of these images stick in your mind. But 'Baker' as a name doesn't give you much to picture, so it's easier to forget. This paradox underscores how when you learn something new, connecting it to images or ideas you already know can help you remember it better. It's a neat trick for studying or remembering people's names—just link them to something more visual in your mind!

Even FDR used visual techniques to remember names. A Washington Post article mentioned that FDR reportedly used visual techniques such as imagining the letters of a person's name written across their forehead, which helped him to remember faces and names.[152] Whether or not that was his actual technique, the memory principle is solid—visually associating a name with a face.

Believe it or not, you can train your memory to remember faces and names with fantastic skill. Imagine attending a dinner party, meeting fifteen new people, and remembering their names. Wouldn't that be great? You can significantly elevate this skill with some techniques, some imagination, and practice. Dominic O'Brien, an eight-time World Memory Champion and author, utilizes special techniques to train and significantly enhance memory. In one of his memory records, O'Brien successfully memorized one hundred faces and names in just fifteen minutes! In his book *Quantum Memory Power*, O'Brien gives tips on remembering faces and names.[153]

For remembering faces better, O'Brien said always to "Give a face a place." Here are some techniques:

Link the face to someone already familiar. If the face reminds you of somebody familiar, associate it. Then, link it to the typical place of that familiar person or even somebody famous. For example, if you meet Rose and she reminds you of your sister, create a mental association the place could be your sister's house. Now, for the name part, you would visually imagine a Rose in your sister's house.

Alternatively, if the person's face doesn't remind you of someone familiar, you could use salient features to remember the person. Maybe somebody has a sizable nose or bright blue eyes. Something must stand out to you. When you focus in on that characteristic, the feature becomes the place. You can even visualize it being made more pronounced or wackier than it is to help you remember the feature better.

Imagination helps with memory. So, if you meet a Rose with a big nose, then you might imagine a rose sticking out of Rose's nose. Though a word of advice: you probably shouldn't share how you remember their names with people. That's just for you.

THAT'S FOR REMEMBERING FACES, BUT WHAT ABOUT NAMES?

Some names have an intuitive image already, such as linking them to an existing person with that name, like Jerry. I will always think of Jerry the Mouse from Tom and Jerry. These associations are highly personal.

However, many names don't automatically conjure visual content. So, the trick is to convert names to visual content. While the name "Rose" is something we can already visualize with an image, some names, like "Steve," have no stock image. "Steve" per se is an abstraction unless you have some link to something or someone already familiar, such as the comedian Steve Martin. Therefore, you must be creative with imageless names and make some visual content representing the name. This process is called *converting a name to a name peg.* The idea is to convert verbal content into something you can visualize (a peg). So, for the name "Steve," we could use the image of a stove because "stove" sounds close enough to "Steve."

If you want to be systematic about building this technique out, I recommend you keep a name peg list somewhere organized, like on a spreadsheet, and build them out for common names. After you meet people for whom you need to invent a new name peg, remember to add their name peg to your name peg list. You don't want to have a different name peg for the same name. So, you do not wish to link one Steve with a stove and another Steve with a staff. Pick one and stick to it.

This method relies on the power of visual memory and association. By linking a person's name to a unique aspect of their appearance through imaginative and vivid imagery, you're more likely to remember their name in future encounters. Practice this with each new person you meet; soon, recalling names will become much more manageable.

Here are some example Name Pegs for some common US names, but you can *create your own associations* for common first names and last names in your part of the world:

- Emily – Sounds similar to "Family." Imagine a happy family scene. You can picture a family crest.

- Chris – Think of a cross. You could visualize a cross.

- Sarah – Picture Sarah Lee cupcakes. Imagine a tray of delicious, freshly baked cupcakes, perhaps with your favorite toppings, to help you recall the name Sarah.

- Laura – Envision laurels, like the ones worn by victors in ancient times. Picture a wreath of green laurel leaves, perhaps placed on someone's head in a ceremony.

- Mike – Think of a microphone.

- Michael – I tend to think of Michael Jordan holding a basketball. Note: Name pegs can be people and things as long as they produce memorable visual content.

One of the most important things you can do is to remember somebody's name. Now, you have learned several techniques for doing so, and you should put them into practice and improve this vital skill.

SKILL 37:
WORKING IN TEAMS

"If you want to go fast, go alone.
If you want to go far, go together"
—African proverb

INTRODUCTION TO TEAMWORK

TEAMWORK IS LIKE A SUPERPOWER THAT TURNS A GROUP OF individuals into a force to be reckoned with. It's not just about gathering a group together; it's about fostering a shared understanding where everyone is aligned, communicating effectively, and bringing their unique skills to the table. Think about it—a team can be like a pop-up squad coming together for a specific mission, or it can be more like a band that sticks together, like a department in a company.

In the world of work, it's teams that make the magic happen. Whether you're launching a rocket or organizing a school event, it's all about teamwork. I've seen this firsthand in my career—being a part of teams, leading them, and juggling several teams simultaneously. When a team is firing on all cylinders, it's incredible what can happen. Combined talents and ideas can outshine what anyone could do solo.

Consider sports, for example. It's one thing to be a star athlete, but it's a whole other game to be part of a team. In a team, it's not just your skills that count but how you gel with others, play off each other's strengths, and push toward a common goal. That's the real game-changer. So, teamwork is about bringing your A-game and blending it with others to score those big wins together, whether on the field or in the office. Everybody has different strengths; let them shine through!

UNDERSTANDING TEAM DYNAMICS

A team typically goes through several stages:

1. **Forming:** Members get acquainted and understand the team's purpose.

2. **Storming:** Differences arise, and members express their opinions more openly.

3. **Norming:** The team establishes norms and finds ways to work together harmoniously.

4. **Performing:** The team reaches its full potential in productivity and problem-solving.

5. **Adjourning:** For temporary teams, this stage involves wrapping up and reflecting on achievements and learnings. *This stage is often left off the list.*

Applying team leadership principles along these stages of team development can immensely improve team growth and success.

Forming Stage

At the beginning of any team's journey, during the Forming stage, there are two game-changing moves to make. First up, building trust. Trust isn't just about getting along; it's about creating a team vibe where everyone feels they can speak up, share ideas, and really connect. Think of it as setting up a trust zone where the team's magic begins. People need to know you have their back, or they will not be as open to making full contributions.[154]

Next, get clear on who does what and why. Nail down roles and goals. It's like having a map for your team adventure—everyone knows their part and where the journey is headed. It's not just about assignments; it's about understanding how each person's role weaves into the bigger picture and contributes to something extraordinary.

By taking these two steps, you're not just forming a team but kickstarting a mighty, purpose-driven crew ready to tackle what lies ahead. It's the groundwork for a journey filled with growth, challenges, and epic achievements.

Storming Stage

Effective communication is especially essential as the team is in the Storming stage. Keep those lines open and clear. It's all about ensuring that every voice is heard and every conflict becomes a stepping stone for growth, not a roadblock. Also, people need to be listened to (see Skill 30) and validated.

Let's bring those conflict resolution skills (see Skill 34) into play. Equip your team with these skills, and you're essentially giving them lifeboats to navigate through stormy waters. These skills are like tools in your team's survival kit, helping to manage tensions and resolve issues without losing sight of the team's goals. Facilitation techniques such as structured brainstorming sessions can help make this process more constructive and less chaotic.

So, in this Storming stage, it's all about harnessing the energy of conflicts for growth, communicating like pros, and mastering the art of resolving clashes. It's challenging, sure, but it's also where some of the most significant growth and team bonding happens. Get this right, and your team will come out of the storm more united and ready for anything.

Norming Stage

The Norming stage is where your team starts to find its groove. Think of it as the phase where everyone's unique superpowers come into play. Here's how to make the most of it:

First up, leverage diversity (see Skill 39). Your team is a melting pot of skills, experiences, and perspectives. Combined, it's like a creative explosion waiting to happen. Encourage each member to bring their A-game and watch as innovative solutions emerge from this rich blend of ideas. Celebrate diverse skill sets and perspectives within the team.

Now, let's talk about accountability. It's not just about doing your part; it's about owning it. Establish a culture where everyone feels responsible for the team's success. Every member is a co-pilot, steering the team toward its goals. When everyone's invested, the sense of collective achievement is just unbeatable. What you measure matters! Set clear, achievable goals and track progress. Pick some meaningful indicators that you can use to gauge whether you are succeeding at your goals.

Shared leadership is a game changer, transforming teams into dynamic, collaborative powerhouses fueled by collective strength.

Imagine a team where leadership isn't just a title held by one, but a role shared by many. Encourage members to lead in areas where they shine. It's about tapping into everyone's strengths and letting them take the wheel when it's their turn to drive. This encouragement not only boosts confidence but also creates a truly collaborative environment.

Jocko Willink, author of *Extreme Ownership: How US Navy SEALs Lead and Win*, advocates for *decentralizing command*, a strategy that involves distributing leadership roles across a team.[155] This approach is a form of shared leadership, allowing leaders to focus on broader strategic objectives while team members manage more immediate tasks and decisions. It empowers individuals, fosters trust, encourages initiative, and enhances the team's ability to adapt quickly to new situations. Decentralizing command is essential in environments where rapid response and flexibility are critical.

So, in the Norming stage, it's all about making the most of your team's diversity, building a culture of accountability, and embracing shared leadership. Get this mix right, and you're on your way to a team that's not just functioning but flourishing.

Performing Stage

In the Performing stage, you're like a well-oiled machine, but the key to staying on top is never to stop fine-tuning. Here's how you keep the momentum going:

First, let's talk about continuous feedback and improvement. It's like being an athlete who never stops training. Always look for ways to improve, both individually and as a team. Encourage ongoing feedback—it's the compass that guides your growth. Open, honest conversations about what's working and what isn't will lead to minor tweaks that make a big difference. Think of it as a cycle of growth that keeps you agile and adaptable. Encourage a culture of feedback and continuous improvement. Establish clear communication channels and regular check-ins.

Now, the spotlight is on achieving results. You've bonded, battled through the storm, found your rhythm, and now it's all about crossing the finish line together. With a cohesive team, the drive to achieve collective results becomes your north star. It's not just about the individual anymore; it's about what you can achieve together. Foster a sense of shared responsibility and collective achievement. Set ambitious goals, and then go get them as a unit. Celebrate each win, learn from setbacks, and push the bar higher.

How feedback is given also matters immensely. I once heard a Disney executive say something that stuck with me. "The celebration of excellence breeds excellence." Taking time as a team to appreciate and recognize the good is a virtual cycle that motivates and inspires more. Notably, the inverse is also true. I've seen managers who liked to throw tempers and point fingers at people about the bad. That style weakened a team because it demoralized and demotivated others. A word of advice: praising in public and criticizing in private is often better. Learn to save face to preserve people's dignity and focus on building constructive team dynamics. Learn to deliver and receive both positive and negative feedback gracefully. However, even negative feedback can be delivered with grace and encouragement rather than blame and shame. But don't forget to give positive feedback as well because that encourages and strengthens.

So, in the Performing stage, it's about harnessing the power of continuous feedback for perpetual growth and keeping your eyes on the prize—achieving those stellar results as a team.

Aligning team practices with these developmental stages helps in understanding the natural progression of a team's growth. It provides a structured approach to fostering a high-performing team from its formation to reaching its peak performance.

In summary, effective teamwork requires a combination of interpersonal skills, structured processes, and a commitment to shared goals. By understanding and applying these principles, you can significantly enhance your team's performance and experience the profound satisfaction of achieving together.

SKILL 38:
RELATIONSHIP BUILDING

"The quality of your life is the quality of your relationships."
—Tony Robbins

QUALITY RELATIONSHIPS ARE ESSENTIAL NOT ONLY TO THE quality of life but also to your overall health. Did you know your social circle might be a secret ingredient to living longer and healthier? Fascinating research has shown a strong link between the quality and extent of our social relationships and our overall health, affecting everything from our mental well-being to our lifespan.[156] One study published in the *PLOS Medicine* journal looked at 308,849 individuals over an average of 7.5 years and found that individuals with adequate social relationships have a 50% greater likelihood of survival than those with poor or insufficient social relationships.

The connections we forge with others do more than just enrich our day-to-day experiences; they also profoundly impact our physical health and longevity. So, when nurturing your well-being, remember that fostering solid bonds with friends, family, and your community isn't just about having fun or feeling supported—it's also a vital part of staying healthy. In a world where we're often focused on personal achievements and material success, this is a heartwarming reminder of the power of human connection.

However, in modern society, the landscape of social relationships is changing dramatically, and it's easier to be socially isolated. Living near or with extended family is becoming less common in many developed countries. You might live on the opposite coast from your relatives or even in a different country (like my family does). There's also a trend among people your age to put off marriage and start a family.

What's more, living alone is becoming increasingly typical across all age groups, leading to a noticeable increase in loneliness. This shift in living arrangements is a crucial aspect of modern life, profoundly affecting how we connect with others and form social networks. That's why investing in quality relationships in all spheres of your life is more important than ever, whether personal or professional. Or even make extra efforts to connect more meaningfully with those you encounter daily, such as that cafe barista or mail delivery person.

MAKING QUALITY TIME FOR PEOPLE

Don't ever get so task-focused that you neglect meaningful relationships. Early in my career, during a summer internship at PricewaterhouseCoopers, I encountered a lesson in the intricate dance between task completion and nurturing relationships—a lesson that has stayed with me ever since. My days involved collaborating closely with a client—a manager from the United States Postal Service named Mike, who became a guide and mentor to me. Our routine included a daily fifteen-minute walk down a corridor bridging two government buildings, a journey necessitated by my lack of an access badge. This walk became our makeshift meeting room, where conversations flowed as freely as the coffee we grabbed along the way. In his wisdom, Mike shared helpful insights that extended far beyond the confines of our project.

Driven by a youthful zeal to innovate, I soon devised a method to automate our data transfer tasks, rendering our daily walks obsolete. It was a small technical triumph but a personal oversight. The efficiency I had gained in task management came at an unexpected cost—the gradual loss of our invaluable coffee-chat interactions. The bureaucratic hurdles that Mike once helped me navigate became more challenging without the ease of his guidance.

This experience crystallized a pivotal realization for me: the essence of life's journey is not solely defined by the milestones we achieve but equally by the relationships we cultivate along the way. It's a delicate balance, ensuring that the zeal for accomplishment doesn't overshadow the value of connection. As I reflect on my career, it's clear that the moments that have truly enriched my path are those shared with individuals whose influence transcends the professional sphere, reminding me that at the heart of success lies the art of cherishing human connections.

Think about how this truth holds, whether in the professional or personal sphere. Sure, nailing a work project feels excellent, but does it compare to the deep satisfaction of quality time with good friends or a heartfelt conversation with family? Life's demands will always be pulling you in a hundred directions, but remember, it's the people in your life who add color to your days.

Investing in relationships isn't just about having fun. It's about building a support network, finding joy, and creating memories. When looking back, these moments and connections stand out, not the endless hours you spent on work tasks.

So, while being dedicated and driven in your work or studies is essential, don't forget to balance it with the warmth of human connections. After all, what's success without people to share it with? Investing time and energy in relationships isn't just fulfilling; it's essential for a rich, well-rounded life.

MAINTAINING RELATIONSHIPS

Relationships grow stale or decay if not maintained with purpose and effort. To keep friendships, family ties, or professional connections vibrant, invest quality time and actively engage in each other's lives. Maintaining relationships involves a balance of shared activities and respecting personal space. Demonstrating thoughtfulness and care is fundamental. Many overlook this due to self-preoccupation or busyness, so it's important to consciously make an effort. *Show you care!*

Effective communication is crucial. Engage in regular, honest conversations and listen actively. Small, consistent gestures, like a quick call or a coffee meet-up, are as significant as grand ones in strengthening bonds. Show appreciation through simple acts like saying thank you, giving compliments, or celebrating special occasions.

Reliability is critical to building trust. Keep your promises and be there for others, especially in times of need. Also, respect the boundaries in each relationship, understanding and honoring personal space and comfort levels.

Remember, relationships are about giving, not just receiving. The continuous nurturing of these bonds brings immense rewards, including belonging, support, joy, and love. The effort invested in relationships significantly enhances our well-being and happiness.

SKILL 39:
VALUING DIVERSITY

"It is not our differences that divide us. It is our inability to recognize, accept, and celebrate those differences"
—Audre Lorde

W<small>E LIVE IN A DIVERSE WORLD. D</small>IVERSITY <small>ENCOMPASSES A</small> spectrum of differences, ranging from cultural and racial to gender, political beliefs, religions, neurotypes, ages, geographical backgrounds, socioeconomic statuses, sexual orientations, and much more.

Illustrative Diversity Dimensions

Race	Ethnicity	Gender	Physical / Mental Abilities	Age
Sexual Orientation	Geographic Location	Education	Communication Style	Work Experience
Parental / Family Status	Personality	Immigration Status	Political	Appearance
Belief system / Religion	Socioeconomic	Neurodiversity	Language / Accent	Marital / Relationship status

Some of these aspects are more visible than others on the surface, but all these deeply affect who we are. If you ever want to see a microcosm of our diverse world, just stroll through New York City. It's amazingly diverse. The coexistence of so much diversity is like a colorful mosaic of humanity. There is so much potential, wisdom, and talent to be tapped from this remarkable diversity.

> **In our interconnected world, embracing diversity enriches our lives and empowers us with a wealth of perspectives and experiences.**

But let's be honest: embracing diversity isn't always straightforward. It's riddled with challenges like stereotypes, biases, and misconceptions, which can erect walls between understanding and acceptance. It's easy for people from different walks of life to be judgmental about "the others" outside their circle. Often, these issues stem from a simple lack of exposure or understanding of different cultures and lifestyles.

Usually, overcoming these hurdles requires proactive efforts—for instance, world travel, diversity workshops, and open dialogues with diverse people, to name a few ideas. Seek more diversity exposure, and learn to step outside your comfort zone. Doing so can broaden your perspective and lead to eye-opening, transformative experiences, and ultimately can help profound personal growth.

A life-changing experience for me was back in high school when I hosted a foreign exchange student from Argentina. Learning about a foreign culture I knew little about then was a joy. The following summer, I leaped out of my comfort zone and became an exchange student in Argentina.

This adventure was fun, but it wasn't easy, as it included a lot of social blunders and misunderstandings. Ultimately, it didn't just broaden my horizons; it reshaped them. I forged global friendships, honed my Spanish skills, and developed a profound appreciation for diverse cultures.

Fast forward to today, and those early experiences with diversity have led me down an extraordinary path. I joined the US Foreign Service, living and working across three continents. That initial step into the world of cultural diversity wasn't just an adventure but the gateway to a life rich with global experiences and perspectives. It's amazing how one decision to embrace a new culture can open doors to a world of possibilities. Now, my three children are experiencing diverse cultures every day as we live overseas, and they have gained their own diverse perspectives they will carry throughout life.

To boost your diversity and inclusion skills, start by actively being more inclusive toward others. Educate yourself on diversity through varied sources and broaden your social circle to encompass different backgrounds, welcoming any discomfort as a learning opportunity. Listen attentively and pose open-ended questions to gain insights into diverse viewpoints. Self-reflect on personal biases and actively seek feedback for growth.

Moreover, engaging in diversity training is beneficial, as is advocating for inclusive behavior and standing against discrimination. Participate in activities that foster inclusivity and cultivate empathy to forge authentic connections. Uphold accountability for inclusive practices in yourself and others, and embrace a lifelong commitment to expanding your understanding of diversity and inclusion.

In conclusion, diversity is a treasure trove of experiences, perspectives, and ideas. Recognizing, accepting, and celebrating our differences enrich our lives and contribute to a more harmonious and vibrant world. The journey toward inclusivity and understanding is continuous, requiring constant learning, empathy, and open-mindedness.

To recap, as a way to remember key concepts from this chapter, remember to LISTEN TRUE (Listening truly, Interpersonal empathy, Self-assertiveness, Talking publicly, Ending harmful conflicts, Networking, Total recall of faces and names, Robust teamwork, Uplifting relationships, Embracing diversity).

These skills are foundational for effective communication, understanding, and collaboration. Enhancing these abilities allows you to navigate social landscapes more confidently and build robust, meaningful connections.

Mastering interpersonal skills and appreciating diversity equips us for successful personal and professional relationships. Next, in Level 6, we'll explore the crucial aspect of financial literacy and independence, building on the foundations we've set.

LEVEL 6:
MASTER MONEY MATTERS

MONEY MASTERY CAN UNLOCK A NEW LEVEL OF LIFE WHERE you call the shots. This chapter is about transforming your approach to personal finances—from making savvy savings to smart investing. It's your playbook for financial independence. Here, we cut through conflicting money advice, providing clear, practical strategies. We'll explore how to create a budget that fits your lifestyle, explore the basics of investing, and lay the groundwork for long-term financial health.

In Level 6, you'll also learn how to navigate the often-intimidating world of credit scores, loans, and insurance. Think of these as tools in your financial toolkit, not hurdles on your path. We'll break down complex concepts into bite-sized, easy-to-understand pieces. Whether you're planning for college, dreaming of travel, or just aiming to make your paycheck stretch further, these money skills are your key to making it happen. And it's not just about the here and now; we're setting you up with the know-how to build lasting wealth, ensuring a future where financial stress is a thing of the past. Ready to turn your financial goals into achievements? Let's get into this!

Self-Assessment

As you enter the realm of financial literacy in Level 6, let's take a moment to assess your current understanding and goals related to money management. Reflect on these key questions to maximize your learning and application of the skills in this chapter. Write down the answers to these questions before starting the chapter.

1. **Wealth Mindset Evaluation:** How do you currently perceive wealth? Is it merely about having money, or does it encompass broader aspects like freedom, happiness, and security?

2. **Financial Self-Awareness:** How would you rate your understanding of budgeting, saving, and investing? Identify specific areas where you feel confident and others where you feel less knowledgeable.

3. **Current Financial Practices:** Reflect on your current financial habits. Do you actively budget? Have you started saving or investing? What practices have you found effective or challenging?

4. **Money Skills Goals:** Identify one specific financial goal you have for yourself. How do you think the skills in this chapter will help you achieve this goal?

5. **Challenges and Solutions:** Consider a financial challenge you've faced recently. How did you address it, and what could you have done differently with the knowledge you hope to gain from this chapter?

Keep these questions in mind as you explore Level 6. They are designed to help you connect your current financial situation with the new skills and knowledge you will acquire, leading to practical and impactful learning.

SKILL 40:
WEALTH MINDSET

---

*"Wealth consists not in having great possessions,
but in having few wants."*
—Epictetus

BEFORE YOU CAN MASTER ESSENTIAL MONEY SKILLS, IT'S CRUcial to understand what it means to be truly wealthy. Too many people confuse wealth with money, which is shortsighted. Money is a tool—a means to an end, not an end in itself. True wealth encompasses much more than just money.

Notice that this skill is not called "Money Mindset" but rather "Wealth Mindset." Wealth often evokes images of financial abundance, but its true essence extends far beyond mere monetary value. This chapter explores various perspectives on wealth, emphasizing that its true value lies in the opportunities and choices it offers us. Wealth isn't just about having substantial financial resources; it's about the freedom and ability to pursue your goals, passions, and a fulfilling life.

QUIZ TIME: WHO DO YOU THINK IS WEALTHIER AMONG THESE DIFFERENT PEOPLE?

A) Jack, the High-Earning but Stressed Banker: Jack earns $450K a year on Wall Street, working eighty-hour weeks. Despite the high income, he faces health issues like a bad back, high cholesterol, substance addiction, anxiety, and is at risk of a heart attack. He has no family and is experiencing burnout.

B) Amelia, the Fulfilled School Principal: Amelia earns $90K a year, working sixty-hour weeks. She has a fulfilling job, a loving family, good health, and looks forward to a pension.

C) Chris, the Peace Corps Volunteer with Purpose: Chris is living abroad, getting by on a small stipend, working in the Peace Corps. He deeply enjoys the work and its impact in the community, and plans to pursue a government job later, showcasing a clear path for future stability.

Each scenario illustrates different aspects of wealth, challenging the notion that financial success alone defines it. In its truest sense, wealth is a blend of financial stability, personal well-being, and life satisfaction.

The right answer is not straightforward because, again, it's not purely about money. We could hopefully agree that in this case, the answer is not the one with the most money. If you think the Wall Street banker, Jack, is the wealthiest, then just wait until he *drops over dead* from an anxiety-ridden heart attack and has nobody to attend his funeral. That's not wealth; that's just sad. Jack is time-poor, health-poor, and relationship-poor. He is not improving his wealth with this money. As to whether Amelia or Chris is "wealthier" is debatable.

Don't confuse money with wealth—money is just one avenue and not sufficient on its own to achieve true wealth.

Wealth is a highly personal, multivariate concept. If we define true wealth as the freedom and ability to pursue goals, passions, and a fulfilling life, we know that not everybody shares the same goals, passions, or views on what it means to have a fulfilling life. I believe there are some major shared factors, though, that increase your life's quality and fulfillment, including:

- Your mindset and outlook on life

- Ability to pursue your life passions or your calling

- Freedom to control your own time and resources

- Physical and mental health and vigor

- Less harmful stress for improved well-being

- Self-development, actualization, and achievement

- High-quality, healthy relationships

- Meaningful, memorable experiences

- Making a difference and leaving a legacy

These factors define what it means to be truly wealthy. It is no coincidence these factors align reasonably well with the chapters in this book.

Real wealth lies in success—it's about refining your skills to enrich yourself and lead a more fulfilling life. We all have a limited number of years on this earth, and you want to make the most of those years. It's all about striking that perfect balance. Don't get too caught up in chasing money at the expense of enjoying life today—after all, who knows what tomorrow holds? But, at the same time, it's important not to put yourself in a situation where you're missing out on options. Thus, planning ahead is essential to living your best life.

MONEY AND HAPPINESS ARE ONLY RELATED TO A POINT

According to the findings from the longest-running happiness study, the Harvard Study on Adult Development, it's clear that money's role in our happiness isn't as straightforward as we might think.[157] Earning enough to meet your basic needs is crucial—that's a no-brainer. But once you hit a certain point, stacking more cash doesn't stack more happiness.

What makes us happier? It's the connections we make in our personal lives and at work. Chasing after career success and material gains, like that next big promotion or luxury car, can leave us pursuing a version of happiness that always seems just a bit out of reach. Instead, investing in experiences that foster genuine connections and regularly reflecting on whether our lives align with our values and goals can lead to more profound, enduring happiness. Remember, it's not about waiting for retirement to find meaning and joy; it's about discovering or creating joy every step of the way. The journey is as important as the destination.

Remember Skill 13, Finding the Good Enough? We were talking about finding balance in your time allocation, but it's also important to find your Good Enough concerning your resource consumption. When Amy and I were young professionals just starting our careers, I was greatly influenced by a book called *Your Money or Your Life* by Vicky Robin and Joe Dominguez.[158] I highly recommend adding that classic to your reading list. One of the concepts they explained well was the Fulfillment Curve, where they explained how important it is to find your point of "enough," or your happiness starts to decline as you overconsume. These works inspired my visuals below.

Finding a point of "enough" in personal spending is akin to the Law of Diminishing Marginal Utility, a key principle of economics. This principle states that the satisfaction gained from each additional unit of a good or service decreases with increased consumption. Similarly, the added satisfaction diminishes when you spend beyond your "enough" point. For example, excessive spending can lead to clutter, which paradoxically detracts from joy and fulfillment. We must recognize this pattern in our spending habits for a more balanced and fulfilling life.

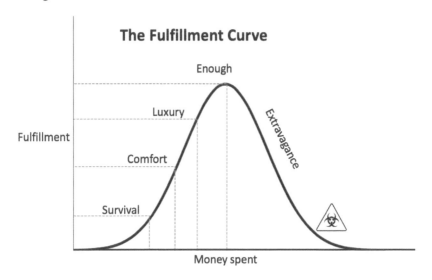

The main point is that there is a limit to how much happiness you will gain from spending money on your own needs and wants. After you have enough, buying more things in extravagance will be the opposite of fulfilling. It's a death spiral. Self-absorption, consumption, and self-involvement only go so far, and then more of it sours and rots your joy like moths destroy old clothes.

However, the *ah-ha* moment came as I learned about an alternative way to reach even higher levels of fulfillment, even after you have reached the top of the fulfillment curve. If you face beyond yourself, you can flip part of your fulfillment curve so it goes up rather than down. If you turn your focus outward toward others, then your fulfillment can ascend beyond the heights of what is reachable by mere consumption. Outward-focused fulfillment is about participation and service and focusing on things such as giving back, being part of a more significant cause, or helping improve the lives of others. There is nothing greater than being part of something greater than yourself.

Here is an alternative path you can take rather than that of extravagance or gluttony. See the dotted line that continues going up when we have found our peak of "enough," and we invest our time or money beyond the mere benefit of ourselves.

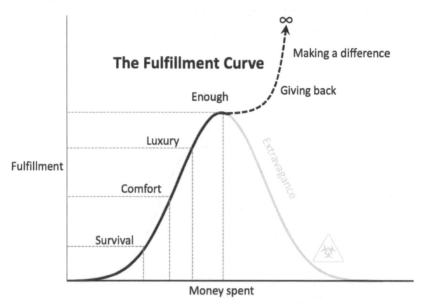

I had an early-in-life realization that there is much more to life than "building your own kingdom." This realization was part of my decision to leave a comfortable six-figure job at IBM in my mid-thirties and take a sizable pay cut to join a foreign service career in international development. I had found enough and wanted to invest my life more in others.

Some people thought I was crazy as I went from a high, well-paid position to an entry-level, low-paying position. But I thought it was worth it because I was pursuing a calling. I've explored the world with my family, helped fight global poverty, and have had many fulfilling experiences. Were there sacrifices? Of course! You will face brutal trade-offs as you make career and life decisions. Money is very important, but it's not always about the money. Whatever you do, try to live your life with no regrets.

Identify your threshold of "enough" in terms of finances, but don't wait until you reach that point to start pursuing life's other fulfilling aspects. Many joys, like skill enhancement and deepening relationships, require time to develop. Engaging in activities such as volunteering or hobbies like painting can provide immense satisfaction, and it's important to start these pursuits now rather than delaying them for an uncertain future. Remember, money is just a tool, not the ultimate goal. Relying solely on financial achievements for fulfillment can lead to disappointment. Now that we have a better understanding of true wealth, let's explore effective money management strategies.

SKILL 41:
ACCOUNTING FOR YOUR MONEY

"Accounting is not just about counting beans;
it's about making every bean count."
—William Reed

YOU CAN ONLY MANAGE YOUR MONEY WELL IF YOU LEARN how to account for it properly. Also, you must learn to think more like a business to grow your money. The first thing you need to know is how much you are worth and how much you are making.

Let's start by determining how much you are financially worth.

Hypothetically, how much would you be worth if you sold everything you own and paid off all your debts? The money left over is your *Net Worth*.

What is an asset and a liability? An asset is something you own or control that has value or brings value. A liability is something you owe, such as a debt. You want to grow your assets and minimize your liabilities to get richer. Businesses use a report called a balance sheet to show the balance of their assets and liabilities, but rather than calling it net worth as we would for a person, they would call it "equity."

Let's create your personal balance sheet to see your net worth.

- **Step 1: Tally Your Assets.** All your bank accounts, investments, retirement accounts, cash on hand (or under your pillow), and the market value of everything you could theoretically sell, like your vehicle, house, equipment, jewelry, technology, and fine art. Put that on a spreadsheet and tally up the value under a column called "Assets."

- **Step 2: Tally Your Liabilities.** All your credit cards, mortgages, loans, and IOUs—tally up the balance and put it under the Liabilities column.

- **Step 3: Calculate your net worth.** Assets minus Liabilities is your net worth.

NET WORTH STATEMENT (SIMPLIFIED EXAMPLE)

Category	Description	Amount
Assets		
Cash and Cash Equivalents	Checking Account	$4,500
	Savings Account	$15,000
Investments	Retirement Accounts (IRA, 401k)	$45,000
	Stock Portfolio	$25,000
	Bonds	$10,000
	Real estate investment property (Current market value)	$250,000
Personal Property	Car (Current Value)	$15,000
	Jewelry	$5,000
	Electronics	$3,000
Other Assets	Art Collection	$7,000
Total Assets		*$380,500*
Liabilities		
Debts	Mortgage Balance for investment property	$180,000
	Car Loan	$10,000
	Credit Card Debt	$5,000
	Student Loan	$20,000
Total Liabilities		*$215,000*
Net Worth	**Total Assets - Total Liabilities**	**$165,500**

As of a specific point in time, this person's net worth is calculated to be $165,500. This table represents a detailed breakdown of the assets and liabilities, clearly showing their financial standing. Understanding and regularly updating this summary is critical for effective financial planning and decision-making.

Keeping track of your balances across multiple accounts can be a hassle because you must log in to different platforms. However, there are helpful tools to make this easier. I recommend using a personal finance aggregator service, which pulls the relevant data from all your accounts and keeps a running, real-time update of your balances. These applications help you manage your money and your budget.

For example, I used Mint.com for many years, which was free, but it closed in early 2024. However, several alternatives are available, and here are a few ideas at the time of this writing: Empower (formerly called Personal Capital), You Need A Budget (YNAB), Monarch Money, and Tiller.[159] One of the reasons I personally like Tiller is if you have strong spreadsheet skills, it pulls your real-time account data into a spreadsheet so you can analyze it however you would like. One caveat, though, is using these features can get rather technical. What I love about Personal Capital's Empower is its excellent analyses, and it has a helpful smartphone app as well. Explore your options and pick an application that suits you.

GROWING YOUR NET WORTH

The way to increase your net worth, is to earn more income than your expenses over time.

Sometimes, you hear about "net income" versus "gross income." Let's distinguish these two concepts. Gross income is the total amount of money earned before any deductions or taxes are taken out. For many people, this equates to hourly wages, salary, commissions, and any bonuses. On the other hand, net income is what remains after all required taxes and deductions, such as health insurance or retirement contributions. Net income is often referred to as your "take-home pay" or "paycheck."

Net Income = Gross Income - Taxes and withholdings

When talking about payroll, taxes and withholdings (also called "deductions") are subtracted from an employee's gross income to determine the net income or paycheck amount. Withholdings are essentially pre-paycheck expenses, such as Social Security taxes and health insurance premiums. However, not all withholdings are expenses in the traditional sense. For example, retirement contributions, such as 401(k)* contributions, are withheld from gross income and deposited into retirement savings accounts. These contributions are not technically expenses because they remain the employee's assets, although penalty-free access to this money is delayed until retirement.

Additionally, retirement contributions are excluded from taxable income for the year, meaning they reduce the employee's current taxable income. While these amounts are not included in the employee's net income, as they haven't yet "come in" to the current spendable accounts, they still represent an important form of deferred income.

Let's understand the concept of liquidity. Money that is liquid is spendable right now. Some money might be able to be pulled out and spent immediately (such as what you have stored in a banking account). Other money might be tied up in a longer-term investment, such as a 401(k), which will be more accessible someday. Money that is more usable now is known as being more "liquid" or has more "liquidity" than money that is usable later. For example, the 401(k) money comes in through your gross salary but is stored in a retirement investment account, which is not liquid until you are of a certain age.

For personal financial management, net income is the equivalent of available cash that comes into your accounts. The difference between net income and cash is more substantial when dealing with business accrual-based accounting. But for our purposes here, you can use net income and cash interchangeably.

---

* In the United States, alternatives to the 401(k) for public sector employees include the 403(b) plan, the 457(b) plan, the Thrift Savings Plan (TSP), and traditional pensions, while individual retirement options such as Traditional and Roth IRAs are also available. Several other countries have similar retirement savings schemes. These include the Workplace Pension in the UK, the Registered Retirement Savings Plan (RRSP) in Canada, Superannuation in Australia, the Riester Rente/Rürup Rente in Germany, the iDeCo in Japan, the Pensioenfonds in the Netherlands, and the KiwiSaver in New Zealand. Each of these schemes offers unique features and tax benefits aimed at helping individuals save for retirement.

CALCULATING YOUR CASH FLOW

Next, let's calculate how much money you earn in a period versus how much you spend. You can think of your financial wealth like water in a sink. If you spend faster than you earn, your money goes down the drain, leaving you with nothing—or worse, with debt! If you earn faster than you spend, your sink will fill with money and soon overflow!

Rule #1 in wealth building: Always live beneath your means! In other words, always spend less than you make. Every time you break this rule, you get poorer.

We are going to determine your personal cash flow, which involves understanding how much money flows into your accounts (or pocket) versus how much goes out due to expenses. Sometimes, people might confuse a personal cash flow statement with a budget, although a budget describes how much cash we *should* spend in a given period. On the other hand, a cash flow statement shows how much cash we *actually* spend in a given period. However, they are two sides of the same coin—personal cash flow information is essential for building your budget baseline.

Step 1: Add up all your sources of net income. Let's categorize income sources into *active* and *passive* income. Here's the difference: Active income comes from the active use of your time, such as a job or freelance work. On the other hand, passive income is earned with little to no effort, regardless of what you do with your time. Later, we will see why this distinction is important because building passive income streams is the key to financial independence. Let's look at these net income types more carefully:

- **Active income:** This includes your net salary (the amount you receive after taxes and benefit deductions). You can also call this your "paycheck." Additionally, this should include any net income from side gigs or freelance work.

- **Passive income:** This includes any interest earned, such as from bonds, savings accounts, bank certificates of deposits (CDs), or royalties. It also includes dividend money paid to you from stock ownership.*

Sometimes, it's tricky to classify something as active versus passive. A good rule of thumb is to consider how much of your time it requires to generate the income. Income from any assets you own that produce money with minimal effort, such as if you receive rental income from a house you are renting out, you could count that as passive unless you find yourself doing a lot of active work to keep it maintained for your renters, in which case it is more accurate to look at it as active income.

Step 2: Add up all your expenses. Some people have different ways of looking at expenses. What we mean by "expense" is when money leaves your accounts or pockets, and you no longer own it.

Let's categorize expenses into *fixed* versus *variable*. Fixed expenses are predictable ones. For example, if you have a monthly car or house mortgage payment using a fixed rate, that's relatively fixed as it will likely not change much over a year. On the other hand, you have variable expenses, which can vary significantly, such as groceries, clothing purchases, entertainment expenses, etc. Here are a few examples, but the categories you pick are going to be very personal to your situation:

Fixed Expenses
• Mortgage or Rent Payments • Car Payments • Student Loan Payments • Insurance Premiums (like health, auto, and life insurance) • Subscription Services (like streaming platforms, gym memberships) • Internet and Cable Bills

---

* Active income is sometimes known as earned income and it comes from your labor. Passive income comes from your capital. Some people make a distinction from portfolio income—that coming from holding a portfolio of investments such as stocks and bonds—from that of passive income, such as investments in real estate where you are not actively using your labor.

Variable Expenses
• Groceries and Dining Out
• Utility Bills (can vary based on usage)
• Gasoline or Public Transportation Costs
• Personal Care Items (like toiletries, haircuts)
• Leisure and Entertainment (movies, hobbies)
• Clothing and Apparel Purchases
• Home Maintenance and Repairs (which can fluctuate)
• Transaction costs such as ATM fees

You will use this information to build your budget baseline as well. Remember, a budget helps you decisively control how much to allocate, whereas your cash flows show what you have actually spent. When building a budget, it's helpful to estimate the monthly cost of fixed and variable expenses by calculating these costs over an extended period, such as twelve months, and then dividing by twelve to get the average monthly expense. When creating a monthly budget, include the monthly equivalent of your expenses.

This approach allows you to set aside money for those expenses when they occur, even if they happen in a future month. For example, suppose you typically pay your tax preparer an annual fee of $600 in April. In that case, you should allocate $50 per month in your budget for tax preparation, adding a note to remind yourself of the future payment date.

Step 3: Calculate what is left over. After adding up all your net income and expenses, calculate your net cash flow to determine the amount of cash coming into your accounts or pocket covering a period of time (such as a specific month, quarter, or year).

Your net cash flow is the amount remaining for savings and investments. If you have a positive net cash flow (excess cash), that amount can be allocated to savings and investments.

PERSONAL CASH FLOW STATEMENT
(SIMPLIFIED EXAMPLE)

Category	Description	Type	Monthy Amount	Annual Total (USD)
Net Income				
Active Income				
Paycheck	Net Pay (after taxes and withholdings)	Active	$5,300	$63,600
Passive Income				
Dividends	From Stock Portfolio, etc.	Passive	$200	$2,400
Rental Income	From Real Estate Investment Property	Passive	$1,200	$14,400
Total Net Income			**$6,700**	**$80,400**
Expenses				
Fixed Expenses				
Housing	Mortgage/Rent (primary residence)	Fixed	$1,200	$14,400
Real Estate Investment	Mortgage (invest-ment property)	Fixed	$1,500	$18,000
Utilities	Electricity, Water, etc.	Fixed	$200	$2,400
Insurance	Health, Car, Home	Fixed	$300	$3,600
Loan Repayments	Student Loan	Fixed	$350	$4,200
Giving	Tithe/charity/donations	Fixed	$670	$8,040
Variable Expenses				
Groceries	Food and Supplies	Variable	$500	$6,000
Transportation	Gas, Maintenance	Variable	$250	$3,000
Entertainment	Movies, Dining Out	Variable	$150	$1,800
Miscellaneous	Clothing, Personal Care	Variable	$100	$1,200
Total Expenses			**$5,220**	**$62,640**
Net Cash Flow	Total Net Income – Total Expenses		$1,480	$17,760

I recommend you habitually distinguish between active and passive income because passive income is the key to financial independence. If you grow your passive income streams to exceed your expenses eventually, you no longer need to work for money if you choose not to actively. That's the definition of financial independence. With active income streams, you are working for money. With passive income streams, money is working for you. This chapter will cover building passive income streams under several upcoming money skills.

In summary, understanding your net worth versus net cash flow are two sides of the financial coin. Understanding both these concepts is crucial. Your net worth shows your overall financial value, while your net income helps track your ongoing financial performance. Together, they provide a comprehensive view of your financial status, guiding your budgeting, saving, and investing decisions.

SKILL 42:
BUDGETING AND SAVING

"Do not save what is left after spending,
but spend what is left after saving."
—Warren Buffett

I N SKILL 41, WE EXPLORED THE CONCEPT OF A PERSONAL CASH flow statement, which, though similar, is not the same as a budget. A budget is a *proactive* financial plan where you outline your future income and expenses, setting specific financial goals. It's like a road-map for your financial journey, guiding you on how to allocate your funds.

On the other hand, a personal cash flow statement is more of a reflective tool. It provides a real-time snapshot of your financial trans-actions, showing the money flow in and out of your accounts. This statement helps you track whether your spending aligns with the plan set out in your budget. Essentially, while your budget sets the course for your financial future, your personal cash flow statement shows you where you currently stand and how well you adhere to your budget.

Budgeting requires you to analyze and make decisions about your financial allocations and craft the equivalent of a personal cash flow statement that is ideal going forward.

Now, let's talk about designing a budget that works for you. It's all about balancing what you *need* (like rent, food, getting around, and staying healthy) with what you *want* (like those epic nights out, the latest tech, or dream vacations). Needs are your must-haves, the essentials you can't live without. Wants, on the other hand, are your nice-to-haves. They make life enjoyable, but you could trim them if you needed to save up more or cut back on expenses.

Nailing down your budget is about finding the sweet spot between these needs and wants. You must cover the essentials and sprinkle in those wants without compromising your financial goals.

When you're making your budget, take a hard look at your spending. Split it into needs and wants and see where your cash goes. Sometimes, you've got to make tough calls, like cutting back on the latest fashion or eating out less, so you can stack up savings or crush that debt. It's about setting up a plan that's real, flexible, and totally in tune with what you want out of life.

For money that you are saving or investing, it's a good practice to allocate that to specific purposes or goals you might have in the future, such as paying for the kid's college fund or retirement. Knowing what you are saving and investing toward is important to ensure you invest enough in each area.

BUDGETING PRINCIPLES

A practical approach to budgeting is the 20-30-50 rule. As the rule goes, allocate 20% of your income to savings and investments, 30% to wants or flexible spending, and 50% to essential needs.

BUDGET ALLOCATION

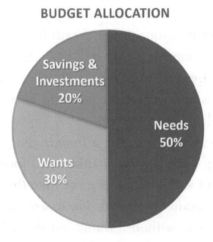

This rule's background lies in its simplicity and ease of application. It is a suitable starting point for those new to budgeting or seeking a basic financial management framework. We already learned above how to define wants versus needs. The 20% for savings and investments is instrumental for building your financial future, including savings, debt repayment, and investments. Prioritizing savings helps build an emergency fund, save for retirement, or achieve other financial goals. You build your wealth through prudent saving and investing.

There are alternative approaches to budgeting than the 20-30-50 rule. Explore them and pick a method suitable for your circumstances and style. The important thing is to apply sound discipline to budgeting, which ultimately leads to your ability to save and invest prudently.

The financial gurus encourage the use of a budgeting method. One such method is the Envelope System, a more hands-on approach where cash for various spending categories is physically divided into different envelopes. Once an envelope is empty, no more spending is allowed in that category until the next budgeting period. Some of our friends have used this system and say it's helpful to see the cash balances physically.

When Amy and I were starting out, rather than using physical envelopes, we preferred to use debit cards rather than cash. Then, we documented every single expense and the corresponding budget categories in a notebook, which worked for us and helped us create transparency and discipline. We eventually got smartphones and moved everything to a digital budgeting process.

Others swear by the merits of using Automated Budgeting, a modern approach that leverages technology and automatic transfers to manage finances, ensuring savings and bill payments are handled without manual intervention. Whatever system you use, just stay on top of your budget. If you use automation, you want to avoid tuning out, lest you undermine your budget vigilance and discipline!

IMPORTANCE OF FRUGALITY AND HOW TO DO IT

Frugality is an important life skill in itself. If we are being frugal, we are extracting the best value from what we have and finding contentment and satisfaction in what we have available. With the support of frugality, living beneath your means is crucial for financial stability. It involves spending less than you earn and saving the surplus. Being frugal doesn't mean compromising on quality of life. Instead, it's about making smart choices, like choosing cost-effective alternatives and avoiding debt traps. Learning to be frugal is essential to living beneath your means, and frugality requires disciplined spending habits.

Frugality isn't about being stingy; it's about maximizing value and making thoughtful spending decisions. To live frugally, learn to do these well:

- Limit unnecessary expenditures.

- Find quality goods at lower prices. Become a savvier consumer.

- Opt for Do-It-Yourself (DIY) solutions where possible.

- Embrace a minimalist lifestyle focusing on simplicity and utility. As an added benefit, this approach also declutters your life and reduces stress.

- Making the best use of what you have at your avail (whether you own it or have use of it)

COST OF HABITS: WHAT IS THAT STARBUCKS COFFEE REALLY COSTING YOU?

When I first started out after college, I lived near Washington, DC. I had a daily ritual of passing by a high-end coffee shop and buying a cappuccino every morning. Starbucks, for me, was like a fishing lure; I would purchase a drink automatically without thinking twice. This habit didn't stop there; I would also get a cappuccino after lunch as a pick-me-up.

At the time, a cappuccino used to cost over $3.00. Nowadays, it is closer to $4.50 for a cappuccino due to price inflation. When you look at the cost of a daily habit over time, it's eye-opening. In today's dollars, the yearly cost of that habit was approximately $3,285 (that is $4.50 per cup x 2 times per day x 365 days)! With the effective tax rate of around 24%, I needed to earn today's equivalent of $4,322 in gross salary (which equates to $3,285 after 24% taxes are removed) just to fund my daily cappuccino habit.

When I was starting out, that expense was a sizable portion of my salary—an expensive habit and even more eye-opening when you look at these habits over many years. Then, I thought about what I could do with that money if I eliminated that habit. That money could help pay for higher education, a vacation abroad, or another goal.

Amy and I were newly married and starting our careers at the time, and we needed to save money. So, we started replacing these habits. Instead of buying an expensive cappuccino, I brewed coffee at home, which was less expensive. I made that my new ritual. We revised lots of expensive habits to increase our savings. After our first year, we saved enough money for a down payment on our first home purchase in Arlington, Virginia. It all literally came down to buying fancy cappuccinos as a perpetual renter versus brewing my own coffee as a new homeowner. We made the right choice because, after a few years, we gained $160,000 of home equity from purchasing our first home.

Watch out for those fishing lures! Be sure to identify your "fishing lures" —those things that make you impulse buy without question. Your fishing lures give you a dopamine hit every time you purchase them, which are ingrained in your primordial brain as a habit purchase. You must identify and rethink those and reengineer your habits (applying Skill 14). Assess your spending habits and discern if they align with your financial goals. Do the math and examine your daily habits and their long-term financial impact. Get control of your impulses!

Besides cutting down on expensive habits, we also became smarter about other purchases, especially large ones like our next car. Using resources like Consumer Reports magazine, we sought to determine the best values for significant investments. Understanding the total cost of ownership was crucial. We evaluated how to maximize the car's lifetime value by balancing several factors: securing a favorable purchase price, choosing a model with low maintenance needs, ensuring efficient fuel consumption, finding affordable insurance, and selecting a vehicle with minimal depreciation. Considering these factors, we aimed to make a well-informed decision that ensured long-term value and cost-effectiveness beyond the initial cost.

WHERE TO STORE YOUR SAVINGS

After effectively learning to budget well, you should live beneath your means, meaning you should have money for savings and investing. I recommend not leaving more than six months' expenses in a low-interest savings account. You want to have enough for a rainy day or an unexpected considerable expense such as finding yourself between jobs, dealing with your car getting totaled, or a significant expense such as the birth of a child. Otherwise, you don't want too much of your money to sit idle when it can be invested in something with higher returns. Shop around for banks with savings accounts with few fees and high yields. Then, put the rest in investments for long-term growth.

Remember, budgeting and saving are not just about cutting costs; they're about making strategic decisions that align with your financial and life goals.

SKILL 43:
INVESTING BASICS

"The stock market is a device for transferring money
from the impatient to the patient."
—Warren Buffett

AFTER YOU CAN BUDGET AND SAVE EXTRA MONEY, YOU NEED to turn your attention to investing to grow your wealth. Investing is a crucial skill for wealth building, distinct from saving due to its higher risk but with the potential for greater return. It involves committing assets like money, time, or talents to earn a positive return on investment (ROI). However, investing also means putting these assets at risk, with the possibility of a negative ROI.

Storing money under the mattress isn't wise due to risks like theft and inflation. Keeping it at home poses risks of loss or damage. Banks offer safer storage, but the value of money in savings can diminish over time due to inflation. For instance, $100 today holds less value than a decade ago due to rising prices, reducing its purchasing power over time.

BEATING INFLATION SO YOUR
MONEY DOESN'T WITHER

Inflation is like a sneaky thief, slowly stealing the value of your money over time. To put this in perspective, the cost of a classic McDonald's hamburger in 1965 was a mere 15 cents in the US, compared to $3.59 in 2024—nearly 24 times the 1965 price! Historically, the US inflation rate has averaged around 2-3% per year, with fluctuations, such as an 8% rate in 2022. To maintain or increase the real value of your money, your investment returns need to beat inflation. Therefore, the inflation rate serves as a minimal benchmark for investment returns.

Your Return on Investment (ROI) should ideally exceed the inflation rate. Another common benchmark is the risk-free rate, often represented by the yield on ten-year US Treasury bonds. As of December 8, 2023, this yield was 4.23%, providing a stable, low-risk annual return. At that rate, you have the option to invest in U.S. Treasury bonds, which are considered to carry very low risk (virtually "risk-free") due to being backed by the U.S. government. Comparing other potential investments to this risk-free rate benchmark helps us assess if higher returns justify the increased risk.

Investing $1,000 at a 4.23% risk-free rate grows your money, but with a 3.2% inflation rate, the purchasing power decreases. Therefore, to understand your *real* investment returns, you need to calculate the *effective rate of return*, which shows the real value of your investment, after accounting for inflation.

The effective rate of return gives us a clearer picture of the real value of our investment returns by considering our purchasing power rather than just the nominal rate of return, which is the return on investment without factoring in inflation. In other words, the effective rate of return reveals our actual return after adjusting for how much prices have risen over time. Remember, this calculation still doesn't include the impact of taxes on your earned interest, which could further affect your net returns.

To calculate this, we use the formula for the effective rate of return, which is:

$$\textit{Effective Rate of Return} = \frac{1 + \textit{Nominal Rate of return}}{1 + \textit{Inflation Rate}} - 1$$

In our example, with a nominal rate of return of 4.23% and an inflation rate of 3.2%, the calculation would be:

$$\textit{Effective Rate of Return} = \frac{1 + 0.0423}{1 + 0.032} - 1$$

$$\textit{Effective Rate of Return} \approx 0.0099 \text{ or } 0.99\%$$

Therefore, the real return on your $1,000 investment, growing at 4.32% after accounting for 3.2% inflation, is approximately $1,010 after rounding. This figure is before considering any potential taxes on the earned interest. Taxes will likely eat more of the positive return away. That's why many people like to invest in investments with higher rates of return, but when we do that, it invites higher levels of risk.

To earn higher returns, often we must invest our money in investments with higher risk levels. Here are some different types of investment asset classes, each carrying different risk and reward profiles:[160]

- **Stocks:** Equity in companies, offering potential for growth and dividends.

- **Bonds:** Fixed-income investments with steady interest payments.

- **Real Estate Investment Trusts (REITs):** Property market investments without direct ownership.

- **Business or Side Hustle:** High risk, potentially high reward. Requires significant time to manage.

- **Other asset classes:** Cash or cash equivalents, certificates of deposit (CDs), index funds, mutual funds, exchange-traded funds (ETFs), commodities, private equity, venture capital, hedge funds, derivatives, cryptocurrencies, etc.

PURSUING HIGHER GAINS WHILE MINDING HIGHER RISKS

Investors search for the best reward-to-risk ratios. That is, they seek investments with a high likelihood of high returns while minimizing their risks as much as possible. One way to reduce risks is not putting all your eggs in one basket.

Diversify your investments to reduce overall risks to your money.

For example, investing in an index fund like the S&P 500 index of stocks is typically less risky than investing in any particular stock.* The risk of an individual company's stock gaining or losing value is generally higher than that of the S&P 500 index, which some people use as a proxy indicator of the "stock market."

According to a stock market analysis by McKinsey, the historical average annual return of the S&P 500 since the 1800s, even after adjusted for historical inflation, has been 6.5%-7% annually.[161] The last 25 years have kept on par with that historical range at around 6.8% annualized returns (adjusted for inflation) from January 1996 to June 2022. Some years are higher, and some are lower. Still, if history were indicative of future expectations, we could expect the S&P 500's returns to be over 6.5% adjusted for inflation as a rule of thumb. The nominal rate of return (not including inflation) has been about 9% per year.

I highly recommend getting good with spreadsheets as they make all these calculations effortless. My first encounter with spreadsheets was during business school, and they quickly became an indispensable tool in my financial arsenal. Being adept at using spreadsheets can transform the way you handle your finances, allowing for more precise tracking, better forecasting, and smarter decision-making.

THE POWER OF COMPOUNDING VERSUS THE HEADWINDS OF INFLATION

If you have money and years to invest, the power of compounding can make you wealthy. Take a look at the table. If you invest $1,000, then at 9% after compounding yearly, it will double after year eight and triple after year thirteen. With compounding, it grows faster and faster, like a snowball rolling downhill and accumulating more snow. However, the real value of that money must account for the effects of inflation, so the real purchasing value of your investment will double after year thirteen (not eight). It will triple after year twenty (not thir-

---

* The S&P 500, or Standard & Poor's 500, is a stock market index that measures the stock performance of 500 large companies listed on the stock exchanges in the US. It is widely regarded as a benchmark indicator of the overall performance of the US stock market.

teen) because after factoring in 3.2% inflation, the real rate of return is closer to 5.6% instead of 9%. But that's still quite a snowball! Those are the sorts of returns people have gotten investing for the longer term in the S&P 500 over the years.

Year	Nominal growth rate		Inflation-adjusted growth rate	
	Value at 9% compound annual growth	Percentage value of original investment	Real value after factoring in 3.2% annual inflation	Percentage value of original investment
0	$1,000.00	100%	$1,000.00	100%
1	$1,090.00	109%	$1,056.20	106%
2	$1,188.10	119%	$1,115.56	112%
3	$1,295.03	130%	$1,178.26	118%
4	$1,411.58	141%	$1,244.48	124%
5	$1,538.62	154%	$1,314.42	131%
6	$1,677.10	168%	$1,388.29	139%
7	$1,828.04	183%	$1,466.32	147%
8	**$1,992.56**	**199%**	$1,548.73	155%
9	$2,171.89	217%	$1,635.77	164%
10	$2,367.36	237%	$1,727.70	173%
11	$2,580.43	258%	$1,824.80	182%
12	$2,812.66	281%	$1,927.35	193%
13	**$3,065.80**	**307%**	**$2,035.67**	**204%**
14	$3,341.73	334%	$2,150.08	215%
15	$3,642.48	364%	$2,270.92	227%
16	**$3,970.31**	**397%**	$2,398.55	240%
17	$4,327.63	433%	$2,533.35	253%
18	$4,717.12	472%	$2,675.73	268%
19	**$5,141.66**	**514%**	$2,826.11	283%
20	$5,604.41	560%	**$2,984.94**	**298%**

Past performance is never a guarantee of future performance, but it is certainly suggestive unless you have better information. There are valid reasons why not everybody invests their money in the S&P 500, including the fact that people don't have ten to twenty years to keep their money invested. Some find the stock market too risky for their risk appetite. There are years when it swings up and down like a rollercoaster, which stresses out some people too much.

Some people get cocky or greedy and think they can beat the S&P 500 with their powers of stock speculation. I don't recommend this approach unless you are a Wall Street professional with a track record or if you can simply afford to lose that speculative money. And there are many other reasons. Also, it's good to diversify across stocks and different asset classes, such as bonds, real estate, or even gold. Why? Because diversification spreads out and reduces your overall risks.

Investing is an essential skill for financial stability and growth. Understanding these basic concepts and carefully assessing risk versus potential return can pave the way to successful financial growth. Remember, every investment carries some level of risk, and it's about making informed decisions that align with your financial goals and risk tolerance.

SKILL 44:
CREDIT AND DEBT MANAGEMENT

"Debt is like any other trap, easy enough to get into,
but hard enough to get out of."
—Henry Wheeler Shaw

CREDIT AS A FINANCIAL SHOCK ABSORBER
AND WORKING CAPITAL TOOL

LET ME START BY REPEATING RULE #1 OF WEALTH BUILDING— always live beneath your means. Credit cards and other forms of credit give you access to cash that is not yours and using credit for longer than a month typically carries a hefty price tag called a debt service fee. Don't get me wrong, credit is handy and important, but it's also dangerous because it allows you to spend beyond your means more easily if you are not careful. Spending beyond your means is a trap leading to poverty and hardship. Don't walk into traps.

So why use credit? Credit, when used wisely, acts as a financial shock absorber. It can provide a buffer in times of unexpected expenses or opportunities, effectively serving as a form of working capital. You can also just use your debit card, which pulls money out of your bank account, versus credit, which lends money out of another bank's account. Use of debit cards or cash is most prudent for most expenses if you have sufficient funds. Credit is helpful for those chunky or unexpected expenses where you need to spread out payments over time. This adaptability is especially crucial for young adults who might encounter sudden needs or opportunities, like a career move or a necessary purchase.

However, the more you spread out your payment, the more debt service you will pay for borrowing that money. All of this can add up substantially if you are not careful.

DIFFERENTIATING BETWEEN GOOD DEBT AND BAD DEBT

Not all debt is inherently bad. Some debts, like low-interest loans for education or a mortgage, can be considered investments in your future or give you access to purchase an asset that can appreciate in value, like a house. These types of debts are often collateralized, meaning they are backed by an asset, which can make them less risky. However, high-interest consumer debt, such as credit card debt, is typically more problematic and should be managed carefully. I strongly recommend that, if you are able, you pay off the entire balance of all your credit cards every month. That way, you avoid paying debt service fees altogether.

Credit cards usually carry high debt service fees, so you want to ensure that any debt using higher interest rates is paid down as quickly as possible. Sometimes, you can finance something with really low-interest rates. I've seen deals where car dealers provide a payment plan with interest rates as low as 0%. That financing is a good deal. It doesn't mean the car is a good purchase, but at 0% interest, it is worth spreading your payments over time because you are not losing anything and are keeping access to your money longer.

Let's say you have a car payment balance for a $20,000 car that has been charging 2% interest for over five years. You have over $20,000 in cash in your account and could pay it off completely. Should you pay off that car? Well, it depends on your options. What else can you do with the $20,000 in your account? Suppose you found a high-interest savings account, for instance, that paid you 4% interest. In that case, it's economically better to park the $20,000 into that higher-interest savings account than to pay off your car payment.

BUILDING TRUST WITH FINANCIAL INSTITUTIONS: THE ROLE OF A GOOD FICO SCORE

How do you get access to credit? Access to credit is mainly dependent on trust from financial institutions, often measured by your FICO score.

A FICO score is a credit score created by the Fair Isaac Corporation (FICO). It's one of the most commonly used credit scores in the United States and is an essential measure used by lenders to assess an individual's creditworthiness. FICO scores range from 300 to 850. A higher score is better, as it indicates lower credit risk to lenders. Generally, a score above 670 is considered good, above 740 is very good, and above 800 is excellent. While the FICO scoring model is specific to the US, the concept of credit scoring is not exclusive to the US, and similar systems exist in other countries. However, they may operate differently and under different names.

A good FICO score, reflecting a history of responsible credit use, is critical to building this trust. Understanding and actively working to improve your FICO score is an essential skill. This score reflects your financial reliability and a higher score can lead to better credit terms.

Here are tips for improving your FICO score:

- **Make Payments on Time:** Timely payments are the most significant factor in your FICO score. Set reminders or automate payments to ensure you never miss a due date.

- **Keep Balances Low:** High balances relative to your credit limits can negatively impact your score. Aim to keep your credit utilization—the ratio of your credit card balance to your credit limit—below 30%.

- **Length of Credit History:** The longer your credit history, the better. So, you should avoid closing old accounts as they contribute to the length of your credit history.

- **Limit New Credit Applications**: Each time you apply for credit, it can cause a slight, temporary dip in your score. Apply for new credit sparingly, especially if planning a significant purchase like a home or a car.

- **Diversify Your Credit Types:** A mix of credit types, such as credit cards, student loans, and mortgages, can positively influence your score. However, don't take on debt you don't need just to diversify your credit.

- **Monitor Your Credit Report:** Regularly check your credit reports for errors. If you find inaccuracies, dispute them with the credit bureau. You're entitled to one free report from the three major credit bureaus each year.

- **Pay Off Debt Rather Than Moving it Around:** Consolidating your credit card debt onto one card or spreading it over multiple cards might not improve your score. The most effective way to improve your score is by paying down your total debt.

- **Avoid Risky Behaviors:** Actions like paying late, having an account sent to collections, or declaring bankruptcy can significantly damage your credit score.

- **Be Patient and Persistent:** Improving your FICO score is a gradual process. Continue practicing good credit habits; your score will reflect this over time.

A strong FICO score is crucial, as it not only helps secure better interest rates and terms for loans and credit cards, saving you money in the long run but also plays a role in non-credit situations like rental and employment screenings. Landlords may use it to assess payment reliability, and some employers check it for positions involving financial duties or sensitive data, although this practice is regulated and varies by state. Thus, maintaining a good credit history is important as it impacts multiple areas of your life.

RESPONSIBLE CREDIT USE: BALANCING SPENDING AND DEBT MANAGEMENT

Effective credit use involves balancing spending with debt management. The key to this is paying off your entire monthly balance to avoid high-interest charges. Regular oversight of your credit score, understanding your debt-to-income ratio, and knowing your debt terms are critical for responsible credit management.

Credit is a powerful tool, but it comes with notable risks. Mismanagement can lead to significant debt and harm your financial stability and credit reputation. Borrow cautiously to avoid excessive debt that could hinder financial independence.

In summary, managing credit and debt requires self-discipline, foresight, and an understanding of your financial limits. Responsible credit use is essential for laying a foundation for a stable financial future.

SKILL 45:
STRATEGIC RISK MANAGEMENT

"By failing to prepare, you are preparing to fail."
—Benjamin Franklin

BE READY FOR LIFE'S SURPRISES

PREPARATION IS THE KEY TO RESILIENCE, SUCCESS, AND PEACE of mind. It transforms the unknown into a manageable challenge and equips us with the tools to face life's uncertainties confidently. In the unpredictable journey of life, being equipped to handle life's uncertainties is a crucial skill. Be prepared for potential risks to your livelihood, whether it's an unexpected job shift, a sudden medical expense, or a dip in the stock market. While this Strategic Risk Management skill is under the money skills chapter, it applies to your overall well-being and livelihood, not just your financial health.

UNDERSTANDING AND MANAGING
DIFFERENT TYPES OF RISKS

Life is inherently risky, and predicting every challenge is impossible. However, developing a strategy to manage these risks is a critical life skill.

Hope for the best, but prepare for the worst.

Another way to think about this is to maximize your potential gains while protecting yourself against potential losses. Don't confuse preparedness for pessimism. Think of it as building a personal toolkit to shield yourself from life's unexpected twists. The key is proactively identifying potential risks—whether in your personal life, career, or finances—and then crafting a contingency plan. This proactive approach doesn't just prepare you for when things go sideways; it empowers you to navigate life's uncertainties with confidence and resilience. By understanding the nature of different risks and preparing accordingly, you can minimize their impact and steer your life in a positive direction, even in the face of adversity.

Risk management in various life areas involves strategic planning and adopting protective measures:

- **Personal and Employment Risks** include job loss, high-interest debt, skill obsolescence, and income dependency. Mitigation involves diversifying income sources, managing debts, continuously developing skills, and maintaining a robust professional network.

- **Health-Related Risks** cover unexpected medical expenses and long-term health issues. Staying healthy, having comprehensive health insurance, and considering disability insurance are key preventive measures.

- **Investment and Market Risks** involve market downturns, inflation, and retirement shortfalls. Protect your investments through diversification, regular portfolio reviews, and a long-term investment approach.

- **Property and Asset Risks** pertain to property damage, asset depreciation, and real estate market fluctuations. Maintaining adequate insurance, regular asset maintenance, and staying informed about market trends help mitigate these risks.

- **Family and Educational Expenses** include high educational costs and changes in family dynamics. Planning with savings vehicles like 529 plans, seeking scholarships, and adjusting financial plans for family changes are essential.

- **Macroeconomic Risks** arise from broader economic factors like recessions and political instability. Building an emergency fund and staying informed about economic developments helps cushion these shocks.

- **Legal and Identity Risks** relate to identity theft and legal disputes. Protecting personal information and considering legal insurance or a savings fund for legal expenses are preventive strategies.

- **Natural Disasters and Crises** demand emergency preparedness, including maintaining a well-stocked emergency kit, having comprehensive insurance coverage, and a clear evacuation plan.

Proactively addressing these risks enhances resilience and secures your future.

SKILL 46:
INSURANCE FUNDAMENTALS

*"It is better to be prepared for an opportunity and
not have one than to have an opportunity and not be prepared."*
—Whitney M. Young Jr.

LET'S FACE IT: LIFE THROWS CURVEBALLS; SOMETIMES, THEY'RE more like fastballs aimed right at your wallet—insurance steps in to cushion the blow. Imagine buying a safety net that catches you when something goes sideways, like a health incident or a car crash. With insurance, you're actively preparing for life's unexpected twists. Insurance is your strategy for staying ahead, from fender benders to health scares.

Think of insurance as a group effort in risk management. It's as if you and a bunch of people pitch in to help out whoever hits a rough patch. If you run into trouble, there's a collective fund to help. That's the essence of insurance. You pay a small amount regularly (called premiums), which goes into a bigger pool. You can access this pool to help cover the costs if something goes wrong.

The premiums you pay are essentially your ticket to peace of mind. The amount varies, primarily based on how likely the insurance company thinks you might need to use that insurance. It's like betting on the weather—the insurance company is guessing whether you'll need that umbrella.

Coverage is what you get in return for your premiums. It's the insurance company promising to cover certain expenses for you, like repairs after a car accident, medical bills, or damage to your home. It's their way of saying, "Don't worry, we've got this covered." Insurance is also helpful against financial risk if you get sued for something, like your responsibility in a car wreck. Insurance is a strategic move to keep your life on track, even when unfortunate surprises come your way. It's about being prepared, staying secure, and knowing that whatever happens, you have a plan in place.

DIFFERENT TYPES OF INSURANCE

Several popular types of insurance cater to different aspects of personal and professional life. Learn about them. Here's a brief overview of some of the many types of insurance available to purchase:

- **Health Insurance:** Covers medical expenses, including doctor's visits, hospital stays, surgeries, and sometimes prescription medications. It's essential due to the outrageously high cost of healthcare in the United States. It is interesting how much healthcare costs differ depending on the country you are in, as well as the quality.

- **Life Insurance:** Provides financial support to beneficiaries (like family members) in case of the policyholder's death. Common types are term life insurance, which covers a specific period, and whole life insurance, which includes an investment component and covers the policyholder's entire life. Usually, you buy life insurance to cover a specific financial goal that can continue to happen without your salary in case you die. Amy and I purchased separate term life insurance on ourselves in case one of us dies so that the other can continue paying off our home mortgage as well as support our kids' future college expenses. We were okay with thirty-year term insurance because we figured our thirty-year mortgage would probably be paid off by then anyway.

- **Car/Auto Insurance:** This type of insurance is mandatory in most places. It covers damages to your vehicle and liability for damages you may cause to others in an accident.

- **Homeowners Insurance:** Protects your home and possessions against damage or theft. It also typically includes liability coverage if someone is injured on your property.

- **Renters Insurance:** Similar to homeowners' insurance, but for renters. It covers personal property within a rented space against risks like theft and fire and often includes liability coverage.

- **Disability Insurance:** Provides income protection if you cannot work due to a disability. It ensures financial stability during such periods.

- **Travel Insurance:** Offers coverage for travel-related risks, including trip cancellations, lost luggage, travel delays, and medical emergencies abroad.

- **Long-Term Care Insurance:** If you or a loved one becomes unable to care for yourself, this type of insurance covers long-term services and supports, including personal and custodial care, often in a variety of settings such as your home, a nursing home, a community organization, or other facilities.[162]

- **Pet Insurance:** Covers veterinary bills for your pets, which can be surprisingly costly, especially for illness or injury.

There are many more types! Each type of insurance mitigates specific financial risks and offers peace of mind, making them popular choices for individuals looking to safeguard different aspects of their lives and assets.

Understanding your insurance options is crucial, as each type serves a distinct purpose. It's about finding the right fit for your unique needs and life stage. Your insurance portfolio should reflect your life to protect your health, car, and home.

> **The more your assets and income grow, the more strategic safeguards you will need, like insurance.**

Remember, while insurance is an expense, it's also an investment in your peace of mind. It's about ensuring restful nights, knowing that you and your loved ones are safeguarded against life's uncertainties. Insurance is a strategic move that lets you stay on course, equipped, and ready for whatever challenges you face. So, get covered, stay informed, and confidently move forward in your life's journey.

SKILL 47:
ENTREPRENEURSHIP

"Don't wait for the right opportunity: create it."
—George Bernard Shaw

PICTURE THIS: YOU'RE TURNING THAT SPARK OF AN IDEA, born from a daydream or a scribble in your notebook, into your venture. The essence of entrepreneurship is that it's a risk-taking journey where individuals like you take the helm, driving their vision forward with passion and determination. Entrepreneurs are pioneers at heart, unafraid to experiment with novel concepts, be it a cutting-edge app, a distinctive online store, or a local café with a unique flair. They see potential where others see the ordinary. *Fortune favors the bold: create, don't wait.*

Yet, entrepreneurship is more than just launching a business. It's an immersive, personal journey involving time, talent, and financial commitment. The rewards can be substantial, offering financial returns and deep personal fulfillment. However, the path involves risks and requires resilience and grit (see Skill 4). Not all ventures succeed, and many entrepreneurs fail several times before they have a breakthrough.

At its core, entrepreneurship is about innovation, risk-taking, and a steadfast commitment to growth, applicable in many settings, from solo ventures to transformative roles within larger corporations. It's about constantly challenging the status quo and striving for betterment. So, if you're contemplating this path, channel your passion into your venture because that's where true entrepreneurial spirit thrives.

RESOURCEFULNESS IS YOUR SUPERPOWER

It's okay to start small. Some people start a side gig or a personal project that grows into a profitable venture. At the College of William and Mary, my college roommate, Sam Dogen, went on to become a Wall Street banker. Later, he transitioned away from a traditional paycheck and achieved significant success by pursuing his own ventures. He started a blog about personal finance as a side hustle. His blog, Financial Samurai, grew like wildfire and became one of the world's most reputable personal finance blogs, helping to fuel the FIRE (Financial Independence, Retire Early) movement.

The FIRE lifestyle approach emphasizes extreme saving and investing to achieve financial freedom and retire much earlier than traditional retirement ages. In 2012, my roommate was able to retire at the early age of thirty-four! His investments eventually generated beyond $200,000 a year in passive income, which freed him up to do whatever he wanted with his time earlier than most people would ever dream of retiring.[163] Sam also published a Wall Street Journal bestselling book, *Buy This, Not That: How to Spend Your Way to Wealth and Freedom.*[164] Sam told me he is currently writing his next book.

Another William and Mary classmate, Anshuman Vohra, went all in on a large entrepreneurship venture not too many years after graduating. Anshuman lived in my freshman dorm in DuPont Hall, and we also had the same business school classes. A few years after we graduated in 2000, Anshuman left a successful career in finance and started a new gin company.[165] Interestingly, my college roommate, Sam Dogen, was one of the early investors in Anshuman's gin company. Sam and Anshuman played tennis together and hit it off. This gin company, BULLDOG Gin, is a premier global gin brand.

It is a small world. In the summer of 2023, I found myself taking shelter in an underground speakeasy-style pub in Ukraine during an air raid, and to my surprise, they were serving BULLDOG Gin. I messaged Anshuman a photo of his global influence. BULLDOG Gin had been sold to Gruppo Campari for approximately $70 million.[166] After that, even though he could have retired, Anshuman decided to start another company called HALO Sport, which makes an advanced electrolyte hydration powder. Sam and Anshuman are doing well for themselves because they had a vision and have pursued it diligently, taking measured risks, which has paid off massively.

At its heart, entrepreneurship is about laying out a vision and then building a path to make it a reality. This path includes solving a lot of problems and coming up and fixing things along the way. Beyond making money, you're also making a difference. Entrepreneurs boost the economy, create jobs, and often lead the way in social change. You're not just building a business; you're creating a legacy.

The world of entrepreneurship is constantly evolving, and so will you. Whether it's the latest tech trend or a new marketing strategy, there's always something new to learn and new ways to level up. Embarking on an entrepreneurial journey is about more than just making money—it's about crafting a lifestyle that's as unique as you are. It's about passion, adventure, and the satisfaction of seeing your dreams become reality. So go ahead, take that leap, and build something incredible.

There are thousands of entrepreneurial possibilities out there to explore. For example, one could start with freelancing by offering skills like writing or programming on platforms like Upwork or Fiverr. The Internet opens doors to online businesses, including e-commerce stores, drop-shipping, or selling unique products on Etsy. I would be remiss not to mention how AI is opening up a new world of possibilities. For those with tech expertise or innovative ideas, tech startups, app development, or creating tech gadgets offer lucrative opportunities. Content creation on YouTube, blogs, or podcasts can generate income through ads and sponsorships.

Consulting services in marketing, finance, or IT can capitalize on your professional expertise. The demand for services like wellness coaching and personal training is growing as people are increasingly interested in coaching and personal development. Eco-friendly product businesses cater to increasing environmental awareness. Personal branding and influencer marketing on social media can also be profitable. Additionally, one could consider starting a local service business, such as a café or a boutique, to serve the community.

Successful entrepreneurship requires enhancing your knowledge, gaining exposure to seasoned entrepreneurs, and accumulating experience, even if initially on a small scale. For example, you could take an online course on entrepreneurship or enrich your knowledge with books and podcasts from successful entrepreneurs. There are ample networking events and conferences for gaining real-world insights. You could participate in entrepreneurial communities, both online and locally, and explore university programs or business incubators. Gain practical experience through internships or volunteering in business roles, start small projects or side hustles, and participate in business plan competitions for valuable feedback. Above all, embrace the learning-by-doing approach; start your own business venture, no matter the scale, to gain hands-on entrepreneurial experience.

Ultimately, entrepreneurship is largely a mindset as much as it is a discipline. It can be fulfilling and profitable, but it requires continuous learning, adaptability, and resilience. Start with an idea you're passionate about, keep learning, and don't be afraid to take that first step.

SKILL 48:
RETIREMENT PLANNING

"Retirement is not the end of the road.
It is the beginning of the open highway."
—Unknown

IT'S NEVER TOO EARLY TO START RETIREMENT PLANNING, BUT too many people either never start or start too late, and they get trapped in work's hamster wheel. Financial freedom is within reach if you plan ahead and apply discipline.

While hardworking, my mother's family came from broken households and poor roots. For as long as I can remember, my grandmother, whom I called Nana, was a cashier for a cafeteria called K&W, which is now out of business. She was exceptional at counting money and could do some pretty fantastic arithmetic in her head. However, Nana would spend all her hard-earned money on her family, saving none. As her grandson, I loved the generous stack of Christmas gifts she gave us; it was her joy. Unfortunately, as her health declined, she was never able to retire before she passed away.

In some ways, Nana's day job kept her active, and she seemed to enjoy it as it gave her a social outlet. But in other ways, it gave her no options to take advantage of her golden years. My grandmother didn't drive either, so my mother and her siblings would take turns taking my grandmother to and from work each day. She worked long hours and was highly dependent on others, with no option but to continue working those long, draining hours. Nana's story is an all-to-common one.

Although, for many, the ultimate dream is to be able to retire and stop working to have essentially a permanent vacation from work obligations. On the other hand, I believe that retirement doesn't suit everyone. Several retired colleagues experienced an initial period of joy, only to feel later bored or miss that sense of purpose they once had in their high-powered careers. Even my roommate, Sam Dogen, who retired at the unusually early age of thirty-four, later said he got bored and started picking up work to fill his time with something meaningful. But more importantly, he had accumulated enough wealth to give him options.

Retirement shouldn't be viewed as an ultimate goal for all; rather, *the ability to retire* should be. The key is having greater control over our time. It is not just important to have more time, but you should also ideally have sufficient health. If work is fulfilling, continue doing it. If there's a desire to explore new avenues or learn new things, and if financial stability allows it, pursue those interests. Retirement is not necessarily the ideal for everybody.

The essence of financial independence lies in making these choices. After all, having choices represents true freedom—because freedom itself is the ultimate goal. The ultimate aim is to have the freedom and ability to live out your worthiest of dreams. Therefore, I'm using "financial independence" interchangeably with "retirement" because when you are financially free, you can comfortably retire if you want to. The option of how you spend your time becomes yours.

You reach true financial freedom when your passive income suffices to sustain your desired lifestyle indefinitely, liberating you from the necessity of active work.

Let's talk about how to get to financial independence. Technically, you are financially independent if you earn sufficient passive income to cover all your expenses for your desired living standard. That's highly personal because one person's desired living standard can vastly differ from another's. One person might have three children and live in an expensive city and a moderate-sized home, so the basic yearly budget to maintain a desirable standard of living could be over $100,000 to $200,000 per year. Another person might be content living in a less expensive town, with a smaller home, and choose not to have children—this cuts their yearly budget in half.

A FIVE-STEP PATH FOR ENGINEERING YOUR FINANCIAL INDEPENDENCE

In some ways, retirement planning is as much an art as a science. But you do yourself a major disservice if you don't approach it with a clear strategy and a rigorous approach. Here are six steps designed to bring clarity and rigor to your financial planning. Given the complexity of financial planning, I recommend considering hiring a financial advisor to help you with your situation. There is also good online software, such as Empower, that can help you with basic retirement modeling. With that said, these five basic steps will help you start thinking through all this.

Step 1: Envision your ideal lifestyle. The first step to engineering your path to financial independence is defining the desired end state so you can work backward in your planning from there. It takes work to clarify your vision and dreams. Fast forward through your ideal life and envision your desirable lifestyle. Think about major goals you would like to achieve (like owning a home, paying for higher education, world travel, etc.), where you would like to live, and what standard of living you would like. Write all this down. Also, discuss it with those close to you.

A word of advice: Identify what "enough" looks like. People who fail to do this run the risk of never being satisfied. The caveat is that it is human nature that our desires grow when fed. You might never be content if your desires and expectations tend to grow faster than your means. Therefore, do some soul-searching and define what good enough looks like as a minimum standard, and then anything above that is icing on the cake. If your standard for good enough grows too much, then potentially nothing will ever be good enough for you, and that means you will never let yourself feel financially independent, but the lack of freedom would be your own doing in that case. Dream big, but don't let greed take hold. Greed is a trap because it robs you of contentment.

Step 2: Draft a budget for your ideal lifestyle. Once you set your vision, you should create a budget for that vision that produces a per-year expense number. For a rough illustration, let's say that you would like to be able to accomplish the following lifestyle:

- Maintain comfortable living expenses, such as a home, car, utilities, food, fitness, entertainment, etc.

- Take some vacation trips with family and friends

- Maintain all health insurance and other insurance policies for peace of mind

- Pay for some major goals like helping with kids' college, weddings, and other rites of passage

- Personal development to keep learning new things, cultivating skills, and exploring hobbies

- Spending quality time with family and friends

- Help out others in need within your means

Imagine your future life—go ahead, you've worked hard for this. This image is unique as your dreams and goals shape it. Now, let's bring some practicality into that vision. How much would it cost to live that life in today's dollars? Pull out your budgeting skills here. Let's say, based on where you dream of living, your annual expenses might start at around $80,000. But remember, living costs vary widely between cities worldwide.

Also, life is full of changes. If you are a young professional starting a family, your budget might lean heavily toward housing and childcare. Fast forward a few years, and the picture might change. Your kids could be more independent, and if you're a homeowner, that mortgage might be an expense of the past. However, as we age, healthcare costs can creep up. It's wise to factor in insurance to manage these unexpected expenses.

All these shifts are crucial in planning your budget. A spreadsheet can be your best friend here. Here is an example of something to try: list significant income and expense categories down the left side and include some life events or goals like paying for your kids' college, etc. Even if you don't have kids yet, plan ahead! Add the years from now through age one hundred on the top row. Then, at the intersection of the expenses and years, estimate those expenses' costs at that point in time. There are different ways to visualize this, but having a visual layout helps you see when and how your financial needs will change. Don't forget there's also handy online software to guide you through this planning process. By mapping out your financial journey, you're setting the stage for a life that's not just dreamt about but also well-planned.

Here's a straightforward method to gauge your retirement needs with a simple thought experiment. Begin by examining your current earnings as a foundational benchmark. Reflect on your current standard of living: Are you satisfied with it, or do you find it somewhat lacking? If you're not entirely happy and things feel tight, then you might consider aiming for a higher retirement income (not considering inflation). Conversely, if you're comfortable and content with your present financial situation, using your current earnings as a baseline for your retirement target could be an effective starting point.

Many people anticipate reduced expenses in retirement, maybe due to a fully paid-off mortgage or grown-up kids who have children who've flown the nest. So, your retirement income might be lower than your working days' earnings. Also, after retirement, you don't need to save anymore if you don't want to. A standard benchmark is about 80% of your pre-retirement income. However, this is just a rough guide.

It is crucial to think through your specific life goals (i.e., your future needs, wants, and wishes) and their costs before locking in a retirement plan. Start with this relative income approach to get a ballpark figure. Then, dive into creating a more detailed retirement budget. Remember, this is a draft. With retirement likely decades away, it's wise to revisit and adjust this plan regularly. Your priorities, hobbies, and life's opportunities will evolve. While it's essential to plan, staying flexible and open to change is equally crucial.

After this exercise, you should have an estimate or at least a low-high range for an ideal yearly post-retirement budget, using the future value amount.* Let's also call this your *target retirement net income* figure. For illustration, let's just say that your target retirement net income figure is $80,000 per year (or if we were projecting 15-years out, it might need to be $128,317 after adjusting up for inflation).

How you end up funding that target retirement net income might come from multiple sources, such as your savings, 401(k), pensions, Social Security, etc. Although pensions are less common today and Social Security isn't guaranteed, these sources can significantly impact your financial planning.

Also, be cautious with relying on Social Security. The US government's Social Security trust fund was predicted to run out of money around 2033.[167] If this happens sometime in your lifetime, you might receive less than expected or possibly nothing from Social Security. Therefore, how much you rely on these income streams in your retirement planning depends on your preference for risk. If you prefer to be more conservative in your planning, you might want to rely less on these uncertain income sources.

Step 3: Adjust your target retirement net income to account for taxes to get the equivalent of a target retirement gross income. When planning for retirement, it's crucial to factor in taxes to understand how much you'll have to spend. It's easy to overlook the impact of taxes on your net worth and the money you'll withdraw in retirement. Remember, a significant portion of your savings might be subject to taxes, reducing the amount you'll have available for spending.

---

*   Keep in mind that because of inflation, money is worth less in the future. Therefore, your target retirement net income figure should use the Future Value (FV) at the point of retirement. So, assuming inflation is 3.2%, that implies that $80,000 today would need to be $128,317 in 15 years from now in order to have the same purchasing power. You can calculate the FV with this formula: FV = Present Value x (1 + inflation rate)^(years from now), or in this case $128,317 = $80,000 x (1.032)^15

Consider different types of retirement accounts. Funds in tax-deferred accounts, like a 401(k), are taxed upon withdrawal. This money was saved before taxes, meaning it hasn't been taxed yet. When you withdraw from these accounts in retirement, the amount gets taxed as regular income based on your federal and state tax brackets.

For instance, if you're a single tax filer in Virginia as of 2023, a gross income of $100,000 would face an effective tax rate of about 20%, combining federal and state taxes. Also, depending on where you live, your age, and your employment status at retirement, you might need to consider other taxes and withholdings. For example, on any non-retirement earned income, the Federal Insurance Contributions Act (FICA)* tax, which is 7.65%, covers Social Security and Medicare and affects your take-home pay. While the FICA tax is technically 15.3%, employers typically cover half. However, you'll be responsible for 15.3% if you're self-employed. In the US, retirees do not pay FICA taxes on retirement income such as Social Security benefits, pensions, distributions from 401(k) plans, and individual retirement accounts (IRAs).

So, when calculating your retirement income, adjust your target to reflect these taxes and get an accurate picture of your gross income. This approach ensures you have a realistic view of your financial situation in retirement.

When planning for retirement, understanding the tax implications of withdrawing from your 401(k) is critical. Withdrawing funds from a 401(k) before you turn 59 ½ years old may result in a penalty fee of 10% of the amount withdrawn. But not all your savings might be in a 401(k). If you've got investments in a stock account with money you've already paid taxes on, withdrawing these funds would subject you to capital gains tax, which differs from income tax. And remember, tax rules can vary based on where you live.

---

*   Many countries have similar taxes fund social security and healthcare benefits. For example, the United Kingdom has National Insurance (NI), Canada has the Canada Pension Plan (CPP) and Employment Insurance (EI), Australia has the Superannuation Guarantee and Medicare Levy, Germany has Social Security Contributions (Sozialversicherungsbeiträge), France has Social Security Contributions (Cotisations Sociales), Japan has Social Insurance Contributions, and the Netherlands has Social Security Contributions (Sociale Zekerheidsbijdragen).

Determining how much of your savings is pre-tax versus already taxed is essential. For instance, 80% of your savings are in a traditional 401(k), while the remaining 20% is in a personal savings account. In this case, you'll eventually have to pay taxes on that 80%.

While consulting a tax professional is ideal for accurate calculations, if you're just looking for a ballpark figure, use your target retirement income from Step 2. Suppose you've set it at $80,000 and estimate your effective tax rate at 20%, combining pre-tax and post-tax income sources. You can calculate the target requirement gross income needed to cover your expenses in retirement like this:

This figure is like your "required retirement salary" (not yet taxed). So, from our example above we have $80,000 / (1 - 20%) simplifying to $80,000 / 80% = $100,000. This amount represents the annual withdrawal rate you'll need from any of your retirement income sources plus your retirement nest egg, which should be planned to grow with inflation. Essentially, this is like setting a gross salary for yourself in retirement, giving you a tax-adjusted target retirement income of $100,000.

Step 4: Determine your target retirement nest egg* savings needed for retirement. Let's determine how much you'll need to set aside in your retirement savings to support your desired lifestyle. As we continue using the above scenario, let's say that your gross target income required is $100,000 in retirement, to be adjusted for inflation. How big does your nest egg need to be to make this happen?

We need to calculate the total amount that you need to save up based on our target retirement gross income requirement. However, before doing so, we can reduce this target retirement gross income required figure by subtracting out the portion that is provided from known alternative income sources such as Social Security, as relevant. For instance, if you knew you expected $18,000 from Social Security,

---

*   A "nest egg" refers to a sum of money saved or invested for future use, especially for retirement. The term is often used to describe savings that are accumulated over time and set aside for a specific purpose, such as providing financial security in later years. The idea behind a nest egg is to build a financial reserve that can be relied upon when regular income is reduced or stops, such as during retirement.

your *adjusted target retirement gross income* for the purposes of calculating a nest egg would be $82,000 (or $100k - $18k).

A commonly used guideline is the '25 times rule', based on the 4% rule. This rule of thumb suggests you need a nest egg 25 times your annual retirement expenses. Withdrawing 4% annually from your retirement savings is widely considered a safe rate to ensure your nest egg lasts. But remember, this rule was more relevant in the 1990s, and today's financial climate, with potentially lower returns on stocks and bonds, might call for an updated approach.[168] Plus, this rule doesn't fully account for taxes and other income sources. Therefore, using your adjusted target retirement gross income, which we had derived from your ideal retirement lifestyle expenses, provides a more nuanced calculation. For a more conversative estimate, you can even use a higher multiple.

Now let's apply this approach to our example. Since our adjusted target retirement gross income amount was $82,000, then a reasonable nest egg for that would be $2.05 million (or $82k x 25). In other words, in this example, you should be aiming to save $2.05 million in some retirement account before you retire. Remember, in this scenario, Social Security is projected to be $18k per year. Using the 25 times rule, that's basically equivalent to having $450k in retirement savings (or $18k x 25); that's an extra $450k you won't need in your nest egg, assuming Social Security still works by the time you retire.

Remember, these are just guidelines. Your retirement strategy should reflect your unique financial situation, future goals, and lifestyle aspirations. It's a good idea to periodically reassess your plan, especially as markets and personal circumstances change.

Step 5: Now figure out how much you need to invest per year to reach your nest egg savings goal. Start early and set aside enough money to reach your nest egg goal.

Let's use a more assertive scenario. For example, say you are twenty-one and need a $3 million nest egg by age 57, the year you wish to retire. If you can invest $31,303 in something like stocks and maintain a yearly 5% compound annual return, you will have $3 million by then. Or better yet, max out your retirement accounts toward that amount. Depending on how much you make, setting aside $31,303 per year could be pretty doable. If you started saving as early as eighteen (three years earlier), you could achieve this goal by setting aside only $26,294 per year. The earlier you start, the more the power of compound interest will work in your favor, helping you reach your nest egg with greater leverage.

I figure this amount out by using a formula. Here is a helpful formula to determine how much you need to invest per year to arrive at your nest egg goal by your target retirement age. Of course, this provides an estimate; it is recommended that you consult a financial advisor to provide a more rigorous estimate, accounting for factors such as your actual rate of return on investments might fluctuate from year to year. Also, check out handy online software to help you figure this out with different inputs and scenarios.

HOW TO CALCULATE YOUR ANNUAL SAVINGS NEEDED FOR RETIREMENT

What You Need to Know:

- **Desired Nest Egg:** This is the total amount you want to save by retirement.

- **Investment Return Rate:** The yearly rate of return you expect from your investments. For instance, if you expect a 5% return, use 0.05 for this number.

- **Years Until Retirement:** How many years do you have until you retire?

The formula:

$$\textit{Annual Savings Needed} = \frac{FV \times r}{[(1+r)^n - 1]}$$

Plugging in the Inputs from Our Example:

- Desired Nest Egg (FV): $3,000,000 (note "FV" stands for "Future Value")

- Investment Return Rate (r): 5% per year or 0.05

- Number of Years Until Retirement (n): 36 years (57 - 21)

$$Annual\ Savings\ Needed = \frac{3,000,000 \times 0.05}{[(1.05)^{36} - 1]}$$

Performing the Calculation Step by Step:

1. Calculate $(1 + r)$: $1 + 0.05 = 1.05$

2. Raise 1.05 to the power of 36: $(1.05)^{36}$ (it is probably best to use a calculator for this)

3. Subtract 1 from the result of step 2: $(1.05)^{36} - 1$

4. Multiply the FV by r: $\$3,000,000 * 0.05 = \$150,000$

5. Divide the result of step 4 by the result of step 3.

This calculation will give you the amount you need to save each year (in this example, $31,302) at the end of the year to reach your goal of $3,000,000 by age fifty-seven, assuming a 5% annual return on your investments.

If you've followed these steps, you should now have a clearer idea of your retirement savings goal. You'll also know the annual contributions needed to reach it and the optimal rate of return for your investments. You must do your homework to find suitable investments for your desired returns. On this, I recommend seeking advice from professionals. Of course, unexpected positives and negatives might happen along the way, so revisit your retirement plan at least yearly and adjust if needed. Applying this knowledge, you will be closer to achieving financial independence as a clearer goalpost and ultimately have a fulfilling life of wealth and freedom to live out your dreams.

As a way to remember the key skill concepts covered in this chapter, remember WEALTHIER (**W**ealth mindset, **E**ssental accounting of your finances, **A**llocating resources through saving and budgeting, **L**ucrative investment, **T**actical debt management, **H**edging of risks, **I**nsurance understanding, **E**ntrepreneurship, and **R**etirement planning).

Understanding financial literacy and developing a wealth mindset prepares us not just for monetary success but for making informed life choices. As we conclude this chapter, we look forward to Level 7, where we'll integrate our learnings and focus on the art of leadership and continuous learning.

LEVEL 7:
LEARN TO LEARN AND LEAD

A LIFELONG LEARNER WITH A CLEAR PURPOSE NATURALLY evolves into a compelling leader. Imagine a world where your capacity to learn isn't just a trait—it's your superpower. Your ability to absorb, adapt, and apply knowledge sets the stage for success and leadership. In Level 7, we'll embrace the dual powers of learning and leadership and learn how to take these skills to the next level.

In this chapter, we'll unpack the essence of lifelong learning, emphasizing its role in accumulating knowledge and cultivating a mindset geared toward exploration, balance, and growth. This journey will illuminate how embracing continuous learning can transform you into a leader who inspires others toward a compelling vision and thrives amidst the complexities of the modern world. By combining the principles of perpetual learning with the art of leadership, this chapter aims to equip you with the insights and strategies necessary to inspire, influence, and leave a lasting impact on your surroundings.

This chapter is more than just a guide; it's a roadmap to elevating your learning and leadership skills for real-world impact. Ready to level up and shape your future?

Self-Assessment

As you begin Level 7, focused on expanding your learning and leadership skills, let's engage in a self-assessment to maximize the impact of these crucial skills. Reflect on these questions to deepen your understanding and application. Write down the answers to these questions before starting the chapter.

1. **Learning Reflection:** Reflect on how the learning techniques from previous chapters have worked for you. Which methods have been most effective and why?

2. **Learning to Learn:** Think about a skill or subject you initially found challenging but eventually mastered. What strategies did you use, and how can they be applied to learning new skills in the future?

3. **Leadership in Action:** Consider a time when you took on a leadership role, formally or informally. What did you learn from that experience about your own leadership style?

4. **Application of Leadership Skills:** Identify an area in your life, such as a project, group activity, or personal goal, where you can apply or enhance your leadership skills. How do you plan to implement these skills?

5. **Continuous Learning Goals:** Set a specific goal for continuous learning or leadership. How will achieving this goal contribute to your personal or professional growth?

These reflective questions are designed to bridge your learning from the previous chapters to the advanced concepts of learning and leadership in Level 7. They will help you apply these skills more effectively in your own life.

SKILL 49:
LEARNING TO LEARN:
THE SKILL OF SKILLS

"Give a man a fish, and you feed him for a day;
teach a man to fish, and you feed him for a lifetime."
—a well-known proverb

YOU HAVE PROBABLY HEARD THIS PROFOUND PROVERB before. You can flip this proverb inward and apply it to the fact you are teaching yourself, and this profound truth still applies from a learning perspective. You can learn a fact and be informed for a moment; learn to learn, and you are empowered for a lifetime. Do this, and now the profundity is in you!

Acquiring specific knowledge or skills is undoubtedly beneficial. However, the ability to learn effectively and independently stands as a far more significant and lasting gift. It's about equipping yourself with the tools to gather information and understand, assimilate, and apply it in various contexts. This skill enables you continuously to grow, adapt, and excel, keeping pace with an ever-evolving world. In essence, learning to learn is not just about accumulating facts or skills; it's about nurturing an adaptable, curious mind that can navigate the complexities and opportunities of life with confidence and agility.

In today's fast-paced world, the ability to learn new things efficiently and effectively stands out as the ultimate life skill. It's the bedrock upon which all other skills are built, the 'skill of skills' if you will. For shaping your future, learning to learn is your most powerful tool in this journey.

Learning is an adventure of self-discovery and exploration. The world is a vast, fascinating place, and there's so much out there that can spark your curiosity and passion. But to truly make the most of this journey, you must start with an open mind. Let go of the need always to be right or to think you know everything. A lack of humility stifles learning.

Humility in learning is like emptying your cup; it makes room for new knowledge and experiences. This process also takes clear, critical thinking (see Skill 24), including shedding our biases as much as possible. Approach each new topic or skill with fresh eyes, as if you're seeing it for the first time, and be ready to challenge your assumptions and embrace the role of a lifelong learner. Embrace the power of wonderment.

The key to mastering the art of learning is not just in what you learn but how you learn. Be curious and ask questions, even about things you presumably already know. Be selective in what you choose to learn; it should resonate with your interests and goals. And remember, learning isn't just about taking in information; it's about understanding and applying it. Develop a systematic approach to your learning journey—set objectives, find efficient study techniques, and regularly review and apply what you've learned.

In the art of learning, quality reading is critical. Diverse materials, ranging from stimulating novels to insightful research, sharpen your mind and broaden your perspectives. Yet, true learning is active—it's about diving into new experiences, from coding to culinary adventures, making theoretical knowledge practical and lively.

Your learning should resonate with your life. Connect it to your passions and goals, turning it into an exciting, personal journey. Organize this journey with clear, achievable goals, ensuring each step is impactful and contributes to your broader aspirations.

The world offers a wealth of knowledge to explore. Follow your curiosity, whether it leads to the intricacies of technology, the depths of psychology, or the elegance of art. Complement this exploration with a dynamic reading list that grows and changes with your interests.

Remember, 'learning to learn' is more than acquiring knowledge; it's a commitment to continuous growth and adaptability, shaping your intellect and entire life approach. Embrace this journey wholeheartedly and witness its transformative power.

One of the best ways to really grasp a topic is to engage with it actively, and it's even more effective when you teach it to someone else. Sharing your knowledge not only helps others but also reinforces your learning. And don't forget the importance of reading—a habit that exposes you to new ideas and perspectives, broadening your horizons.

Perhaps you might be wondering, "What should I learn next?" The answer is anything that piques your interest and contributes to your life goals. Whether technology, arts, sciences, or social issues, the world is your oyster.

Learning to learn is an ongoing process that continues throughout your life. It's about staying curious, being open to new experiences, and never being afraid to step out of your comfort zone. So, embrace this journey with enthusiasm and an open mind. The skills and knowledge you acquire will not only help you navigate the complexities of adulthood but also enrich your life in ways you've never imagined. Happy learning!

SKILL 50:
LEARN TO LEAD

"Leadership is not about being in charge.
It is about taking care of those in your charge."
—Simon Sinek

W E'VE REACHED A PIVOTAL MOMENT—SKILL 50, THE ES-
sence of leadership. Leadership transcends mere titles, roles, or methods. It is an intricate art that harnesses your passion, talent, and wherewithal to create an influential force that inspires, empowers, and drives change. It is a huge responsibility, but one that can be profoundly fulfilling.

There are a ton of self-proclaimed leadership gurus out there, each with their own take on leadership. Some offer insightful perspectives, while others—not so much.

Once upon a time, in a tale as enlightening as it is ancient, a group of blind men encountered an elephant for the first time. Eager to comprehend this majestic creature, each man reached out, touching a different part of the elephant's body. One grasped its solid side, another its sharp tusk, a third its sinuous trunk, while others explored a sturdy knee, an enormous ear, and the swishing tail. From these fragments of experience, each man drew a confident conclusion about the essence of an elephant. To the man who touched the trunk, the elephant was akin to a thick snake; to another feeling its leg, it seemed as sturdy as a tree.

This parable strikes a chord, particularly when reflecting on the landscape of leadership philosophies that populate our world today. Much like those blind men, many leadership gurus tend to illuminate just one facet of leadership, holding it up as the whole truth. Some sing praises of personal charisma as the cornerstone of effective leadership; others tout the paramount importance of results, vision, goal setting, or unwavering commitment. Yet, true leadership, in its fullest expression, encompasses the entire elephant. It's an intricate dance of qualities, a balance that calls for a comprehensive approach.

The real magic happens when you carve out your unique leadership philosophy and refine it through the crucible of experience. It's about blending your skills, knowledge, and experiences to elevate yourself, uplift others, and create ripples of positive change. Your approach to leadership can redefine boundaries and transform lives. If helpful, I will share my perspective on balanced leadership while encouraging you to develop your own unique leadership philosophy.

A BALANCED LEADERSHIP PHILOSOPHY: HARMONIZING PEOPLE, PASSIONS, NEEDS, AND SKILLS

Over the years, I've gained valuable insights from serving on and leading teams. These experiences have helped to shape my own leadership philosophy that continues to evolve, much like life itself. Having a leadership philosophy helps simplify a complex matter, giving you a better sense of what to do.

My leadership philosophy drew inspiration from personal experience and the modified *ikigai* concept (see Skill 7), but it is distinct. I call it *Balanced Leadership*. As a leader, there is always chaos and competing tensions you are trying to resolve as you move a vision or strategy forward. A successful leader brings clarity and order to the chaos and inspires others to move forward in synchronicity.

To do this, a leader must make sure people, passions, needs, and skills come together in harmony for impactful outcomes. Inspired by but distinct from the *ikigai* depiction, this leadership perspective emphasizes a dynamic interplay where each element contributes to and enhances the others, fostering an environment of collective growth and success.

Balanced Leadership
Clarify, Develop, and Harmonize these:

PASSION

COMMITMENT ENGAGEMENT

PEOPLE BALANCED LEADERSHIP **SKILLS**

SERVICE IMPACT

NEEDS

People: Identifying and Developing

Without people, there is no leadership. A leader values the diverse individuals involved, such as team members and those they are helping. It consists of being in tune with others' motivations, talents, and needs. Also, it requires identifying everyone's unique strengths and potential and fostering their development. This process includes maintaining healthy relationships and ensuring everyone is actively engaged, valued, and understood. At the intersection of people and their needs is service. When people are aligned with passion, there is commitment.

Passions: Clarifying and Channeling

Without passion, leadership is lifeless. Passion is the fuel that drives both individuals and teams toward excellence; it is the stuff of influence, which is the very soul of leadership. A leader's role is to clarify these passions in alignment with an inspiring vision and goals. As a leader, continuously keep the team focused on the bigger picture (the why). Make sure to channel individual passions to contribute to a collective purpose, ensuring everyone works effectively and with authentic commitment. Bring the right people to the table, and it is important that they are passionate about the shared vision and adequately equipped to make a difference. When passions align with skills, productive engagement and flow are possible at the highest levels.

Learn to cultivate your charisma. Charismatic leaders inspire with a compelling vision and passion, maintaining approachability. They authentically connect through confidence and empathy, leveraging emotional intelligence to deeply engage and communicate clearly. This approach builds trust and motivates teams effectively.

Needs: Understanding and Addressing
Without meeting needs, leadership is pointless. Leadership involves a keen understanding of the real needs of both the individuals within the team and those whom the team serves. Doing this means continually assessing and addressing these needs (with the right people applying the right skills and passions), ensuring that the team's efforts effectively solve real problems and make a meaningful impact. When skills meet needs, you get impact.

Skills: Equipping and Leveraging
Without skills, leadership is ineffective. A leader not only identifies the existing skills of team members but also works on unlocking their latent talents. It's crucial to equip team members with the necessary tools, training, and opportunities to develop and use their skills effectively. I also would group systems with skills because it's powerful to establish solid systems. It's about bringing the right talent to the table and aligning skills with the team's objectives and the broader needs they aim to meet.

HARMONIZING THESE ELEMENTS

A leader takes responsibility for clarifying, developing, and harmonizing all these components (people, passions, needs, and skills) and more. As you steer through life, never undervalue the impact of sharing your knowledge. Engaging in activities like mentoring, volunteering your skills, or offering counsel cements your understanding and fosters robust, supportive communities.

A true leader doesn't just chase personal achievements; they lift others along their journey. This means understanding and cultivating the strengths of those around you, providing encouragement and support for their development, and rejoicing in their triumphs.

Crafting your unique leadership philosophy is instrumental in finding your own voice. Your approach must be authentic. Reflect on your personal interpretation of leadership, your core values, and the kind of influence you aspire to have. This philosophy will act as your guiding light, influencing your choices and actions.

Remember, leadership is a skill that is continually developed and refined. According to John Maxwell, "Successful leaders are learners. And the learning process is ongoing, a result of self-discipline and perseverance."[169] Depending on the situation, different leadership facets may need to be brought to the forefront. Dedicate time to exploring various leadership approaches and theories. Learn from the journeys of exemplary leaders. Resources like books, podcasts, workshops, and mentors are invaluable.

To master leadership, you must employ all the skills you've learned and a genuine spirit of service. Successful leadership also requires integrity and trust, clear vision and goals, the ability to bring out the best in others, and adaptability to learn. This mastery paves the way for your success and serves as a powerful instrument to make a lasting impact in the world.

One of the most effective ways to solidify your learning is to share it. Talk about the concepts and skills from this book with friends, family, or colleagues. Teach others. Engaging in dialogues about these topics deepens your understanding and helps disseminate this wisdom.

The ultimate aim of leadership is to forge a better world. While this task might appear overwhelming, remember that significant changes often start with bold ideas and small steps. Each positive action you take, every individual you inspire, and every initiative you lead adds to a larger impact. As a leader, your capacity to drive change is limitless.

FINAL WORDS

AS WE REACH THE END OF THIS BOOK, LET'S PAUSE AND AP-preciate the ground we've covered.

We discovered the essence of being FOCUSED, realizing that remarkable achievements are within reach when one ASPIRES toward greatness, prioritizes WELLNESS, and boosts brainpower by putting on their BRIGHTS. By extending this understanding to others, we LISTEN TRUE, uncovering a deeper sense of being WEALTHIER, far beyond the confines of financial wealth. Let us seize every chance to *LEARN & LEAD*, forging paths toward a richer, more fulfilling life.*

As we close this chapter—both literally and metaphorically—on an excursion that has woven through landscapes of developing a winning mindset, achieving worthy goals, bolstering health, fostering strong relationships, mastering finances, and so much more, remember this: cultivating a habit of continuous learning and self-improvement builds on itself, continually expanding what is possible for yourself and others. Make every moment count.

The important thing is to get into the arena and live life to its fullest. You will have good times and challenging times, but remember to celebrate your achievements and learn from failures, continuing forward with vigor and purpose. I share one of my favorite quotes of

---

*   *All the capitalized words in this paragraph are acronyms of the 50 game-changing life skills recapped at the end of each book chapter, apart from LEARN & LEAD, since Level 7 only included two skills.*

all time from Theodore Roosevelt from a famous speech he delivered in 1910, but rings as inspirational and true today:

> It is not the critic who counts; not the man who points out how the strong man stumbles, or where the doer of deeds could have done them better. The credit belongs to the man who is actually in the arena, whose face is marred by dust and sweat and blood; who strives valiantly; who errs, who comes short again and again, because there is no effort without error and shortcoming; but who does actually strive to do the deeds; who knows great enthusiasms, the great devotions; who spends himself in a worthy cause; who at the best knows in the end the triumph of high achievement, and who at the worst, if he fails, at least fails while daring greatly, so that his place shall never be with those cold and timid souls who neither know victory nor defeat.[170]

Congratulations on reaching this milestone! Your commitment to mastering these fifty game-changing life skills will yield significant benefits, leading to a more meaningful and impactful life. May your journey be filled with lifelong learning, personal achievements, and the profound joy of sharing your insights and experiences with others. As you progress, let your successes inspire and light the way for others, creating a ripple effect of positive change.

My hope for you is an abundant life, rich in experiences, surrounded by people who matter, and dedicated to making a difference to the greater cause that is your unique calling. The true wealth you accumulate extends far beyond the financial, leaving a legacy of impactful contributions. As you turn the last page of this book, step forward with determination to thrive, transform, and leave a legacy that resonates for generations. May your life be filled with growth, sharing, and enduring impact. Now, go ahead and level up, thrive, and make your mark!

With all my love,

Steve

LEAVE A REVIEW

Thank you for reading! Your feedback would mean so much to me and would help others discover this book. Please take a moment to leave a review by scanning the QR code or visiting the link below. Your review makes a big difference and is greatly appreciated.

http://stevemscott.com/review-paperback

NOTES

1. Inspired by the wisdom of Philippians 4:8 (English Standard Version), from a let-ter written by the Apostle Paul around AD 62. This verse not only provides sound guidance for life but also aligns with psychological principles, suggesting that our thought life can significantly impact our emotional well-being and behavior. It highlights the power of our thoughts in shaping our experiences and character, encouraging a mindset that fosters a fulfilling and mentally healthy life.

2. Oren Harari, *The Leadership Secrets of Colin Powell*, 1st ed. (McGraw Hill Profes-sional, 2002), https://books.google.com/books?id=kstneA_TbiQC.

3. Translated by Benjamin Jowett, adapted by Miriam Carlisle, Thomas E. Jenkins, Gregory Nagy, and Soo-Young Kim, "Plato, The Apology of Socrates" The Cen-tre for Hellenic Studies (December 12, 2019), https://chs.harvard.edu/primary-source/plato-the-apology-of-socrates-sb/.

4. World Bank Group, "New Malawi Economic Update Calls for Urgent Action to Address Macroeconomic Imbalances and Increase Energy Access," World Bank (July 18, 2023), https://www.worldbank.org/en/news/press-release/2023/07/19/new-afe-malawi-economic-update-calls-for-urgent-action-to-address-macroeco-nomic-imbalances-and-increase-energy-access.

    In 2018, when my family was in Malawi, it was estimated that 11% of Malawian's had access to electricity. Fortunately, due to tremendous international develop-ment efforts, this figure has climbed since then, but it is still one of the lowest in the world.

5. Jon Kabat-Zinn, "Jon Kabat-Zinn Teaches Mindfulness and Meditation," online course, MasterClass, https://www.masterclass.com/classes/jon-kabat-zinn-teach-es-mindfulness-and-meditation.

6. "Meditation for Improving Emotional Intelligence," *Mindfulness and Meditation* (July 26, 2023), https://mindfulness-and-meditation.com/blog/meditation-for-improving-emotional-intelligence.

7.   Dan Buettner, "How to Live to 100," TED Talk, accessed December 29, 2019, https://ikigaitribe.com/ikigai/podcast05/#tve-jump-18bd0fb5a2f; "Marc Winn on Merging Ikigai With the Venn Diagram of Purpose," The Ikigai Podcast on *Ikigai Tribe* (December 29, 2019), https://ikigaitribe.com/ikigai/podcast05/#tve-jump-18bd0fb5a2f; "How The Andrés Zuzunaga Venn Diagram Became Ikigai," The Ikigai Podcast on *Ikigai Tribe* (January 29, 2020), https://ikigaitribe.com/ikigai/podcast07/; Nicholas Kemp, *IKIGAI-KAN: Feel a Life Worth Living* (Tokyo: Ikigai Tribe, 2020), Kyle Kowalski, "The True Meaning of Ikigai: Definitions, Diagrams & Myths about the Japanese Life Purpose," *Sloww*, n.d., accessed January 29, 2020, https://www.sloww.co/ikigai/; Jim Collins, *Good to Great: Why Some Companies Make the Leap... and Others Don't* (New York: HarperBusiness, 2001), Héctor García and Francesc Miralles, *Ikigai: The Japanese Secret to a Long and Happy Life* (New York: TarcherPerigee, 2017); Mieko Kamiya, *Ikigai-ni-Tsuite (What Makes Our Life Worth Living)* (Tokyo: Misuzu Shobo, 1966).

Understanding more about ikigai and the genesis of the famous diagram provides a fascinating case study about the power of the confluence of different ideas among different people and cultures. The result can be far-reaching when ideas come together powerfully, like the famous *Ikigai* Venn Diagram. *Ikigai* became popular in the West primarily in the early 2000s, largely due to American researcher Dan Buettner. Buettner, known for his work on Blue Zones and longevity, identified *ikigai* as a key factor for greater longevity in Japan. He mentioned the concept in his TED Talk "How to Live to 100" and other writings.

The Western interpretation of *ikigai*, particularly the *Ikigai* Venn Diagram, was further popularized by Marc Winn, an entrepreneur from the small island nation of Guernsey. Inspired by Buettner's Ted Talk, Winn created a blog post in 2014, merging the concept of *ikigai* with a Venn diagram of purpose. The Venn diagram itself wasn't even Winn's idea. It originated from Andrés Zuzunaga, a Spanish astrologer and author. Winn borrowed the visual concept and changed the center word into *ikigai* after creating a visual mashup for a blog article. His version of the *Ikigai* Venn Diagram went viral. It resonated with the masses, popularizing the Japanese word *ikigai* in the Western world.

The famous Zuzunaga/Winn Venn diagram, which focused on balancing one's passions, skills, financial viability, and societal needs, gained meme-like popularity on social media. While highly perceptive, this interpretation diverges significantly from the traditional Japanese understanding of *ikigai*. According to Japanologist Nicholas Kemp, for the Japanese, *ikigai* is more about a feeling (like the zest for life) and less about a pursuit or achievement, underscoring the cultural nuances and different perspectives.

Interestingly, the concept of *ikigai* has a much longer history in Japanese culture. Japanese psychiatrist Mieko Kamiya first spotlighted it in her 1966 book Ikigai-ni-Tsuite (What Makes Our Life Worth Living). This book, which has yet to be translated into English, presents *ikigai* within the context of Japanese culture and psychology.

8. Stephen R. Covey, *The 7 Habits of Highly Effective People: Powerful Lessons in Personal Change*, Rev. ed. (Free Press, November 9, 2004).

9. Kirill Tšernov, "How Leaders Make Decisions Using 80/20 Rule," *Weekdone* (March 24, 2022), https://blog.weekdone.com/how-leaders-make-decisions-using-8020-rule/.

10. Richard Koch, *The 80/20 Principle: The Secret to Achieving More With Less* (Crown Currency, October 19, 1999).

11. David A. Kalmbach et al., "Genetic Basis of Chronotype in Humans: Insights From Three Landmark GWAS," *Sleep* 40, no. 2 (December 9, 2016), https://doi.org/10.1093/sleep/zsw048.

12. Francesco Cirillo, *The Pomodoro Technique: The Acclaimed Time-Management System That Has Transformed How We Work* (National Geographic Books, 2018), https://www.goodreads.com/book/show/18482790-the-pomodoro-technique.

13. Simon Kemp, "Digital 2024: Global Overview Report — DataReportal – Global Digital Insights," DataReportal – Global Digital Insights (January 31, 2024), https://datareportal.com/reports/digital-2024-global-overview-report.

14. Doug Bolton, "The Reason Steve Jobs Didn't Let His Children Use an iPad," *The Independent* (November 1, 2017), https://www.independent.co.uk/tech/steve-jobs-apple-ipad-children-technology-birthday-a6893216.html.

15. Praveen Pankajakshan, "MULTITASKING AND THE BRAIN," *Brighter Minds* (January 1, 2020), https://www.brighterminds.org/post/multitasking-and-the-brain; Wikipedia contributors, "Infomania," *Wikipedia* (December 1, 2021), https://en.wikipedia.org/wiki/Infomania#cite_note-:1-4; Will Knight, "'Infomania' Dents IQ More Than Marijuana," *New Scientist* (April 22, 2005), https://www.newscientist.com/article/dn7298-info-mania-dents-iq-more-than-marijuana/.

16. Torkel Klingberg, "The Overflowing Brain," *ResearchGate* (September 2023), https://doi.org/10.1093/oso/9780195372885.001.0001; MPG, "Information Overload: Memory and Focus Are at Risk," Morris Psychological Group (November 7, 2014), https://www.morrispsych.com/information-overload-memory-and-focus-are-at-risk/.

17. Cassiano Ricardo Alves Faria Diniz and Ana Paula Crestani, "The Times They Are A-changin': A Proposal on How Brain Flexibility Goes Beyond the Obvious to Include the Concepts of 'Upward' and 'Downward' to Neuroplasticity," *Molecular Psychiatry* 28, no. 3 (December 27, 2022): 977–92, https://doi.org/10.1038/s41380-022-01931-x.

18. James Clear, *Atomic Habits: An Easy & Proven Way to Build Good Habits & Break Bad Ones* (Avery, October 18, 2018).

19. Phillippa Lally et al., "How Are Habits Formed: Modelling Habit Formation in the Real World," *European Journal of Social Psychology* 40, no. 6 (July 16, 2009): 998–1009, https://doi.org/10.1002/ejsp.674.

20. BJ Fogg, *Tiny Habits: The Small Changes That Change Everything* (Harvet, February 1, 2020).

21. BJ Fogg, "Behavior Model," *Behavior Model,* accessed December 5, 2023, https://behaviormodel.org/.

22. "Guatemala: Nutrition Profile," US Agency For International Development (2018), https://2017-2020.usaid.gov/sites/default/files/documents/1864/Guatemala-Nutrition-Profile-Mar2018-508.pdf.

23. Molly Warren et al., "State of Obesity 2023: Better Policies for a Healthier America," TFAH (November 22, 2023), https://www.tfah.org/report-details/state-of-obesity-2023/.

24. Sally Wadyka, "The Link Between Highly Processed Foods and Brain Health," *The New York Times* (May 4, 2023), https://www.nytimes.com/2023/05/04/well/eat/ultraprocessed-food-mental-health.html.

25. Mark Schatzker, *The Dorito Effect: The Surprising New Truth About Food and Flavor* (Simon & Schuster; 2nd ed., May 5, 2015).

26. World Health Organization: WHO, "The Top 10 Causes of Death" (December 9, 2020), https://www.who.int/news-room/fact-sheets/detail/the-top-10-causes-of-death; "Leading Causes of Death," Centers for Disease Control and Prevention (May 2, 2024), https://www.cdc.gov/nchs/fastats/leading-causes-of-death.htm.

27. University of Turku, "Eating Triggers Endorphin Release in the Brain," ScienceDaily (August 28, 2017), https://www.sciencedaily.com/releases/2017/08/170828102719.htm.

28. Alexandra C. McPherron et al., "Increasing Muscle Mass to Improve Metabolism," *Adipocyte* 2, no. 2 (April 1, 2013): 92–98, https://doi.org/10.4161/adip.22500; Kedryn K. Baskin, Benjamin R. Winders, and Eric N. Olson, "Muscle as a 'Mediator' of Systemic Metabolism," *Cell Metabolism* 21, no. 2 (February 3, 2015): 237–48, https://doi.org/10.1016/j.cmet.2014.12.021.

29. Irena Djuricic and Philip C. Calder, "Beneficial Outcomes of Omega-6 and Omega-3 Polyunsaturated Fatty Acids on Human Health: An Update for 2021," *Nutrients* 13, no. 7 (2021): 2421, https://doi.org/10.3390/nu13072421.

30. Tommaso Filippini et al., "Potassium Intake and Blood Pressure: A Dose-Response Meta-Analysis of Randomized Controlled Trials," *Journal of the American Heart Association* 9, no. 12 (2020): e015719, https://doi.org/10.1161/JAHA.119.015719.

31. Louis D. Brown et al., "Cholesterol-lowering Effects of Dietary Fiber: A Meta-analysis," *National Library of Medicine* 69, no. 1 (January 1999): 30–42, https://doi.org/10.1093/ajcn/69.1.30.

32. Vikas Kapil et al., "Dietary Nitrate Provides Sustained Blood Pressure Lowering in Hypertensive Patients," *Hypertension* 65, no. 2 (February 2015): 320–27, https://doi.org/10.1161/hypertensionaha.114.04675.

33. Russell J. de Souza et al., "Intake of Saturated and Trans Unsaturated Fatty Acids and Risk of All Cause Mortality, Cardiovascular Disease, and Type 2 Diabetes: Systematic Review and Meta-Analysis of Observational Studies," *BMJ* 351 (2015): h3978, https://doi.org/10.1136/bmj.h3978.

34. Yash Patel and Joshua Joseph, "Sodium Intake and Heart Failure," *International Journal of Molecular Sciences* 21, no. 24 (2020): 9474, https://doi.org/10.3390/ijms21249474.

35. Laila Al-Shaar et al., "Red Meat Intake and Risk of Coronary Heart Disease Among US Men: Prospective Cohort Study," *BMJ* 371 (2020): m4141, https://doi.org/10.1136/bmj.m4141; Karen J. Murphy et al., "Effects of Eating Fresh Lean Pork on Cardiometabolic Health Parameters," *Nutrients* 4, no. 7 (2012): 711-723, https://doi.org/10.3390/nu4070711; Muhammad M. Abdullah et al., "Recommended Dairy Product Intake Modulates Circulating Fatty Acid Profile in Healthy Adults: A Multi-Centre Cross-Over Study," *British Journal of Nutrition* 113, no. 3 (2015): 435-444, https://doi.org/10.1017/S0007114514003894; Paul J. Nestel and Trevor A. Mori, "Dairy Foods: Is Its Cardiovascular Risk Profile Changing?" *Current Atherosclerosis Reports* 24, no. 1 (2022): 33-40, https://doi.org/10.1007/s11883-022-00984-1.

36. Thad Wilkins and Jacqueline Sequoia, "Probiotics for Gastrointestinal Conditions: A Summary of the Evidence," *PubMed* (August 1, 2017), https://pubmed.ncbi.nlm.nih.gov/28762696/.

37. Paul Cronin et al., "Dietary Fibre Modulates the Gut Microbiota," *Nutrients* 13, no. 5 (2021): 1655, https://doi.org/10.3390/nu13051655.

38. Zhen Song et al., "Effects of Ultra-Processed Foods on the Microbiota-Gut-Brain Axis: The Bread-and-Butter Issue," *Food Research International* 167 (2023): 112730, https://doi.org/10.1016/j.foodres.2023.112730.

39. Jotham Suez et al., "Non-caloric Artificial Sweeteners and the Microbiome: Findings and Challenges," *Gut Microbes* 6, no. 2 (2015): 149-155, https://doi.org/10.1080/19490976.2015.1017700.

40. Lynda Frassetto et al., "Acid Balance, Dietary Acid Load, and Bone Effects—A Controversial Subject," *Nutrients* 10, no. 4 (2018): 517, https://doi.org/10.3390/nu10040517.

41. Heather J. Leidy, Peter M. Clifton, Arne Astrup, Thomas P. Wycherley, Margriet S. Westerterp-Plantenga, Natalie D. Luscombe-Marsh, Stephen C. Woods, and Richard D. Mattes, "The Role of Protein in Weight Loss and Maintenance," *The American Journal of Clinical Nutrition* 101, no. 6 (2015): 1320S-1329S, https://doi.org/10.3945/ajcn.114.084038.

42. Yujin Wan et al., "Association between Changes in Carbohydrate Intake and Long Term Weight Changes: Prospective Cohort Study," *BMJ* 382 (2023): e073939, https://doi.org/10.1136/bmj-2022-073939.

43. Kevin D. Hall et al., "Ultra-Processed Diets Cause Excess Calorie Intake and Weight Gain: An Inpatient Randomized Controlled Trial of Ad Libitum Food Intake," *Cell Metabolism* 30, no. 1 (2019): 67-77.e3, https://doi.org/10.1016/j.cmet.2019.05.008. Erratum in: *Cell Metabolism* 30, no. 1 (2019): 226; Erratum in: *Cell Metabolism* 32, no. 4 (2020): 690.

44. Vasanti S. Malik, Matthias B. Schulze, and Frank B. Hu, "Intake of Sugar-Sweetened Beverages and Weight Gain: A Systematic Review," *American Journal of Clinical Nutrition* 84, no. 2 (2006): 274-288, https://doi.org/10.1093/ajcn/84.1.274.

45. John L. Sievenpiper, "Low-Carbohydrate Diets and Cardiometabolic Health: The Importance of Carbohydrate Quality Over Quantity," *Nutrition Reviews* 78, suppl. 1 (2020): 69-77, https://doi.org/10.1093/nutrit/nuz082.

46. Gregory Traversy and Jean-Philippe Chaput, "Alcohol Consumption and Obesity: An Update," *Current Obesity Reports* 4, no. 1 (2015): 122-130, https://doi.org/10.1007/s13679-014-0129-4.

47. David O. Kennedy, "B Vitamins and the Brain: Mechanisms, Dose and Efficacy— A Review," *Nutrients* 8, no. 2 (January 27, 2016): 68, https://doi.org/10.3390/nu8020068.

48. Lena Braunschweig et al., "Oxygen Regulates Proliferation of Neural Stem Cells Through Wnt/B-catenin Signalling," *Molecular and Cellular Neurosciences* 67 (July 2015): 84–92, https://doi.org/10.1016/j.mcn.2015.06.006. The findings are mixed, indicating the need for further research.

49. Misty Hawkins, Natalie Keirns, and Zachary Helms, "Carbohydrates and Cognitive Function," *Current Opinion in Clinical Nutrition and Metabolic Care* 21 (2018): 1, https://doi.org/10.1097/MCO.0000000000000471; Andrew Smyth et al., "Healthy Eating and Reduced Risk of Cognitive Decline: A Cohort from 40 Countries," Neurology 84, no. 22 (2015): 2258–2265, https://doi.org/10.1212/WNL.0000000000001638; Heather Francis and Richard Stevenson, "The Longer-Term Impacts of Western Diet on Human Cognition and the Brain," Appetite 63 (2013): 119-128, https://doi.org/10.1016/j.appet.2012.12.018.

50. J. Snel and M. M. Lorist, "Effects of Caffeine on Sleep and Cognition," Progress in Brain Research 190 (2011): 105–17, https://doi.org/10.1016/B978-0-444-53817-8.00006-2.

51. Neal D. Barnard et al., "Saturated and Trans Fats and Dementia: A Systematic Review," *Neurobiology of Aging* 35, suppl. 2 (2014): S65–S73, https://doi.org/10.1016/j.neurobiolaging.2014.02.030.

52. Letizia Vannucci et al., "Calcium Intake in Bone Health: A Focus on Calcium-Rich Mineral Waters," *Nutrients* 10, no. 12 (2018): 1930, https://doi.org/10.3390/nu10121930.

53. Ian R. Reid, Mark J. Bolland, and Andrew Grey, "Effects of Vitamin D Supplements on Bone Mineral Density: A Systematic Review and Meta-Analysis," *Lancet* 383, no. 9912 (2014): 146-155, https://doi.org/10.1016/S0140-6736(13)61647-5.

54. Ailsa A. Welch, Jane Skinner, and Marcella Hickson, "Dietary Magnesium May Be Protective for Aging of Bone and Skeletal Muscle in Middle and Younger Older Age Men and Women: Cross-Sectional Findings from the UK Biobank Cohort," *Nutrients* 9, no. 11 (2017): 1189, https://doi.org/10.3390/nu9111189; Stella L. Volpe, "Magnesium and the Athlete," *Current Sports Medicine Reports* 14, no. 4 (2015): 279-283, https://doi.org/10.1249/JSR.0000000000000178; Forrest H. Nielsen and Henry C. Lukaski, "Update on the Relationship Between Magnesium and Exercise," *Magnesium Research* 19, no. 3 (2006): 180-189.

55. Hee Ahn and Young Kyun Park, "Sugar-Sweetened Beverage Consumption and Bone Health: A Systematic Review and Meta-Analysis," *Nutrition Journal* 20, no. 1 (2021): 41, https://doi.org/10.1186/s12937-021-00698-1; Anne M. Bennett et al., "Prospective Associations of Sugar-Sweetened Beverage Consumption During Adolescence with Body Composition and Bone Mass at Early Adulthood," *Journal of Nutrition* 152, no. 2 (2022): 399-407, https://doi.org/10.1093/jn/nxab389.

56. Johns T. Johnson, Mohammad Anwar Hussain, Kripa Elizabeth Cherian, Nitin Kapoor, and Thomas V. Paul, "Chronic Alcohol Consumption and its Impact on Bone and Metabolic Health – A Narrative Review," *Indian Journal of Endocrinology and Metabolism* 26, no. 3 (May–June 2022): 206-212, https://doi.org/10.4103/ijem.ijem_26_22.

57. Anitra C. Carr and Silvia Maggini, "Vitamin C and Immune Function," *Nutrients* 9, no. 11 (November 3, 2017): 1211, https://doi.org/10.3390/nu9111211.

58. Inga Weßels, Martina Maywald, and Lothar Rink, "Zinc as a Gatekeeper of Immune Function," *Nutrients* 9, no. 12 (November 25, 2017): 1286, https://doi.org/10.3390/nu9121286.

59. Nima Shomali et al., "Harmful Effects of High Amounts of Glucose on the Immune System: An Updated Review," *Biotechnology and Applied Biochemistry* 68, no. 2 (2021): 404-410, https://doi.org/10.1002/bab.1938.

60. Esra'a Keewan et al., "Are Fried Foods Unhealthy? The Dietary Peroxidized Fatty Acid, 13-HPODE, Induces Intestinal Inflammation in Vitro and in Vivo," *Antioxidants* 9, no. 10 (September 27, 2020): 926, https://doi.org/10.3390/antiox9100926.

61. Guoyao Wu, "Dietary Protein Intake and Human Health," *Food & Function* 7, no. 3 (2016): 1251-1265, https://doi.org/10.1039/c5fo01530h.

62. Katarzyna P. Dzik and Jan J. Kaczor, "Mechanisms of Vitamin D on Skeletal Muscle Function: Oxidative Stress, Energy Metabolism and Anabolic State," *European Journal of Applied Physiology* 119, no. 4 (2019): 825-839, https://doi.org/10.1007/s00421-019-04104-x; Michał A. Żmijewski, "Nongenomic Activities of Vitamin D," *Nutrients* 14, no. 23 (2022): 5104, https://doi.org/10.3390/nu14235104.

63. Flore Depeint et al., "Mitochondrial Function and Toxicity: Role of the B Vitamin Family on Mitochondrial Energy Metabolism," *Chemico-Biological Interactions* 163, no. 1-2 (2006): 94-112, https://doi.org/10.1016/j.cbi.2006.04.014.

64. Justyna Godos et al., "Effect of Brazil Nuts on Selenium Status, Blood Lipids, and Biomarkers of Oxidative Stress and Inflammation: A Systematic Review and Meta-Analysis of Randomized Clinical Trials," *Antioxidants (Basel)* 11, no. 2 (2022): 403, https://doi.org/10.3390/antiox11020403.

65. Alannah K.A. McKay, David B. Pyne, Louise M. Burke, and Peter Peeling. "Iron Metabolism: Interactions with Energy and Carbohydrate Availability," *Nutrients* 12, no. 12 (November 2020): 3692, https://doi.org/10.3390/nu12123692.

66. Leif Hallberg, Mats Brune, and Lena Rossander, "The Role of Vitamin C in Iron Absorption," *International Journal of Vitamin and Nutrition Research Supplement* 30 (1989): 103-108, https://pubmed.ncbi.nlm.nih.gov/2507689/.

67. Lidia Minguez-Alarcón et al., "Fatty Acid Intake in Relation to Reproductive Hormones and Testicular Volume Among Young Healthy Men," *Asian Journal of Andrology* 19, no. 2 (March–April 2017): 184-190, https://doi.org/10.4103/1008-682X.190323; D. M. Ingram, F. C. Bennett, D. Willcox, and N. de Klerk, "Effect of Low-Fat Diet on Female Sex Hormone Levels," *Journal of the National Cancer Institute* 79, no. 6 (1987): 1225-1229, https://europepmc.org/article/med/3480374.

68. Susan M. Shirreffs and Michael N. Sawka, "Fluid and Electrolyte Needs for Training, Competition, and Recovery," *Journal of Sports Sciences* 29, suppl. 1 (2011): S39-S46, https://doi.org/10.1080/02640414.2011.614269. Christopher Gaffney, "Crash Diets May Work Against You – and Could Have Permanent Consequences," *The Conversation* (January 2, 2024), accessed May 12, 2024, https://theconversation.com/crash-diets-may-work-against-you-and-could-have-permanent-consequences-219045.

70. Izabela Sadowska-Bartosz and Grzegorz Bartosz, "Effect of Antioxidants Supplementation on Aging and Longevity," *Biomed Research International* 2014 (2014): 404680, https://doi.org/10.1155/2014/404680.

71. Alexander Panossian and G. Wikman, "Evidence-Based Efficacy of Adaptogens in Fatigue, and Molecular Mechanisms Related to Their Stress-Protective Activity," *Current Clinical Pharmacology* 4, no. 3 (September 1, 2009): 198–219, https://doi.org/10.2174/157488409789375311.

72. Ramesh Chormare and Manoj A. Kumar, "Environmental Health and Risk Assessment Metrics with Special Mention to Biotransfer, Bioaccumulation and Biomagnification of Environmental Pollutants," *Chemosphere* 302 (2022): 134836, https://doi.org/10.1016/j.chemosphere.2022.134836; Rajbir Kaur et al., "Pesticides: An Alarming Detrimental to Health and Environment," *Science of the Total Environment* 915 (2024): 170113, https://doi.org/10.1016/j.scitotenv.2024.170113.

73. Joel Fuhrman, "The Hidden Dangers of Fast and Processed Food," *American Journal of Lifestyle Medicine* 12, no. 5 (September 2018): 375–81, https://doi.org/10.1177/1559827618766483.

74. Francisco José Díaz-Galiano et al., "Cooking Food in Microwavable Plastic Containers: In Situ Formation of a New Chemical Substance and Increased Migration of Polypropylene Polymers," *Food Chemistry* 417 (August 2023): 135852, https://doi.org/10.1016/j.foodchem.2023.135852.

75. Shari R. Lipner and Richard K. Scher, "Biotin for the Treatment of Nail Disease: What is the Evidence?" *Journal of Dermatological Treatment* 29, no. 4 (2018): 411-414, https://doi.org/10.1080/09546634.2017.1395799.

76. B. J. Thomsen, E. Y. Chow, and M. J. Sapijaszko, "The Potential Uses of Omega-3 Fatty Acids in Dermatology: A Review," *Journal of Cutaneous Medicine and Surgery* 24, no. 5 (2020): 481-494, https://doi.org/10.1177/1203475420929925.

77. Merve Akdeniz et al., "Does Dietary Fluid Intake Affect Skin Hydration in Healthy Humans? A Systematic Literature Review," *Skin Research and Technology* 24, no. 3 (2018): 459-465, https://doi.org/10.1111/srt.12454.

78. Steven A. Greenberg, "Diet and Skin: A Primer," *Cutis* 106, no. 5 (2020): E31-E32, https://doi.org/10.12788/cutis.0143.

79. Gary D. Goodman et al., "Impact of Smoking and Alcohol Use on Facial Aging in Women: Results of a Large Multinational, Multiracial, Cross-sectional Survey," *Journal of Clinical and Aesthetic Dermatology* 12, no. 8 (2019): 28-39, https://pubmed.ncbi.nlm.nih.gov/31531169/.

80. Kongkiat Roengritthidet et al., "Association Between Diet and Acne Severity: A Cross-sectional Study in Thai Adolescents and Adults," *Acta Dermato-Venereologica* 101, no. 12 (2021): adv00611, https://doi.org/10.2340/actadv.v101.569.

81. Tamara Searle, Fahad Ali, and Firas Al-Niaimi, "Zinc in Dermatology," *Journal of Dermatological Treatment* 33, no. 5 (April 18, 2022): 2455–58, https://doi.org/10.1080/09546634.2022.2062282; Mrinal Gupta et al., "Zinc Therapy in Dermatology: A Review," *Dermatology Research and Practice* 2014 (July 10, 2014): 1–11, https://doi.org/10.1155/2014/709152; Joyce Wright, Toby Richards, and Surjit K. S. Srai, "The Role of Iron in the Skin and Cutaneous Wound Healing," *Frontiers in Pharmacology* 5 (July 10, 2014), https://doi.org/10.3389/fphar.2014.00156; Kjersten Nett, RDN, LD, "What You Eat Promotes Radi-

ant Hair, Skin and Nails Naturally," Mayo Clinic Health System, May 26, 2022, https://www.mayoclinichealthsystem.org/hometown-health/speaking-of-health/get-radiant-hair-skin-and-nails-naturally; S. Sato, "Iron Deficiency: Structural and Microchemical Changes in Hair, Nails, and Skin," *Seminars in Dermatology* 10, no. 4 (1991): 313-319, https://pubmed.ncbi.nlm.nih.gov/1764360/.

82. Joanne L. Slavin and Beate Lloyd, "Health Benefits of Fruits and Vegetables," *Advances in Nutrition* 3, no. 4 (July 1, 2012): 506–16, https://doi.org/10.3945/an.112.002154.

83. Barry M. Popkin, Kristen E. D'Anci, and Irwin H. Rosenberg, "Water, Hydration, and Health," *Nutrition Reviews* 68, no. 8 (August 2010): 439–58, https://doi.org/10.1111/j.1753-4887.2010.00304.x.

84. John C. Saari, "Vitamin A and Vision," in *Sub-Cellular Biochemistry/Subcellular Biochemistry*, 2016, 231–59, https://doi.org/10.1007/978-94-024-0945-1_9.

85. Carlos Rocha Oliveira, Emille Tejo Viana, Thainá Ferreira Gonçalves, and José Roberto Mateus-Silva, "Therapeutic Use of Intravenous Selenium in Respiratory and Immunological Diseases: A Narrative Review," *Advances in Respiratory Medicine* 90, no. 2 (January 31, 2022): 134–42, https://doi.org/10.5603/arm.a2022.0018.

86. Thomas A. Mezzacca et al., "Ubiquity of Sugary Drinks and Processed Food Throughout Food and Non-Food Retail Settings in NYC," *Journal of Community Health* 45, no. 5 (2020): 973-978, https://doi.org/10.1007/s10900-020-00815-x.

87. D. V. Parke and D. F. Lewis, "Safety Aspects of Food Preservatives," *Food Additives and Contaminants* 9, no. 5 (1992): 561-577, https://doi.org/10.1080/02652039209374110.

88. The US Department of Health and Human Services, "Physical Activity Guidelines for Americans," 2nd ed., health.gov (2018), accessed May 26, 2024, https://health.gov/sites/default/files/2019-09/Physical_Activity_Guidelines_2nd_edition.pdf .

89. Dominique Gummelt, "When It Comes to Your Health, Something Is Better Than Nothing" (December 12, 2018), https://www.acefitness.org/education-and-resources/professional/expert-articles/7167/the-importance-of-proper-nutrition-for-gym-success/; "Dietary Supplements for Exercise and Athletic Performance," National Institutes of Health (April 1, 2024), https://ods.od.nih.gov/factsheets/ExerciseAndAthleticPerformance-HealthProfessional/; Arlene Semeco, "Post-Workout Nutrition: What to Eat After a Workout," Healthline Media (September 20, 2016), https://www.healthline.com/nutrition/eat-after-workout.

90. Kristi Wempen, RDN, "Assessing Protein Needs for Performance," Mayo Clinic Health System (July 17, 2023), https://www.mayoclinichealthsystem.org/hometown-health/speaking-of-health/assessing-protein-needs-for-performance.

91. Carla S. Möller-Levet et al., "Effects of Insufficient Sleep on Circadian Rhythmicity and Expression Amplitude of the Human Blood Transcriptome," *Proceedings of the National Academy of Sciences of the United States of America* 110, no. 12 (February 25, 2013), https://doi.org/10.1073/pnas.1217154110; Rachel R. Markwald et al., "Impact of Insufficient Sleep on Total Daily Energy Expenditure, Food Intake, and Weight Gain," *Proceedings of the National Academy of Sciences of the United States of America* 110, no. 14 (March 11, 2013): 5695–5700, https://doi.org/10.1073/pnas.1216951110; Peter Meerlo, Andrea Sgoifo, and Deborah Suchecki, "Restricted and Disrupted Sleep: Effects on Autonomic Function, Neuroendocrine Stress Systems and Stress Responsivity," *Sleep Medicine Reviews* 12, no. 3 (June 2008): 197–210, https://doi.org/10.1016/j.smrv.2007.07.007; Masahiko Kato et al., "Effects of Sleep Deprivation on Neural Circulatory Control," *Hypertension* 35, no. 5 (May 1, 2000): 1173–75, https://doi.org/10.1161/01.hyp.35.5.1173.

92. Molly E. Zimmerman et al., "The Effects of Insufficient Sleep and Adequate Sleep on Cognitive Function in Healthy Adults," *Sleep Health*, January 16, 2024, https://doi.org/10.1016/j.sleh.2023.11.011.

93. "About Sleep." *Centers for Disease Control and Prevention*, Centers for Disease Control and Prevention, accessed May 26, 2024, http://www.cdc.gov/sleep/about/; M. Hirshkowitz, K. Whiton, S. M. Albert, et al., "The National Sleep Foundation's Sleep Time Duration Recommendations: Methodology and Results Summary," *Sleep Health* 1, no. 1 (2015): 40–43, https://doi.org/10.1016/j.sleh.2014.12.010; N. F. Watson, M. S. Badr, G. Belenky, et al., "Recommended Amount of Sleep for a Healthy Adult: A Joint Consensus Statement of the American Academy of Sleep Medicine and Sleep Research Society," *Sleep* 38, no. 6 (2015): 843–844, https://doi.org/10.5665%2Fsleep.4716.

94. Yijia Zhang et al., "Association of Magnesium Intake With Sleep Duration and Sleep Quality: Findings From the CARDIA Study," *Sleep* 45, no. 4 (April 11, 2022), https://doi.org/10.1093/sleep/zsab276.

95. Raphaël Vallat and Perrine Ruby, "Is It a Good Idea to Cultivate Lucid Dreaming?," *Frontiers in Psychology* 10 (November 15, 2019), https://doi.org/10.3389/fpsyg.2019.02585.

96. Mayo Clinic Staff, "Water: How Much Should You Drink Every Day?," Mayo Clinic (October 12, 2022), https://www.mayoclinic.org/healthy-lifestyle/nutrition-and-healthy-eating/in-depth/water/art-20044256.

97. Sophie C. Killer, Andrew K. Blannin, and Asker E. Jeukendrup, "No Evidence of Dehydration With Moderate Daily Coffee Intake: A Counterbalanced Cross-Over Study in a Free-Living Population," *PloS One* 9, no. 1 (January 9, 2014): e84154, https://doi.org/10.1371/journal.pone.0084154.

98. Jennifer Stone, "How to Calculate How Much Water You Should Drink," University of Missouri System (2022), https://www.umsystem.edu/totalrewards/wellness/

how-to-calculate-how-much-water-you-should-drink; Janet Helm, MS, RDN, "How Much Water Should You Drink in a Day?," *US News & world Report* (June 26, 2023), https://health.usnews.com/health-news/blogs/eat-run/2013/09/13/the-truth-about-how-much-water-you-should-really-drink; Yuri Elkaim, "The Truth About How Much Water You Should Really Drink," *US News & World Report* (September 13, 2013), https://www.yahoo.com/news/truth-much-water-really-drink-204954236.html; Howard E. LeWine, MD, "How Much Water Should You Drink?," Harvard Health (May 22, 2023), https://www.health.harvard.edu/staying-healthy/how-much-water-should-you-drink.

99. Leann Poston, MD, "7 Ways to Lose Weight Without Cardio," Invigor Medical (March 3, 2022), https://www.invigormedical.com/invigor-medical/7-ways-to-lose-weight-without-cardio/.

100. Ronald J. Maughan and James D. Griffin, "Caffeine Ingestion and Fluid Balance: A Review," *Journal of Human Nutrition and Dietetics* 16, no. 6 (December 16, 2003): 411–20, https://doi.org/10.1046/j.1365-277x.2003.00477.x.

101. "Covid-19 and Mental Health: A Growing Crisis," Mental Health America (October 20, 2020), https://mhanational.org/research-reports/covid-19-and-mental-health-growing-crisis.

102. Gülfidan Kurt Aktaş and Vesile Eskici İlgin, "The Effect of Deep Breathing Exercise and 4-7-8 Breathing Techniques Applied to Patients After Bariatric Surgery on Anxiety and Quality of Life," *Obesity Surgery* 33, no. 3 (December 8, 2022): 920–29, https://doi.org/10.1007/s11695-022-06405-1.

103. Christyn L. Dolbier and Taylor E. Rush, "Efficacy of Abbreviated Progressive Muscle Relaxation in a High-stress College Sample.," *International Journal of Stress Management* 19, no. 1 (2012): 48–68, https://doi.org/10.1037/a0027326.

104. Susan Hallam, "The Power of Music: Its Impact on the Intellectual, Social and Personal Development of Children and Young People," *International Journal of Music Education* 28, no. 3 (August 23, 2010): 269–89, https://doi.org/10.1177/0255761410370658.

Andrea M. Scheve, "Music Therapy, Wellness, and Stress Reduction," in *Advances in Experimental Medicine and Biology*, 2004, 253–63, https://doi.org/10.1007/978-1-4757-4820-8_19.

105. US Department of Health and Human Services, "Seasonal Affected Disorder," National Institutes of Health (2023), NIH Publication No. 23-MH-8138, https://www.nimh.nih.gov/health/publications/seasonal-affective-disorder.

106. Xuan Li et al., "The Effects of Tai Chi and Qigong Exercise on Psychological Status in Adolescents: A Systematic Review and Meta-Analysis," *Frontiers in Psychology* 12 (November 24, 2021), https://doi.org/10.3389/fpsyg.2021.746975.

Dana Sparks, "Mayo Mindfulness: Tai Chi Is a Gentle Way to Fight Stress," Mayo Clinic News Network (October 31, 2018), https://newsnetwork.mayoclinic.org/discussion/mayo-mindfulness-tai-chi-is-a-gentle-way-to-fight-stress/.

"The Health Benefits of Tai Chi and Qi Gong," Piedmont Healthcare, n.d., https://www.piedmont.org/living-real-change/the-health-benefits-of-tai-chi-and-qi-gong.

107. Cleveland Clinic, "Forest Bathing: What It Is and Its Potential Benefits," Cleveland Clinic (December 5, 2023), https://health.clevelandclinic.org/why-forest-therapy-can-be-good-for-your-body-and-mind.

Qing Li, "Effect of Forest Bathing Trips on Human Immune Function," *Environmental Health and Preventive Medicine* 15, no. 1 (March 25, 2009): 9–17, https://doi.org/10.1007/s12199-008-0068-3; Duane Steffens, "Forest Bathing, Shinrin Yoku: What Is It, and How to Practice It.," *Born As The Earth Zen Academy* (October 12, 2023), https://www.bornastheearth.com/zen-and-meditation-blogs/forest-bathing-shinrin-yoku.

108. Aspen Avery, "How Nutrition Impacts the Brain and Mental Health - the Whole U," *The Whole U* (March 2, 2020), https://thewholeu.uw.edu/2020/03/02/nnm-2020-nutrition-and-the-brain/.

109. Charles H. Hillman, Kirk I. Erickson, and Arthur F. Kramer, "Be Smart, Exercise Your Heart: Exercise Effects on Brain and Cognition," *Nature Reviews. Neuroscience* 9, no. 1 (January 2008): 58–65, https://doi.org/10.1038/nrn2298; Ruchika Shaurya Prakash et al., "Physical Activity and Cognitive Vitality," *Annual Review of Psychology* 66, no. 1 (January 3, 2015): 769–97, https://doi.org/10.1146/annurev-psych-010814-015249; Andreas Ströhle, "Physical Activity, Exercise, Depression and Anxiety Disorders," *Journal of Neural Transmission* 116, no. 6 (August 23, 2008): 777–84, https://doi.org/10.1007/s00702-008-0092-x; Yu-Kai Chang et al., "The Effects of Acute Exercise on Cognitive Performance: A Meta-Analysis," *Brain Research* 1453 (2012): 87-101, https://doi.org/10.1016/j.brainres.2012.02.068. Erratum in: *Brain Research* 1470 (2012): 159; Teresa Liu-Ambrose, "Resistance Training and Executive Functions," *Archives of Internal Medicine* 170, no. 2 (January 25, 2010): 170, https://doi.org/10.1001/archinternmed.2009.494; Lorenza S. Colzato et al., "The Impact of Physical Exercise on Convergent and Divergent Thinking," *Frontiers in Human Neuroscience* 7 (2013): 824, https://doi.org/10.3389/fnhum.2013.00824.

110. Eva Selhub, MD, "Nutritional Psychiatry: Your Brain on Food," Harvard Health (September 18, 2022), https://www.health.harvard.edu/blog/nutritional-psychiatry-your-brain-on-food-201511168626.

111. "Nutrition and Healthy Eating," Mayo Clinic (November 21, 2023), https://www.mayoclinic.org/healthy-lifestyle/nutrition-and-healthy-eating/basics/nutritional-supplements/hlv-20049477.

112. Ab Latif Wani, Sajad Ahmad Bhat, and Anjum Ara, "Omega-3 Fatty Acids and the Treatment of Depression: A Review of Scientific Evidence," *Integrative Medicine Research* 4, no. 3 (September 2015): 132–41, https://doi.org/10.1016/j.imr.2015.07.003.

113. Sebastião Aguiar and Thomas Borowski, "Neuropharmacological Review of the Nootropic Herb Bacopa monnieri," *Rejuvenation Research* 16, no. 4 (2013): 313-326, https://doi.org/10.1089/rej.2013.1431.

114. Kamil J. Synoradzki and Paweł Grieb, "Citicoline: A Superior Form of Choline?," *Nutrients* 11, no. 7 (July 12, 2019): 1569, https://doi.org/10.3390/nu11071569; Steven E. Bruce et al., "Improvements in Concentration, Working Memory and Sustained Attention Following Consumption of a Natural Citicoline–caffeine Beverage," *International Journal of Food Sciences and Nutrition* 65, no. 8 (July 21, 2014): 1003–7, https://doi.org/10.3109/09637486.2014.940286; Erin McGlade et al., "The Effect of Citicoline Supplementation on Motor Speed and Attention in Adolescent Males," *Journal of Attention Disorders* 23, no. 2 (July 15, 2015): 121–34, https://doi.org/10.1177/1087054715593633.

115. Hee Jin Kim, Pitna Kim, and Chan Young Shin, "A Comprehensive Review of the Therapeutic and Pharmacological Effects of Ginseng and Ginsenosides in Central Nervous System," *Journal of Ginseng Research/Journal of Ginseng Research* 37, no. 1 (March 2013): 8–29, https://doi.org/10.5142/jgr.2013.37.8.

116. Fiona Limanaqi et al., "Potential Antidepressant Effects of Scutellaria Baicalensis, Hericium Erinaceus and Rhodiola Rosea," *Antioxidants* 9, no. 3 (March 12, 2020): 234, https://doi.org/10.3390/antiox9030234; S Akhondzadeh, "Attention-Deficit/Hyperactivity Disorder and Herbal Medicine: An Evidenced Based Approach," *Journal of Medicinal Plants* 17 (February 7, 2018), https://jmp.ir/browse.php?a_id=2081&slc_lang=en&sid=1&printcase=1&hbnr=1&hmb=1.

117. Sarah Docherty, Faye L. Doughty, and Ellen F. Smith, "The Acute and Chronic Effects of Lion's Mane Mushroom Supplementation on Cognitive Function, Stress and Mood in Young Adults: A Double-Blind, Parallel Groups, Pilot Study," *Nutrients* 15, no. 22 (November 20, 2023): 4842, https://doi.org/10.3390/nu15224842; Koichiro Mori et al., "Improving Effects of the Mushroom Yamabushitake (Hericium Erinaceus) on Mild Cognitive Impairment: A Double-blind Placebo-controlled Clinical Trial," *PTR. Phytotherapy Research/Phytotherapy Research* 23, no. 3 (March 2009): 367–72, https://doi.org/10.1002/ptr.2634; Benchao Li et al., "The Relationship Between Mushroom Consumption and Cognitive Performance Among Middle-aged and Older Adults: A Cross-sectional Study," *Food & Function* 14, no. 16 (August 14, 2023): 7663–71, https://doi.org/10.1039/d3fo01101a.

118. Puei-Lene Lai et al., "Neurotrophic Properties of the Lion's Mane Medicinal Mushroom, Hericium Erinaceus (Higher Basidiomycetes) From Malaysia," *International Journal of Medicinal Mushrooms* 15, no. 6 (2013): 539–54, https://doi.org/10.1615/intjmedmushr.v15.i6.30.

119. Qing-Ping Chu et al., "Extract of Ganoderma Lucidum Potentiates Pentobarbital-induced Sleep via a GABAergic Mechanism," *Pharmacology, Biochemistry and Behavior* 86, no. 4 (April 2007): 693–98, https://doi.org/10.1016/j.pbb.2007.02.015.

120. Wachtel- Galor S et al., "Ganoderma Lucidum (Lingzhi or Reishi): A Medicinal Mushroom," *Europe PMC* (May 18, 2012), https://europepmc.org/article/med/22593926#_ch9_sec20_.

121. Rajesh Kumar et al., "Cordyceps Sinensis Promotes Exercise Endurance Capacity of Rats by Activating Skeletal Muscle Metabolic Regulators," *Journal of Ethnopharmacology* 136, no. 1 (June 2011): 260–66, https://doi.org/10.1016/j.jep.2011.04.040.

122. Yūko Kikuchi et al., "Chaga Mushroom-induced Oxalate Nephropathy," *Clinical Nephrology* 81, no. 06 (June 2014): 440–44, https://doi.org/10.5414/cn107655.

123. Emily M. Paolucci et al., "Exercise Reduces Depression and Inflammation but Intensity Matters," *Biological Psychology* 133 (March 2018): 79–84, https://doi.org/10.1016/j.biopsycho.2018.01.015.

124. George Ziegelmueller and Jack Kay. *Argumentation: Inquiry and Advocacy*, 3rd ed. (Alyn & Bacon, January 1, 1997).

125. Alexa Erdogan, "Building Palaces of Memories: A Glimpse at the Method of Loci," *Grey Matters* (March 30, 2014), https://greymattersjournal.org/building-palaces-of-memories-a-glimpse-at-the-method-of-loci/.

126. While exploring the memory palace technique, I decided to hone my skills. So, I took a course by Anthony Metivier, a modern-day memory expert and founder of the Magnetic Memory Method. His approach to constructing memory palaces is quite comprehensive, and he offers unique insights into creating more effective Palaces with more vibrant and associative imagery, which greatly enhanced how I used them. There is a whole underworld of competitive memory experts who teach and practice memory skills. I then got my hands on dozens of books by several other memory experts and found them extremely interesting. Some have great YouTube videos as well. To name a few, if you want to look them up: Alex Mullen, Nelson Dellis, Ron White, Dominic O'Brien, Henry Lorayne, Jonas von Essen, Joshua Foer, Ben Pridmore, and Luis Angel.

127. Jim Kwik, "The Five Foes of Successful Reading," *Medium* (April 23, 2023), https://kwikbrain.medium.com/the-five-foes-of-successful-reading-93d5e1f6216a.

128. Hermann Ebbinghaus, *Memory; a Contribution to Experimental Psychology* (Martino Fine Books, September 12, 2011).

The original publication by Hermann Ebbinghaus in 1885, where he presented his findings on the forgetting curve, is titled "Über das Gedächtnis," which was later translated into English as "Memory: A Contribution to Experimental Psychology."

129. Wikipedia contributors, "Leitner System," Wikipedia (January 5, 2024), https://en.wikipedia.org/wiki/Leitner_system.

    The Leitner System is a widely used method for efficient learning, particularly effective for memorizing large amounts of information, like vocabulary or facts. Developed by the German scientist Sebastian Leitner in the 1970s, this technique is based on the concept of spaced repetition, a learning process that involves increasing intervals of time between subsequent reviews of previously learned material.

130. Shane Mooney, "Spaced Repetition for All: Cognitive Science Meets Big Data in a Procrastinating World," Quizlet (March 10, 2017), https://quizlet.com/blog/spaced-repetition-for-all-cognitive-science-meets-big-data-in-a-procrastinating-world.

131. Michael Michalko, *Thinker Toys* (Berkeley: Ten Speed Press, 1991), 97.

132. Wikipedia contributors, "Lateral Thinking," Wikipedia (May 2, 2024), https://en.wikipedia.org/wiki/Lateral_thinking.

133. Viorica Marian and Anthony Shook, "The Cognitive Benefits of Being Bilingual," *Cerebrum: The Dana Forum on Brain Science* vol. 2012 (2012): 13, https://pubmed.ncbi.nlm.nih.gov/23447799/; Anat Prior and Brian MacWhinney, "A Bilingual Advantage in Task Switching," *Bilingualism* 13, no. 2 (December 17, 2009): 253–62, https://doi.org/10.1017/s1366728909990526.

134. "Latin and English," *Cogitatorium*, n.d., https://rharriso.sites.truman.edu/latin-language/latin-and-english.

135. Knowledge at Wharton Staff, "Why AI Is the 'New Electricity,'" *Knowledge at Wharton* (November 7, 2017), https://knowledge.wharton.upenn.edu/article/ai-new-electricity/.

136. Charley Grant "AI Is Driving 'the Next Industrial Revolution.' Wall Street Is Cashing In.," *Wall Street Journal* (May 27, 2024), https://www.wsj.com/finance/stocks/ai-is-driving-the-next-industrial-revolution-wall-street-is-cashing-in-8cc1b28f.

137. Rosetta Stone, "TruAccent: Learning With Rosetta Stone - Rosetta Stone," Rosetta Stone (September 24, 2021), https://blog.rosettastone.com/truaccent-learning-with-rosetta-stone/.

138. Lory Gil, "Lifesum Adds A.I. Food Recognition to Its Diet and Health Tracking App," *iMore* (March 7, 2018), accessed May 26, 2024, https://www.imore.com/lifesum-adds-ai-food-recognition.

139. Mariko Oi, "Neuralink: Musk's firm says first brain-chip patient plays online chess," *BBC* (March 20, 2024), https://www.bbc.com/news/business-68622781.

140. Mara Van Der Meulen et al., "Genetic and Environmental Influences on Structure of the Social Brain in Childhood," *Developmental Cognitive Neuroscience* 44 (August 2020): 100782, https://doi.org/10.1016/j.dcn.2020.100782; Matheus Fer-

rero, "Study Finds That Genes Play a Role in Empathy," University of Cambridge (March 12, 2018), https://www.cam.ac.uk/research/news/study-finds-that-genes-play-a-role-in-empathy.

141. Julio Plata-Bello et al., "Empathy Modulates the Activity of the Sensorimotor Mirror Neuron System During Pain Observation," *Behavioral Sciences* 13, no. 11 (November 17, 2023): 947, https://doi.org/10.3390/bs13110947.

142. Erin Waish and David Waish, "How Children Develop Empathy," *Psychology Today* (May 9, 2019), https://www.psychologytoday.com/us/blog/smart-parenting-smarter-kids/201905/how-children-develop-empathy.

143. Heyuan Zhu, "How Cultural Factors Influence Empathy Levels in Specific Contexts: A Comparision Between Individualism and Collectivism," *Journal of Education, Humanities and Social Sciences* 10 (April 2023): 169–75, https://doi.org/10.54097/ehss.v10i.6913.

144. Malala Yousafzai and Christina Lamb. *I Am Malala: The Girl Who Stood Up for Education and Was Shot by the Taliban* (Little, Brown and Company, October 8, 2013).

This memoir by Malala herself provides a firsthand account of her experiences.

145. Daniela Renger et al., "Voicing One's Ideas: Intragroup Respect as an Antecedent of Assertive Behavior," *Basic and Applied Social Psychology* 41, no. 1 (January 12, 2019): 34–47, https://doi.org/10.1080/01973533.2018.1542306.

Much of literature on assertiveness seems focused on assertive behaviors while overlooking key underlying attitudinal factors. Social psychology research from Daniela Renger et al. indicates that intragroup respect (including self-respect and respect of others) is an antecedent of more assertive behavior and yields higher group performance in dyadic intragroup discussions.

146. Geoffrey Brewer, "Snakes Top List of Americans' Fears," Gallup.com (March 19, 2001), https://news.gallup.com/poll/1891/snakes-top-list-americans-fears.aspx.

147. J. B. Harvey, "The Abilene Paradox: The Management of Agreement," *Organizational Dynamics* 3, no. 1 (1974): 63-80, https://doi.org/10.1016/0090-2616(74)90005-9, https://www.aspeninstitute.org/wp-content/uploads/files/content/upload/16-Harvey-Abilene-Paradox-redacted.pdf.

148. Roger Fisher, William Ury, and Bruce Patton. *Getting to Yes: Negotiating Agreement Without Giving In*. 3rd Revised ed., (Penguin Books, May 3, 2011).

149. Marshall Rosenberg, PhD, Nonviolent Communication: A Language of Life (PuddleDancer Press: September 1, 2015).

150. Wikipedia contributors, "Oprah Winfrey," Wikipedia, accessed May 26, 2024, https://en.wikipedia.org/wiki/Oprah_Winfrey.

151. Ira Hyman, PhD, "Large Mocha Without a Name," *Psychology Today* (February 24, 2010), https://www.psychologytoday.com/intl/blog/mental-mishaps/201002/large-mocha-without-name.

152. Special to The Washington Post, "Remember People's Names," *The Washington Post* (February 11, 2006), https://www.washingtonpost.com/archive/2006/02/12/remember-peoples-names/e058ae27-4554-4cc7-8e78-ca2c6f51b3ee/.

153. Dominic O'Brien, *Quantum Memory Power: Learn to Improve Your Memory With the World Memory Champion!* (New York: G&D Media, 2020).

154. Sehoon Kim, Heesu Lee, and Timothy Paul Connerton, "How Psychological Safety Affects Team Performance: Mediating Role of Efficacy and Learning Behavior," *Frontiers in Psychology* 11 (July 24, 2020), https://doi.org/10.3389/fpsyg.2020.01581.

155. Jocko Willink and Leif Babin, "How U.S. Navy SEALs," (November 21, 2017), "Extreme Ownership," online course, MasterClass, https://www.masterclass.com/classes/critical-leadership-training-with-navy-seal-officer-jocko-willink-continuous-cut/.

156. Julianne Holt-Lunstad et al., "Social Relationships and Mortality Risk: A Meta-Analytic Review," *PLoS Medicine* 7, no. 7 (2010): e1000316, https://doi.org/10.1371/journal.pmed.1000316.

157. Chris Taylor, "What the world's longest happiness study says about money," *Reuters* (February 6, 2023), https://www.reuters.com/markets/wealth/what-worlds-longest-happiness-study-says-about-money-2023-02-06/.

158. Joe Dominguez and Vicki Robin, *Your Money or Your Life: Transforming Your Relationship with Money and Achieving Financial MORE* (Penguin Books: October 1, 1993).

159. Financial Samurai, "Best Mint Alternatives for Budgeting and Money Management," n.d., *Financial Samurai*, https://www.financialsamurai.com/best-mint-alternatives/.

160. "Guide to the Markets," J.P. Morgan Asset Management, n.d., https://am.jpmorgan.com/us/en/asset-management/adv/insights/market-insights/guide-to-the-markets/.

See Asset Class Returns chart. When you visualize different asset class returns and their volatility over time it helps to see why having a diversified portfolio is a recommended strategy.

161. Vartika Gupta et al., "Prime Numbers: Markets will be markets: An analysis of long-term returns from the S&P 500," McKinsey & Company (August 4, 2022), https://www.mckinsey.com/capabilities/strategy-and-corporate-finance/our-insights/the-strategy-and-corporate-finance-blog/markets-will-be-markets-an-analysis-of-long-term-returns-from-the-s-and-p-500.

162. Taylor DeJesus, "Nursing Home Costs," *Money* (September 26, 2023), https://money.com/nursing-home-costs/.

163. Financial Samurai, "How to Build Passive Income for Financial Independence," *Financial Samurai* (February 19, 2024), https://www.financialsamurai.com/how-to-build-passive-income-for-financial-independence/.

164. Sam Dogen, *Buy This, Not That: How to Spend Your Way to Wealth and Freedom* (Portfolio: July 19, 2022*)*.

165. Brad Japhe, "Interview With Anshuman Vohra: Craft Gin Founder Turned Sports Drink Guru," *Forbes*, November 6, 2018, https://www.forbes.com/sites/bradjaphe/2018/11/06/interview-with-anshuman-vohra-craft-gin-founder-turned-energy-drink-guru/?sh=5089f6e76981.

166. Bulldog Gin, "Gruppo Campari Acquires Super-premium BULLDOG Gin," *PR Newswire*, February 2, 2017, https://www.prnewswire.com/news-releases/gruppo-campari-acquires-super-premium-bulldog-gin-300401458.html.

167. Greg Iacurci, "Social Security's trust funds are running dry. Here are 4 things to know," *CNBC* (September 11, 2023), https://www.cnbc.com/2023/09/11/social-securitys-trust-funds-are-running-dry-heres-what-to-know.html.

168. Financial Samurai, "Net Worth Targets by Age, Income, and Work Experience for Financial Freedom Seekers," Financial Samurai (February 13, 2024), https://www.financialsamurai.com/net-worth-targets-by-age-income-work-experience/.

An alternative perspective comes from Financial Samurai, suggesting financial independence is achievable when you've saved 20X your annual gross income or can generate enough passive income to cover your living expenses. Applying this guidance would imply for example a target net worth of $2.5 million to sustain a $100,000 annual income through retirement.

169. John C. Maxwell, *The 21 Irrefutable Laws of Leadership: Follow Them and People Will Follow You* (Thomas Nelson: January 1, 1998).

170. Theodore Roosevelt, "Citizenship in a Republic and the Man in the Arena: Speech at the Sorbonne, Paris, April 23, 1910" (Independently published: March 27, 2020).

ACKNOWLEDGMENTS

I OWE A DEBT OF GRATITUDE TO THE MANY INDIVIDUALS WHO helped bring this book to life. Thank you to the remarkable team at American Real Publishing for transforming my manuscript into the final book. Special thanks to Olivia Stalvey, Associate Editor, for the excellent edits; Roger Harvey, for the visual enhancements of the cover graphics; Katie Ressa for proofreading; Tara Monaco, for the warm welcome to the AR publishing process; and Roger Brooks, CEO, for being a generous sounding board and creative problem solver.

Thank you to Rocío Martín Osuna for your skillful cover design and original artwork; George Miroshnichenko for your extraordinary hand-drawn illustrations; Dr. Nour Hassan, certified and registered nutritionist and medical physician, for carefully reviewing and providing professional insights within several sections of Level 3; Dr. Kathryn Wilson, Ph.D. in clinical psychology, for providing an expert review and refining the psychological insights throughout these pages; Naty Barry for your expert suggestions on conflict resolution and Nonviolent Communication (NVC); and Sam Dogen, my former college roommate and bestselling personal finance author, for reviewing parts of Level 6 on Mastering Money Matters.

To my USAID and Embassy colleagues on the front lines, your daily dedication to helping others around the world to level up inspires me deeply. To my Ukraine colleagues and friends, your unwavering commitment and indomitable spirit during these most challenging times have been heroic. A special acknowledgment to my friends and colleagues in Guatemala, Malawi, Central Asia—including Kazakhstan, the Kyrgyz Republic, Tajikistan, Uzbekistan, Turkmenistan, plus Afghanistan—and Washington, DC; our unforgettable adventures will forever hold a special place in my heart.

A thank you to all the countless authors, mentors, educators, experts, and friends who inspired me—they are too numerous to mention. As a first-generation college-bound kid, I often found the path unclear. I'm grateful to the many influential friends, mentors, and educators during my young adult years who significantly impacted my outlook and path. I have not forgotten their invaluable guidance. A special shout-out to Betsy McClearn of Salem High, who encouraged me to pursue the International Baccalaureate program during a pivotal time in my life. I also want to thank the caring and committed mentors in the Upward Bound program who were dedicated to helping young people level up. Also, thanks to those I knew at PwC and IBM who profoundly shaped my perspectives on mentorship, leadership, and impactful work.

To my parents, your constant encouragement and work ethic are the foundation upon which I built this book. To my sisters, Tammy and Missy, who, after many years of enduring my near-endless mischief, became educators dedicated to skilling up future generations—I learned a ton from both of you and deeply admire your dedication.

To my incredible family for your love and support. Zachary, David, and Hannah, your feedback and thoughtful insights throughout this book-writing journey were nothing short of extraordinary. After all, you were my original inspiration for this book, and I hope the skills within will guide you as you seize all that life has to offer.

Lastly, to my wife, Amy, your patience and wisdom have been a true blessing. Amidst designing and successfully launching the trailblazing Central America Service Corps (Jóvenes con Propósito) and being the best life partner one could ask for, you found the time to read draft after draft, offering guidance and insights that were crucial to shaping this work. Your dedication to remarkable, life-impacting endeavors for youth and others is profoundly inspiring.

Thank you for being my unwavering source of strength, motivation, and inspiration. This book is a testament to kindred spirits. Onward and upward!

INDEX

Symbols

ABOUT THE AUTHOR

Steve M. Scott is a US diplomat and former management consultant dedicated to lifelong learning and personal growth. Raised in Virginia's Blue Ridge Mountains, he has traveled to over fifty countries, collecting a wealth of life lessons. Currently posted to Guatemala with his family, Steve is passionate about creating strategies and tools for unlocking talent.

To learn more and keep in touch with Steve, visit **http://stevemscott.com**.